THE ETERNAL WE

THE ETERNAL WE

Harold J. Green

LOYOLA UNIVERSITY PRESS

Chicago

Printed in the United States of America

Loyola University Press
3441 North Ashland Avenue
Chicago, Illinois 60657

Library of Congress Cataloging in Publication Data
Green, Harold J.
The eternal we.
1. Interpersonal relations—Religious aspects.
2. Man (Theology)
3. Philosophical anthropology.
I. Title.
BL53.G74 1986 233'.5 86-10332
ISBN 0-8294-0535-6

Design by C.L. Tornatore

To Martin Buber and
Ferdinand Ebner

"Let the work continue. . . ."

Contents

TO THE READER

Introduction and Way In

What does it mean to be a person? Where is the ground of personal existence? The following work addresses these questions from theological, philosophical and psychological perspectives. It concerns the nature of persons, human and divine. The specific focus is on "persons-in-relationship," or just as accurately, on "relationships-between-persons." For persons and relationships are inseparable, and the center of attention throughout the book is the "between" rather than the "within" of persons. In truth, persons arise in relationships, and relationships are the ground of persons. We do not just "have" relationships; rather, who we are and where we live as persons emerge from and ever abide in those primal relationships wherein we have taken our stand, wherein we have known and been known by those "significant others" who have been determinative of our personal meaning and identity.

The essential relationship of persons is that of *language*. "In the beginning was the Word." The who, the what and the why of personal existence—both divine and human—are first revealed and forever have their foundation in Word and language. Word and Spirit are one.

Our *objective existence* as persons rests in the *language* we share. And our *subjective existence* abides in the *love* and *mutuality* which represent the contextual ground of the common word between us. Word, spirit and person are one, distinguishable but indivisible. Together they constitute the dialectic of totality, the whole, the beginning, the way and the end of all persons and events, all things and states of affairs.

This book offers a unified vision of the whole of reality. It proceeds from the top down, from the nature of God to the consequential nature of the all of creation. A vision of God, of the End toward which the whole is moving, determines the way in which the book develops. It begins with the fact of Word, of divine speech, as recorded in John 1:1: "In the beginning was the Word, and the Word was with God, and the Word was God." That means: prior to the Word-event of creation, and in a mode quite beyond our "post-Word" or creation-bounded apprehension, there was divine speech. Call it the "personal dialogue" of God, that speech which does not leave the personal orb of the Holy, spoken of God to God and through God.

Should we term this pre-creation intra-divine speech "dialogue" or "monologue"? Our view of the whole of reality hinges upon the answer to that question. If we assume that divine and human speech are analogous—indeed, as analogous as divine and human persons—, and if we subsequently allow language to speak for itself, taking the word at its word, so to speak, the answer to this question becomes inescapable. For language spoken and living is essentially dialogue. That means: *word manifests an irreducible tri-unity.* The process of speech consists of three elements: a speaker, a listener, and the speech itself. Someone says something to someone. And continuous with that, someone hears and responds. It is a word-relationship in which two subjects or persons exist for and with each other—at least during the time of the dialogue.

Through Word or language itself, therefore, the essential threefoldness of the "Person" of God becomes manifest. Three vital pronouns depict the relational state of affairs of God in and through the Word: *You, I,* and *We*. From the vantage point of the One spoken to—and this book can be written only from that point of view—the primal Speaker is the *You* ever over against all others. From that same vantage point, the One who listens is the *I* of consciousness. And just as importantly, the Speech itself, which constitutes the mutual speaking and listening, thus the very context and shared content of the relationship, is the *We* of Their togetherness.

Through the Word, therefore, the essential triplicity of God becomes manifest. And through the Word of creation, that is, through the actual event of the "issuing" or "externalization" of the Word from the Life of God, giving rise to that which is somehow outside or over against the Persons of God, the irreducible threefoldness of God is carried over into the whole of creation. The "logic" of the Word dialectically carves into the whole of creation the personal lines of demarcation of the divine relationality. Thus from the divine You, I and We does creation consist of the three dimensions of *externalaity, internality* and *mutuality,* respectively, or the without, the within and the between of all persons and things.

Human creation is in the "image" of God. Thus, in accordance with the nature of the speech event, *to be human means to participate in the threefold You, I and We of God.* And it means to do so in and through language. The divine Word of our creation is the inner Source and ever-flowing spring for the human word. As the first sections of the work will make clear, the human person comes into being through the Word of address, and is therefore essentially a being of, in and for Word. Person and Word are one.

It is of the utmost importance that we now come to see that all three dimensions of the human person are equally real, and thus that love and mutuality cannot be reduced into the I of the psyche. Behold, love is more than a "feeling"! Rather than merely within You and I, it is between us—indeed, it is Us—and in it we take our stand and find our very persons, our persons-together. Love is our being-together in person, word and spirit.

A place for the spirit, that is, for the sphere of the "between," must be made in our conceptual and historical Zeitgeist. It is time for the "Me first" mentality to be overcome by the "We first" realization of our inescapable inter-dependence. Not to do so would preclude our redemption and eventuate in our self-destruction. For our coming salvation signifies our entrance into the Eternal We of God. The We *is* the Kingdom of God. And the time of the Kingdom is at hand. Now is the time for the discovery of the We literally in our midst.

✠

This book addresses simultaneously the fields of philosophy, psychology and theology with an insight into the reality of the "We" of human experience. It offers a kind of "metaphysic of mutuality," and seeks to break new ground in our understanding of the nature of Spirit, human and divine.

In terms of philosophy, the book builds above all on the work of Martin Buber, specifically on his "I-You" insight into human relationships. Where Buber focused almost exclusively on the I-You poles of relationship, this work centers on the relationship as such, the We, the sphere of the "between." Buber's dialogic of persons is integrated with the dialectic of spirit of Georg W.F. Hegel. The "essential triplicity" of Hegel's dialectical process is applied to the realm of persons: I, You and We.

With Hegel, I begin with the Trinity. And like the fourth Gospel, I begin with the Word. The Word manifests the Trinity. The "three Persons in one Substance" of the creedal formula signifies the You, the I and the We in the Word. As the book demonstrates in a myriad of contexts, Word, Person and Spirit are not only inseparable, but arise simultaneously from the same event. And from the divine relational dimensions of the without, within and between, respectively, the architecture of the whole is determined. All this happens by virtue of the immutable nature of the Word, of the speech event, whether divine or human or divine-human. This book in fact rests on the faith in the legitimacy of the analogy between divine and human language—as well as between divine and human persons. From Word comes word, as from Person person, and in unfathomable paradox they are continuous.

The book also seeks to sketch in a preliminary way the possible parameters for a philosophy—and spirituality—of language, combining the perspectives of Ludwig Wittgenstein and Ferdinand Ebner. For Wittgenstein, language is ultimately "something animal," understandable only within the context of its living usage. For Ebner, language is ultimately identifiable with spirit. Hence, etymology represents the archeology of spirit; the content and context of the origination of a word reveals its true spirit and relation to the Spirit.

The present work suggests that *language, as identifiable with the We, is* ultimately *a "spiritual animal,"* that is, something—or "someone"—

real between persons, in and through which they live and have their individual being, at least for the course of the dialogue. With God the dialogue is unending—thank heavens! For its ending would signify ours as well.

In terms of psychology, the book links up with the "interpersonal theory" of psychiatry of Harry Stack Sullivan and the "We psychology" of Fritz Kunkel. Indeed, the book asserts that a We-psychology is the proper psychology for our time. Simply stated, *I seek to demonstrate that the We is just as real and essential to the meaning of being a person as the I and the You.* Therefore psychological reduction of the sphere of the between into that of the within, of the inter-human to that of the intra-psychic is both experientially unjustified and conceptually "ill-logos-full," as it were. For apart from clear and consistent reference to the We, psychology cannot see the I aright. Also included is a "psychology of evil," building on the important insights of Rollo May and F. Scott Peck.

The book is above all a work of theology. A theology of the We is developed from the first unto the final sentence. It is a work of faith and for faith. And at the center of that faith is the conviction that *the We constitutes a major*—if not *the* major—*hermeneutical tool for both Biblical and Comparative Religions interpretation.*. Serious exegesis is conducted to demonstrate the central importance of the concept of the We in certain biblical texts. Where Buber maintained that the Hebrew Bible represented the primary and primal record of divine-human dialogue, the "I-You" of persons over against one another, I assert that *the Bible,* especially the New Testament, *represents above all the revelation and fact of divine-human dialectic,* that is, the "We" of persons in mutuality, Spirit and covenant.

Further, and very importantly, the work carries on the "post- Holocaust" Christian theology of such current figures as Paul Van Buren and Krister Stendahl. It offers an *apologia* for Israel in the original sense of the term, that is, a defense or justification of the ongoing role of Israel in the divine plan. Further, a new approach to the essential and complementary relationship between Israel and the Church is presented. The category of the We makes both enterprises not only possible but needful.

✠

The book has three major divisions. The first is "The Eternal You: Creation and the We of Nature." The second is "The Eternal I: Revelation and the We of Humanity." And the third is "The Eternal We: Redemption and the Divine-Human We." The first is the more philosophical, the second the more psychological and the third the more theological in nature and scope. Yet, all three spheres of discourse are interwoven throughout the book.

As the book has more than one purpose and addresses more than one audience, so also are there variations in the style, tone and temper of the writing. Multiplexity of message requires multiplexity of form. At points I am as technical and exacting in succinct elocution as I am able; at other times I am as personal and open as I dare be for public discourse. The book presents a totality; hence, it does so through a totality of modes of expression. My heart speaks herein as fully as my mind. I seek not only to describe but to convince, not only to demonstrate but to persuade the reader to act on what is apprehended.

The opening section of the first major division of the book, entitled "The Architecture of Creation," is the most technical and difficult of the whole work. Yet it needs to be first because it addresses what happened at the beginning! It depicts the "architecture" of God and creation, laying thereby the groundwork for all that follows. What I am trying to do in this first section is to sketch the nature of the whole on the basis of the actual event or moment of the Word of creation. It is as if a physicist were attempting to describe the nature of the cosmos on the basis of the actual instant of the "big bang" of the beginning of the universe.

The reader is therefore strongly advised *not* to begin the book with the opening section of the first division on "The Architecture of Creation," but rather either to proceed straightaway to the second section of the first division, entitled "The Person," or to begin reading the second major division on "The Eternal I: Revelation and the We of Humanity." At a later time, when at least this middle division has been digested, the reader may go back and walk slowly through the architectural maze of the beginning.

One final word about the organization of the book. It is consistently aphoristic and suggestive in style. It is not a systematic theology or philosophy or psychology that is being presented, point by point, but rather probings and soundings into a primal insight about the nature of persons. The essential idea must be repeated again and again, and then lines of consequences laid out like railroad tracks, each needing further development and refinement. The "trueness" of the rails will be determined if and when the trains of the respective disciplines addressed proceed down them.

I lift up and question, turn quickly to a subject and just as quickly away from it to something else. An issue is raised, a point made and the matter left. Within the chapters, this "change of pace," as it were, is demarked by the symbol "✠," which serves to separate paragraphs. When the reader comes upon the symbols, that means that what immediately follows is related to what preceded it, and falls conceptually within the subject of the chapter heading, but is coming at the matter from a different angle. Perhaps the best thing the reader can do at that point is simply to take a fresh breath, and continue.

Above all, I hope that the reader will indeed persevere to the end. And not only to the end of the book, but to the destined end of our common pilgrimage to the Eternal We.

Prologue

In the beginning was the Word.
And the Word was with God and to God.
Behold, the Word was God.
That means: in the beginning was the Address.
And that means: in the beginning was the Relationship.
From the first stood revealed in the Word
The Addresser, the Addressed and the Addressing
In unchanging tri-unity.

God the Addresser
Speaks God the Addressed;
and between Them abides God the Addressing.
In the Addressing,
God the Addresser is the *Eternal You*
To God the Addressed.
In the Addressing,
God the Addressed is the *Eternal I* of response.
In the Addressing,
In the One Word-Spirit between Them,
God the Addressing is the *Eternal We* of holy mutuality.
The Persons of the Addresser and of the Addressed
Are One in the Spirit of the Addressing.

In the Word between the Eternal You and I
Creation was spoken;
In the Word and the Spirit-ground thereof,
The All received life and being and meaning.
From the Eternal We was issued the temporal It;
From the wholly, holy Subject,
Came forth the wondrous Object.

And in the fullness of time,
Behold, a second Word was spoken:
The Word became flesh
And dwelt among us,
Full of love and grace and truth.
Behold, the eternally Addressed
Was spoken in and to creation.
Paradox of paradoxes:
God spoke the Holy I,
The eternal Subject of God's own Address,
Into being with us
And as one of us.
The eternally Addressed
Entered into our body, our life and our history
That we might enter into God's Life,
Into the mutual address of God,
In and through and with the Eternal I.

Behold, the Ultimate I of humanity was in the world.
But the world knew not its own Source;
It was blind and deaf to its own Destiny.
Yet all who truly heard,
All who opened and responded to God's address,
Received authority to become children of God,
And power to be born anew
Through God's will
And in Spirit and Truth.

Prologue

All who entered into the light of God's address
Received the Way to become one with God
In the Eternal I,
One with the Eternal You
Through the Eternal We
Of Their common Life.

No one has ever seen the Eternal You;
Only the Eternal I,
Who dwells in the perfect unity
Of the Eternal We,
Has made God's Person known.

The Eternal You
Creation and the We of Nature

THE ARCHITECTURE OF CREATION

In the Beginning

In the beginning, God. Unfathomable yet speaking. God: emerging as Person in address, in an event—*the* event—of Word, of *logos*. God: Being inseparable from language, the act of speech from the Person who speaks. The Person and the Word of God arise together from the abiding Mystery. Before the foundations of the world, behold, God and Word lived in mutuality.

In the beginning is the Word. That means: in the beginning is the *relationship*. For the Word exists and is meaningful only *between* Persons; It inescapably intends a mutuality. Word issues from One who speaks, and necessarily extends toward One who listens. The relationship of Word is thus an essential tri-unity or triplicity, a three-in-one, or a "difference-in-unity." For the Word reveals three irreducible components: the Speaker, the Spoken to, and the Speaking. Within the eternally fixed context of the relationship itself, that means: the Addresser, the Addressed and the Addressing.

God speaks, and behold, God listens. Nothing is lost; the Word is never empty or meaningless. The speaking and the listening constitute the mutual or common between the divine poles of Addresser and Addressed. Addressing includes both speaking and listening, utterance and reception. God is an eternal sharing. The Word and the Spirit of the Word represent God's mutuality; the Addresser and the Addressed live and move and have Their Being in the Addressing between Them.

In the beginning is the Address. That means: in the event of Address, Person and Word are one. For there is no object or content of the Word save the Person intended by the primal pronoun of Address—the "You." The Original Subject addresses the Other with the Subject's own name or self-designation. The You applies to both and lives equally between Them. That is, to both the Addresser and the Addressed, the Other is the You each is ever over against.

In being Addressed, the I of God emerges and has objective existence vis-a-vis the One who Addresses. For the Persons of the Addresser and the Addressed come to stand objectively in the Word and subjectively in the Spirit of their mutual intention. The I of the Addressed is mediated through the You of Address, and is thus linked forever to the latter. The I-consciousness of the Addressed awakens in the hearing of the Address and arises in the initial response thereto, as intended by the One who first speaks. Conferred in address, the I is confirmed in response.

The eternally Addressed eternally Responds with the selfsame Word of You to the Addresser. The Spirit of the Address is present—but unspoken—in this mutual You of address and response. And in the Spirit of this holy mutuality lies the inner meaning or purpose of the address itself. The You that is shared bespeaks the We of the relationship. And the We is Their common life, Their oneness, Their love Itself.

The address of Being is present in the address of Word. In the Word, the Person is put forward. But without the Word, neither the Spirit nor the intention, neither the form nor the content of that presence would be determinable. Without the Word, the relationship of presence would be consigned to an eternal incompleteness, and sharing reduced to the silent if mutual appraisal of a chasm between the Persons present to each other. Apart from the Word there is no knowledge of the "personality" of Person. Thus, the "personality" of God cannot be known apart from the speaking, apart from the Word of God's own choosing.

In sum, the Eternal I is God the Addressed, the Eternal You is God the Addresser, and the Eternal We is God the Addressing. And in Their perfect unity, the I is mediated to the Addressed through the Word, just as the You is mediated back to the Addresser though the selfsame Word. From the vantage point of the Addressed, God the Addresser is the Eternal You, the ever overagainst, who may only be addressed, and only by virtue and means of the primal Word of address, wherein the I is conferred in call and confirmed in response. The I and the You of God take Their stand in the We of the Word and the mutual Spirit thereof. It is the We which constitutes the life and the mutual being of the I and the You of God. The common is the eternal ground of the unique.

✠

What of the I of the Original Speaker, the Eternal You? If I-consciousness exists in and by virtue of the Word of Address, then the "consciousness of internality" could be said to move both ways, that is, be shared in some sense by both participants in the Word. Yet behold, the I—indeed, the very Person—of the eternally Addressed exists only in and by virtue of the Word-event of the original Address, whereas, the same cannot be said of the Eternal Addresser. God is greater than the Word. The Mystery of the Person of the God the Creator abides forever. And abides in paradox: holy and wholly Other, yet in the Word, Person to and "personality" with the One graced by Address.

✠

"In the beginning was the Word." Thus opens the Prologue of the Gospel of John, the Gospel of the ultimate relationship, the Eternal We. The term for "Word" in the Greek, "*logos,*" has far greater significance in the Greek than can be translated by one word in English. *Logos* means "word, language, logic, wisdom, reason, mind, and spirit." As used by John and the early church, all these meanings—and more—were operative. Also, as used throughout this work, Word or logos is to be understood as containing all of the above meanings.

✠

In the beginning is the Word, the *logos*. And the *logos* is threefold in accordance with the threefoldness of God: the Word *intends, denotes* and *connotes*. The Word reveals the intention of the will of the One who speaks. The deepest mystery of the Word abides here, in the inner purpose of Its utterance. The Word event Itself is formed by and thus manifests the unseen "law" or "logic," so to speak, of the Person of God. In a real way, therefore, the "substance" of Person is manifest in and identifiable with the Word. To be Person means first of all to speak. And apart from the Word, the mind of God cannot be known. God's aim or *telos* is one with the Word that bespeaks it. That is, the intention of the Word constitutes Its immediate though hidden inner *past* and *purpose* in coming to be stated. The intention thus signifies the *subjective* dimension of the Word.

The Word also denotes: It addresses and/or depicts a specific state of being. That is, the denotation is bifurcated into the *intrinsic You* of address, and the *extrinsic It* of expression. The You is ever the end of the Word; the It is never the end but always the content of the Word. In address, however, the You is both content and end. And when addressed, the You bespeaks the I of the Addresser as well. For when the I says "You," the I who is also a You to the One being addressed, something of the being of the I is expressed in the address as well. And if the Addresser should say "I" to the Other, the I of the latter is indirectly included—technically "connoted"—in the spoken I of the former. Whether through addressing or depicting, the denotation of the Word signifies the concrete presence of an *objectum*, of someone or something over against the Speaker. The denotation therefore, concerns the immediate and manifest external *presence* of what is coming to stand in the Word. The denotation thus signifies the *objective* dimension of the Word.

The Word which intends and denotes also connotes. The connotation or "co-notation" of the Word signifies the totality of meanings present but not actually stated *between* the Speaker and the Addressed. Where the intention of the Word manifests the will and "personality" of the Speaker, the union of Word and Person as it were, and the denotation bestows the content of the utterance, the connotation opens up the *context* or ground-of-meaning of the Word, the concrete setting of It's life. The connotation thus represents the mutuality or commonality of meaning which exists between the participants in the speech-event. It is the shared context which makes communication possible and meaningful. The connotation is the Spirit of the Word and of the mutual presence of the Speaker and the Addressed to each other. As such, the Spirit is present and meant, but not stated, not objectified or addressed directly. It is nonetheless just as real and powerful as the subjective and objective dimensions of the Word. Call It the *"inter-subjective"* sphere of the Word, which ties together the intention of the past and the denotation of the present with the immediate implications of the *future*. For the Spirit is ever open-ended and future oriented; and in being present but not stated, the Spirit contains the motive power which may give rise to Word in any subsequent moment.

It cannot be overemphasized, however, that the Word is a triunity of meaning, one dimension being inseparable from the other two. The three dimensions constitute a unity of meaning, a totality of linguistic substance, at once personal, impersonal and inter-personal in nature.

✠

The Three Words

There are three divine Word events in accordance with the threefoldness of God: *creation, revelation* and *redemption.* Creation is the Word of the Eternal You, ultimately echoing God's own name in human creation: *"Be You."* Revelation is the Word of the Eternal I, ultimately leading to the disclosure of the human self in the divine: *'I Am."* The Word of Redemption is the yet-to-be-spoken Word of the Eternal We, which will mean the actual attainment of ultimacy for the human person, God being all in all: *"We Are."* The locus of the first Word is the past, the second the present, and the third the future. Yet inasmuch as God is One and the Word One, and God is the same "yesterday, today and forever," all three Word events are united and operative, if in an incipient way, from the very beginning. The whole sweep of divine Life is present and active in the intention of the original Word of Address.

The Word of creation centers upon the You of the Creator. That means the focus is on *otherness,* or *externality.* The Word of revelation centers upon the I of the Revealer. Hence, at the heart of this event is *identity,* or *internality.* The coming Word of redemption will center upon the We of the Redeemer and the redeemed. That is, the attention will at last be upon *commonality,* or *mutuality.*

These three Words also designate three relationships, three spheres of the We. The We of creation, the We of revelation and the We of redemption emerge in and through their respective speech events. Only in the third relationship, however, is the presence and reality of the We as such to be addressed and realized. Only in the third does the ground of mutuality come to be apprehended, and in its very consummation. The We of creation is the ground of being of the past; the We of revelation is the ground of being of the present; the We of redemption is the ground of being of the future.

The three Word-relationships constitute the three primal divine-human relationships. In the Word of creation, the human is addressed as You, thus being granted not only life, but the divine image of the Eternal You. The Word of creation is thus the giving of the I, mediated through the You of address. The transformation of the You into the I begins in the initial hearing of the address, and in the immediate movement toward response. The Word of revelation is first the discernment of the You of God over against the I, mediated through the speaking I. That is, the I of creation initiates revelation in saying "I am" to the divine Addresser, thus indirectly addressing God as You. The Word of redemption is the gifting of the We, mediated through the joint recognition of the mutuality of being together between the I and the You.

Though successive, these three Word-relationships are One and represent the unfolding of a continuous divine-human history. Hence, the Word of creation melds with the Word of revelation at the point at which the You of the addressed comes back upon the You of the Addresser; that is, when the creation responds to the Creator with the selfsame Word of address. And the Word of revelation merges with the Word of redemption when the "I am" of humanity is confirmed with ultimacy by the "I Am" of God; that is, when the Creator responds to the creation with the offer of eternal mutuality: "You and I are One."

✠

The three Words or *logoi* each have their own "logic" of unfolding life and relationship. The logos of creation is *law,* of revelation is *liberty,* and of redemption is *love.* The basis of law lies in the intention of the Original Addresser; the basis of liberty lies in the response of the eternally Addressed; the basis of love lies in the twofold movement of the Word between Them. Each logic builds upon and is for the sake of the one which precedes it. Thus, liberty requires law, and is the precondition for language itself. And liberty is granted by the Word of address as such, enabling true response and dialogue. Further, not only language, but love is not possible without liberty. Love is the union of law and liberty; more than their unification, love is their very purpose and goal.

Law is the given of the past; liberty is the giving of the present; love is the gift of the future, in breaking into the present and consummating the longing of the past. And in the human person, all three logics are present and operative. Law sustains human nature; liberty underwrites human history; love bestows human meaning and destiny.

The three Words or logoi also represent three spheres of language, to which three dimensions of reality correspond. The language of creation is *nature* or *physis;* the language of revelation is *person* or *psyche;* the language of redemption is *spirit* or *pneuma.* The modus operandi of nature is law, and as such is *monologic.* The operative principle of person is liberty, and as such is *dialogic.* The modus vivendi of spirit is love, and as such is *dialectic.* The monologic mode is determined solely by the Speaker. The dialogic mode is initiated by the addressed in hearing and responding, and therefore signifies a beginning of mutuality and co-determination. The dialectic mode unfolds through reciprocity and the discernment of common being. Hence, where the monologic bespeaks a *univocal* mode of being, the dialogic manifests the bipolar interaction of two persons, therefore of an *either/or.* In the dialectic, however, the opposition or overagainstness of the participants gives way to their apposition. The either/or is transformed into a *both/and* wherein the whole comes to be seen as gift to the parts, where nothing is lost, but everything fulfilled in the true life of unity and mutuality.

In the monologic We of nature, the relationship between the parts is always external to the parts themselves. Unity means mere totality, like an umbrella covering the whole. In the dialogic We of persons, however, the relationship is intrinsic to the participants themselves. Their relationship is a "unity-in-difference." The sparks of personal being fly in and through the mutual resistance and otherness which typifies their meeting together. In the dialectic We, the relational situation reverses: the participants represent a "difference-in-unity." The whole is gift to the parts; the truth is the whole; the parts find their being and difference rooted in and supported by the common ground between them.

✠

The Essential Triplicity

The *essential triplicity* of God is that of *Person, Word* and *Spirit*. The Person of God comes to stand in the Word of Address. The Word is "You." The movement of address ends in the hearing of the Word. The One who is so addressed in Word and hence as Word, hears, and in opening begins to respond and echo back to the Original Addresser the selfsame "You." From the twofold movement of the You, first in being addressed and then in responding, springs forth the I. Unstated but present in and as the twofold movement itself, is the Spirit of shared Person, of the mutuality of the You and the I existing between the Partners. The Spirit is the We of the Speaking as such, the actional ground of the Person who addresses and the One addressed in and as Word. The Spirit is the yet-to-be-spoken or addressed intention of the Word-event, originating in the primal Addresser but planted within the One addressed through the Word itself. The three Persons of God are, therefore: the You of address, the I of response and the We of language. And a special "coherence"— as regards both cohesion and logic—obtains between Person and the You, between Word and the I, and between Spirit and the We.

This essential divine triplicity is repeated throughout all creation. In the beginning is the whole. The whole gives birth to the parts, yet in a real way continues to abide entire therein. Greater than their sum, the whole is gift to the parts. The whole and the parts mutually necessitate each other. The tri-unity of God thus sets forth the "canon" for the whole of creation.

The whole of creation consists of three irreducible dimensions, in accordance with the threefoldness of God: *nature* or *physis, person* or *psyche,* and *spirit* or *pneuma.* The physical, psychical and spiritual spheres may be distinguished, but must not be separated. For they constitute a unified whole, grounded in the unity of God itself. And all spheres came into being and have their life in the one Word. Yet each has its specific character of being; each contributes uniquely to the whole.

God spoke the universe: "Let there be . . .". The physical cosmos is God's *language,* from the micro depths to the macro heights, from the immeasurably small to the awe-fillingly immense. Not addressed as You, but summoned forth as It, the physical world has its being and lawfulness grounded in the hidden intention of the holy Speaker. The mystery of creation is that of the *whatness* of time/space *substance.* The mystery concerns the *givenness* of the past, and the incarnation and depth of the Word seeded into the heart of all matter. What is life; what is ultimate reality? The physical sphere manifests the *without* of things, *otherness* and *externality.* The physical as body or *soma,* strains toward its completion or *teleios* in the realm of the psyche.

The psychical world came into existence subsequent to the speaking of the physical, and is built upon—and into—the latter. Behold, the human person was addressed out of that which was spoken. That is, humanity was first spoken then addressed, first object of then subject for the Word. God said, "Be You!" To be human means to be both spoken as creation and addressed as You, means to belong to both the objective and the subjective spheres of being. In other words, the human person is not only a creature of the Word or logos in the command "Let there be . . .," not only a full participant of nature, but also an agent of the logos in the address to "Be *You,*" one in whom the Word spawns the word, the logos gives birth to *language.*

The mystery of the human person concerns that address and its relationship to having also been spoken. As the physical sphere opens up the dimension of otherness or externality, the psychical manifests the additional dimension of the *within* or *internality.* The mystery of the psychical realm is thus that of the *whoness* or *identity of being.* Who am I? What does it mean to be human? The question of identity raises that of ultimacy: who is the Ultimate Person? Who or what is the justifying and confirming ground of personal being? The psychical world bespeaks the *"givingness"* of language, the mystery of the present, and the ongoing Word-event of revelation. Building upon the depth dimension of nature, the sphere of person adds that of transcendence and height. And as the body of nature strains toward the psyche for its completion, so the psyche seeks the spirit for its wholeness.

The spiritual world comes into existence through the response of the human person to the address of God and of creation itself, including both the physical and the psychical domains. The spiritual world constitutes the sphere of the *between* or *mutuality.* The mystery of the spiritual domain concerns the *giftedness* of the *future,* of redemption, and the final goal or end of all things. For the spiritual dimension is that of *meaning* or *"whyness."* Why is there something instead of nothing? Why am I here? What is ultimate meaning? Building upon the depth dimension of nature and the height dimension of the psyche, the spirit completes the triplicity with the dimension of breadth or expanse. And where the body of nature strains toward the completion in and with the psyche, and the psyche toward the wholeness of the spirit, the spiritual reaches toward holiness and groundedness in God.

✠

The sphere of persons is that of the You and the I. The sphere of spirit is that of the We. The sphere of nature is that of the It. In grammatical terms, the first person singular and second person singular and plural represent the sphere of persons. The first person plural constitutes the sphere of spirit. And the third person, singular and plural, signifies the sphere of nature. Where nature is impersonal or non-personal, spirit is transpersonal or inter-personal.

To each sphere belongs a special "season" of time, a *kairos,* though not in a sense exclusive of the others. Rather, the center of time for each is the *when* of its logos, that is, the time of its actual happening as event. Nature thus belongs to the past: creation has been spoken and continues to operate in accordance with that first Word. Persons belong to the present: though their creation is of the past, persons are now speaking; the present is time for dialogue and discovery. Spirit constitutes the future: it is the yet-to-be-spoken, though it addresses us even now, in its presence in with and under the Word. Spirit is unfolding in a dialectical process which may be glimpsed through nature and persons, through creation and history—especially religious history. For religion represents the history of the concrete interchanges between the human person and Spirit, wherein the dialectic of the latter has broken through the dialogue of the former.

✠

Person is the one who speaks and the one who is addressed. Nature is the spoken. Spirit is both the speaking and the yet-to-be-spoken. Note the unity here: person shares with nature the status of *objectum*, of coming to be in the Word, whether of address or of command. As the speaking itself, spirit underlies both nature and person. Spirit is the ultimate connotation, the true context of being of nature and person. Further, person shares with spirit the status of unspoken presence, in that persons may be present to each other without speaking, on the one hand, and that even in the speaking there is always much that is unexpressed but meant by the speaker, on the other. In short, the three abide in interconnected unity in the event of speech, of word.

At what point, however, does the physical world evolve into the psychical, nature into person? Perhaps at the point at which law becomes language—for they share a common logos. In a sense, language is law that is conscious of itself, law in self-dialogue rather than univocal determination.

✠

The world of nature and of person came into being through the Word. Nature or *physis* was spoken, whereas person or *psyche* was both spoken and addressed. The Word for the former is "Let there be. . . ."; the Word for the latter is "Be You!"

That means: nature exists in and for itself, but person exists in and for response. The Word for nature is "Be"; the Word for humanity is "Be with and before Me." Nature is thus called into being but not yet addressed. Is it then up to humanity to address and thus to redeem nature? Is it for the human person to bring creation into the Word, to bring the It into the orb of the divine-human We?

✠

God and the Three Forms of Life

God is in the Word God has spoken. That means: God is "immanent" to the sphere of nature, of *physis*, yet without being thereby material. "The heavens are declaring the glory of God"—the glory or "weight" of the Person of the Speaker is to be sensed through the *objectum* of the Word of creation. Yet the Person of God, as the Eternal You, is the ever transcendent, ever over against the cosmos which has been called into being. As Spirit, however, which is present in and with the Word, a *mutuality* could be said to exist between the Person of the Speaker and the It of the Word. That is, through the Spirit a real "connotation" exists between the Speaker and the Spoken, hence, a true *inclusivity* of being together in the one Word.

The Speaker is present in the Word, and in the unspoken yet operative Love which is the deepest intent and Spirit of that Word. And the creation is *responsive* to its Creator. Though unable—through divine design—to speak, the creation nevertheless responds to the presence of the Spirit of God with a kind of "presence of being." A *We of nature,* a shared spirit in this relationship of the mutual presence of being, could therefore be said to exist between God and *physis.* And the spirit of that We is the mutuality between the participants, wherein, though each contributes toward the composition of the whole, something has come into being which cannot be reduced to the life of either, or to the mere sum of both. Behold, a We between God and physis has come into being, a relationship. And its name? The wondrous term in Greek: *bios. Bios*: the life of nature in presence to itself and to the Creator present to it.

As spoken, the human person belongs to the physical world. Humanity thus participates fully in the We of *bios,* in the relationship of the presence of being. Yet as addressed, the human person also lives in and by virtue of language proper. Over and above the presence of being in the Word of creation, God is present as Person, as *You* to humanity in the Word of address. And the term for this mutual presence of person? *Psyche.* It is of the utmost significance that in Greek "psyche" means not only "soul" but "life" as well. Psyche therefore means "soul-life," that is, the specific and peculiar yet mutual life of person. From language springs forth the psyche or "soul-life" of the human person—in direct response to the Word of address of the divine Speaker. Language itself, therefore, constitutes the spirit between God and humanity, and both witnesses to and manifests our life together. Person and language are one in the common psyche between God and humanity.

Bios represents God's life with nature, *psyche* God's life with humanity. And in their respective life-forms, the essence of nature and humanity are contained. Hence, bios *is* nature and psyche *is* humanity. Yet behold, the human person participates not only in the life of nature and in the life of language, but also in the life of God. Whereas in the two life-forms of creation, God could be said to be present to and in a kind of mutuality with nature and humanity, in the third life-form, humanity could be said to be participating in the life of God. The third and divine life-form is that of spirit, of *pnuema* proper. And the word for the mutual life of God? *Zoe.* In the Greek New Testament, *zoe* comes to mean the life of Spirit, God's own Way of Being. *Zoe* signifies the primal and ultimate life-form of pure mutuality and oneness, the eternal life of God, offered as salvation to humanity. *Zoe* is God's life of Love.

To be human, then, means to participate in three life-forms in accordance with the threefoldness of God and of the Word. From creation arises the life of bios, from revelation the life of psyche, and from redemption the life of zoe. That means, the human person consists of body, soul and spirit. And each dimension signifies a kind of mutuality and participation in a specific life-form. As body, the human person shares in the We of the presence of being, of law and substance, of physical time and space. As soul, the human person shares in the We of the presence of person, of language and liberty, of personal time and space. As spirit, the human person shares in the We of the presence of God, of love and grace, of the eternal present.

It must be emphasized that these three distinct spheres of mutuality, bios, psyche and zoe, have their life and unity in the one Word. They build upon and interpenetrate each other, like overlapping circles of being together. Thus the mutuality of bios is that of the presence of being, of overagainstness and externality, of the You and the It. The mutuality of psyche is that of the presence of word, of the I and the You, of internality. The mutuality of zoe is that of the presence of love and meaning, of the world between persons, of the We as such. Where bios constitutes the world of objectivity, and psyche the world of subjectivity, zoe represents the *union* of the two domains, of intersubjectivity, of "objective subjectivity" or "subjective objectivity," as it were. In German philosophy, these three worlds have been called the *Umwelt,* the *Eigenwelt* and the *Mitwelt,* respectively: the world around, within and between us. Together, they constitute the whole.

✠

Behold, the human condition: as psyche, we are caught or placed in between two open-ended seas of mutual life, bios and zoe. We are thus like a mysterious isthmus between the two, fragile and ever vulnerable to being overwhelmed by a flood from the one or the other. What then is our purpose but to unite the spheres in our own life, to participate in the unification of bios with and therefore consummation in zoe, in the life of God?

✠

The Three Modes of Love

To the three spheres of creation, the physical, the psychical and the spiritual, there correspond three relational life-forms, that of *bios, psyche* and *zoe*. And the three life-forms operate out of three respective modes of *love*. These three laws or principles of love are, in Greek: *eros, philia* and *agape. Eros* is the driving energy of love in and for the physical world, *philia* in and for the psychical world, and *agape* in and for the spiritual. The drive of eros is that of passion and desire, of need and want. It is the love's law of incompleteness seeking self-completion, preservation and gratification. Eros represents the powerful need to *receive* what one desires but does not have. Philia, however, signifies above all the psychic need to *share* what one is and seeks to be with other persons. Philia means friendship, mutuality and reciprocity. Agape, as the highest principle of love, is the profound need to *give* what one is and has to others. It thus represents benevolence and charity.

Each mode of love constitutes a kind of *union*: the unity of *receiving*, of *sharing* and of *giving*. *Self-receiving* is the end of eros and the love-principle of the physical world; *self-sharing* is the end of philia and the love-principle of the psychical world; *self-giving* is the end of agape and the love-principle of the spiritual world. What then is the pulsating urge of eros? *Attaining, becoming one*—that is, gaining actual physical union with what one seeks for self-completion, and sharing in the monologic of desire. The movement is from deprivation to fulfillment. What then is the driving power of philia? *Meeting, becoming whole*—that is, a concrete union of persons in dialogue, in a mutuality of physical and linguistic presence. The movement of philia is from partiality to wholeness, from isolation to the finding of oneself in and through the other. For apart from the You, the I has no true presence—of time or being.

What then is the élan vital of agape? *Abandonment, becoming holy*—a union of person with spirit through self-surrender. Agape signifies the total giving of oneself, not only to the other but to the relationship as well. It means the merging with the spirit of love itself, holding nothing back, but living entire in the holy sphere between the partners. The movement of agape is thus from wholeness to holiness, from attaining and having to a letting go, and in the giving of all, the gaining of All. For nothing is lost in agape; to die as mere individual is to be born anew in the shared Spirit-love of the holy ground of mutual life and being together. This is true Life; this is ultimate destiny.

Behold, the three dimensions are one, even as love is one. It is love itself which is an eternal receiving, sharing and giving, all revealed in the Word. The being of person is received in creation, shared in revelation and given in redemption. Eros is determined by the nature of what it lacks and the need thereof. Philia is determined by the nature of what it shares and discovers therein. Agape is determined by the nature of what it gives away and attains therewith. Oneness, wholeness and holiness, these are the respective ends of eros, philia and agape.

Music

How can we describe music without music itself being our guide? As with light, music is what music does. And also as with light, music reaches into all spheres of life; music pervades the body, the soul and the spirit. Music indeed brings about a unification of the three spheres; it harmonizes the law of the physical, the liberty and language of the psychical, with the love of the spiritual world. Universal in scope and impact, music is divine in origin, just as language and love. As such, it carries the physical over into the psychic and spiritual realms, and in its own unique life, grants a foretaste and even a form of their coming unification—that is, of the coming redemption.

The melody is the life of music, just as the whole is the life of the parts. Behold a paradox: the melody is both greater than the sum of the notes, yet each note adds a real and irreplaceable quality to the melody. Take out or change a note, and the whole is changed. Yet the life is the whole, the "melodic We," as it were, a reality greater than the notes, in which each takes its stand and has its existence. Melody is spirit; it is meaning and purpose for the parts.

Single notes are incomplete in themselves; they belong in a composition, a melodic We. They may, of course, be utilized in more than one melody. For the horizons of the notes are as endless as those of the melodies themselves. An analogy presents itself here: the human psyche, like the note, belongs in the We of a communal composition. And like the note, the person is not to be swallowed up but rather founded and fulfilled in the We. Further, neither the note nor the person can be simply identified with a particular melody or We, respectively, but lives in and through many such compositions. Yet the melody gives life to the note; just so, the We is the life of the I.

Music is thus a shared reality, a mysterious We, a totality wherein each member makes a contribution to the whole. And it draws us into itself not only as creators and participants, but as listeners and lovers of its life. Music begins as a spiritual form over against the composer, shared somehow by that person and the unseen presence of the original Composer behind it. It is for the human soul to accept and to resonate with it, and finally, to bring it across into the world.

And woe to those of us who are addressed by the singing heavenly sphere, but say No to bringing it across and sharing it with the world of humanity! What is such a life but a torment of unanswered call, of a hearing but refusing to respond. And what does that mean but a refusal to become the one God addressed us to be?

✠

Music originates in heaven and shall find its ultimate purpose and consummation there. As with the Word, music seeks to return to the sphere of its true belonging. But in the hell of this life, and the one that is to follow, there will be no music. Hell will not be silence but sound, over-much and never ceasing. Instead of harmony there will be discord, a cacophony instead of a symphony of voices. Voices—that will be the only sound, Everywhere will be echoed the disunified selfish sound of anger beyond resolution, the moaning anguish of despair unredeemably malevolent. The We of music has no place there. Hell is the abode for souls who have refused forever to be welded into the chorus of spirit. Hell is the end point of the rejection of mutuality.

THE PERSON

The Creative Address

In the beginning is the address: "Be You!" The human person comes into existence and attains being in the divine Word of address. The Eternal You addresses the human person into God's own "Youness." "Be You"—that means, "I grant You a likeness unto Myself by bestowing My own name on You, by calling You, *You*!" The image of God is the You with which God has addressed the human person. The image is therefore fundamentally linguistic: God's Word producing language in us. God speaks God's own personal name to and into us; we exist in and by virtue of God's own "personality." *Personality* signifies the *Who* of God as made manifest in the concrete peculiarity of the actual Speaking.

God speaks and behold, we are. And our very I is bestowed through the event of being addressed as You by God; for the I is the end point of the divine address, the content of the Word, the intended one. The I emerges at the precise moment when the You of address *hears,* and in hearing *turns to respond* to the One who calls. The human I is born of and in response to the divine Word-summons. Hence, the human I is essentially Word, not only utilizing language, but actually *being* language, belonging to God's own personal language.

The human person is created through address and response. That means: we arise through a primal relationship of mutual address. The mutuality is as real as the divine You and the human I. The mutuality of address is the sharing of presence and overagainstness, of externality and mystery. As such, it is a "unity-in-difference." For the response of the human person to the divine You is "I am." In hearing "Be You!", the human person responds with an unexpected and yet unanswered "I am!" And this "I am" initiates the second divine-human relationship, that of revelation. The human person goes in quest of the meaning and confirmation of being an I. And the human "I am," this earthbound response to the divine address, takes a whole life to utter. We answer God with our substance and daily existence. There is no other acceptable response or communicative shortcut.

To be a person, then, means to participate in all three dimensions of the primal speech-event. I am an addresser, addressed, and find my life and being in addressing, in the communicative spirit. That means: through the medium of language, I enter into the image and likeness of the threefold Person of God. I am at once an I who speaks, a You of address and a partner in a linguistic and ontic We.

✠

God not only addressed us in our creation. At the same time God *spoke* us: "*Be* You!" We are both subject and object to God, addressed as partner yet called into being as creature. I am therefore both gift to myself and task to be carried out, both complete and unfinished. The paradox and tension of my creation emerges precisely here in my simultaneous participation in the subjective and objective domains, in being both a who and a what, a person and a thing among other things. Only to be addressed by God would mean to participate exclusively in the Eternal I of God the Addressed; only to be spoken by God would mean to participate exclusively in the temporal It, the objective time-space cosmos of divine expression.

An unbridgeable gap opens wide here between the divine and the human persons, as indeed between the Creator and the creation itself. God may be addressed but never spoken. We cannot "speak" God as *objectum,* or in any sense contain God in our language—nor in our thoughts, dreams or even in our memories. Our memories may unshakably attest to the *that* of a past God-experience, but not the *Who* of the encounter. Our words may seem to point toward God, but without objectifying the One to whom we seek to refer. God may be sensed in the Speaking but not in the spoken. We may apprehend God directly as the One who addresses us, and as the One we address, and, in the "mystical" moment, as the mutual ground or context of our dialogue—that is, as the We of our dialectic.

✠

In our "addressibility" lies our divinity. And in our divinity lies our ability to be co-creative with God. For with God, we are also speakers, we are also agents of the Word. We are speakers in and through the same Word with which we have been addressed and have our existence. And the Word in us would speak to the One who uttered it. The Word lives restless in us until it can return to it's Source and true Home. And it would take us thither.

The Way back is through *response*. We are created to live before the Face, to *answer* God's creative address. Yet behold, the human condition has become the human predicament: we do not respond, we refuse to answer. We remain silent and hidden, even to the divine plea, "Where are You?" Why do we not answer? Why do we struggle so to restrain the Word within us from responding to its Source? The spirit of language gives us deep insight into this mysterious communication breakdown in the etymological relationship between answering and answering *for*, that is, between *responding* and *responsibility*. The latter two terms share the same Latin root: *respondere*, meaning to respond. To answer opens us or makes us liable to answer for. Conversely, where there is no response, responsibility may be denied.

Our response to God does indeed engender a climate for responsibility—first of all for our response itself. And responsibility leads to accountability, and accountability to the need to justify oneself. And when that need presents itself, who can stand before God without guilt? What hidden sin or fear, therefore, lies within us that so strongly resists self-disclosure? What fundamental weakness or selfishness abides in our hearts that turns from the offer of true life in order to escape the shared responsibility for it?

✠

The Psyche

The *psyche* is the person created by the Word of address, a being, therefore, of language. In the original Greek, *psyche* was derived from the verb *psychein*, meaning "to breathe, blow or cool." How significant is the spirit of language here! It is as if the psyche were the direct result of the "breath" of God in the actual event of creative address, thus the "cooled down" air—meaning also "pneuma" or spirit—of the Word itself.

The term "psyche" came to mean both "soul" and "life." Hence, it is our "soul-life"; it is the unique and non-repeatable person called into being through the direct action of God's Word. We both are and have only one "soul-life." If we deny or deface or prostitute or reject it, we can forfeit our very life and extinguish the light of personal being. "What does it profit a person to gain the whole world and lose their psyche?" Thus asked Jesus. Only by yielding our psyche to God and to the Kingdom of Heaven can we receive it for all eternity.

Each of us, as a psyche, manifests a peculiar soul-life, a unique élan vital or life-force, which leaves an imprint upon the souls of those we encounter, not unlike our fingerprints on a physical object. Indeed the uniqueness of our fingerprints, as well as our voices and other bodily aspects, are in fact signs and symbols of the unique psyche which is both our special gift from God, and our gift to each other.

We have been addressed by God; in that event our unique being emerges and finds its temporal and eternal foundation. In saying "You" to us as individuals, God has addressed us in the way we are to address God. In uttering "You," God bestowed on us a kind of divinity in God's own eyes, as it were. Thus, we belong to God's *"Family Spirit"*; our true home is God's heavenly mansion. Could we but see ourselves as God sees us in our creation, in the holy moment of our address, of our springing forth, our hearts imbued with the divine intention, the intention of who we are to become, we would be in awe of the wondrous way we have been formed. We would burn with the realization of the love with which we have been loved.

We are already whom God has called us to be, a gift to be unwrapped and developed. And until we actualize, until we bring to maturity, completeness, and "perfection" (teleios) that which God seeks from us, we will know no peace. For peace is a divine gift of standing in right relation to God. And it is offered when we move in the direction of God's will for us. We can receive the peace of God long before we have completed the work we are here to do, for peace is to guide us on the Way. And the whole of our life is a pilgrimage to the holy city. That awareness gives us peace, and a capacity to let go and let life be.

Yet those who fight God's intention, the call of creation, in truth war against their very soul-life. They are at odds with themselves, and live with an inescapable unrest and inner turmoil. They know only distress, depression and conflict—including the unresolvable conflict of whether to confront or to repress the conflict itself. For they violate the law of their own creation. And God's will is implanted within them as the inviolate law of their personal existence, there either to give life and direction, or to block, frustrate and strive to turn them from their self-defeating ways. Grace or estrangement, the choice is ours, and begins with our response to, our acceptance or rejection of our psyche.

✠

As we belong to the *Family Spirit* of God, so also are we birthed into a human "family spirit," a specific and unique mutuality and configuration of persons. While we are *created* in and for the eternal Family Spirit, we are *conditioned* by and *built* into this corporate human image of the divine reality. The human family cannot create the *psyche*; rather, it is for this spiritual body to confirm or to confound, to clarify or to confuse the self, the soul-life. Only the Spirit of God can create or re-create the soul-life of the human person.

The heart of redemption, therefore, is the renewing, the recreating, the reviving, the regeneration, and the transforming resurrection of our original creation. It is *this* creation, *this* psyche that is to be redeemed. For God's purposes do not change regarding the intention of our creation. The new creation is to be the old creation fulfilled. *This* soul-life was loved into being and *this* soul life shall be saved, made holy and perfect, completed and consummated—and all as this soul-life. The fingerprints will remain; the same voice will continue to address the Holy One as You.

✠

Person, Word and Spirit

What then is "personal being"? And in what sense can it be shared? It is the being who lives in and by virtue of primary relationships. The I first receives its concrete and peculiar life as an *actual presentness between* the I and the divine You of creative address. Then through specific meetings with the You of humanity, the givenness of the I comes to be revealed once again as a presentness between the I and the You. Revelation emerges from mutuality. Only subsequently does the I *internalize* what has been revealed in the common ground of meeting. "Self-image" arises as the partly perceptual, partly conceptual picture the I constructs of its own nature and place in the world of humanity. Self-concept is therefore mediated by otherness; it is refracted through the prism of the perceived response of the one over against it.

Mutuality is thus the ground of person, in and through which the I attains self-consciousness, understanding and actualization. In the beginning is the relationship: the I and the You individuate on the basis of primal relationality, of the creative We. The We is the ground and the life of the I and the You—not the converse, as if the I and the You first entered into the We rather than emerged from it. The I and the You do not exist as such prior to the event of the We. It is the We which is the home and guarantor of the personal being of the I and the You. Personal uniqueness has its root in commonality; only in the mutuality of love may the univocality of the individual be finally seen and affirmed and confirmed. Only love can tell us who we are.

Person and Word are one. We come into existence in and through Word; our true life is that of address and response. Beneath the I is the "You-Word" of address, the ground of which is in turn the "We-Spirit" of creation. As persons we do not just *have* language, but we *are* language, and must speak in order to live and to know who we are. "Speak that I may see You! Let the word which lies on your heart be voiced that I may know You—that we may know You." Word is of our essence and substance; and word is spirit. And Spirit is eternal relationship, the eternal We.

Person is the agent of speech. How then can "person" be defined? For the person does the defining and cannot therefore be equated with the definition. And what is "definition" but an instance of address and response, a form of dialogue? The agreed upon meaning of a word *is* its meaning and life. Its *use* in a "language game" *is* its substance, emerging from and ever dependent upon the common context of those who live in that language. Thus, definition and meaning are intrinsically mutual and belong to the sphere of spirit. The common, the *koinonia* determines the meaning and substance of language. And the agreed upon definition includes as well the meaning of being a person. For all definitions stand upon the threefold "personality" of speech events: speaker, spoken and spoken to. Yet, "person" is not really "in" the content of any definition, but is rather shared among the definers.

Word is of person and person is of word. The syntax of language is of the very logic—logos—of person. Behold, the person is the soul of language, as it were, and language the body of spirit, and spirit in turn the life and meaning of language. Language is to spirit as figure is to ground, or as notation and score to the music and the performance thereof. Person, language and spirit are one.

Is language, then, public or private? It is both. It is a shared dialectic between us. An innate structure is given on the biological level through creation, an inbuilt syntactical-linguistic pattern, a "protolanguage without words," a psychic code of dialogue arising from yet transcending the physical code of monologue. This innate capacity is activated by the inbreaking spirit-language of a people as mediated through the family of origin. As law is an operational given on the physical level, so language is a given on the psychical. The creative use of language presupposes its givenness from a common source. Language is a shared fact before it is appropriated by the individual. And it is assimilated as a shared reality, as the common life itself. Meaning is a common, a given before being modified by the unique perspective of the individual. And if the new meaning diverges too far from the common use, communication breaks down. Your meaning and my meaning emerge out of our meaning. And the thread of our meaning must be maintained at all costs. For a breakdown in communication can eventuate in a rending asunder of the common world of humanity itself.

✠

The Spirit is the "yet-to-be-spoken," but present and meant. The dynamic life of God is One-in-Three: Speaker, Speaking and Spoken to. Hence, when Spirit is finally spoken, it shall be revealed to be one with the Word, the Word which is also one with the Speaker. Further, the life of Spirit, even before it becomes Word, exists dialectically already within the Word. In the one Word of creation the past event of the Creator speaking can still be sensed—much like the original sound of the "big bang," of the actual moment of the creation of the universe can still be heard by means of a proper receiving instrument. So also the future event of the speaking of Spirit is already present in both the Word of creation and the Word of revelation. And the life of Spirit is unfolding through creation and revelation, all in anticipation of the coming consummation. That which is yet to be spoken lives dialectically in the Word of revelation which is now being spoken; the Person and the Spirit of the Speaker abide in the one Word. Behold, the past and the future meet in the dialogue of today.

Language participates in this union of time, for the roots of language extend deeply into the mysterious and living ground of its past and history, the extraordinary process of its syntactical solidification—not unlike the solidification of the earth from molten lava, so that the life already present within in it as intention and seed, as purpose and goal, could begin to actualize itself, could finally carry out the divine mandate, the law of its creation. Further, the language event of revelation presages and anticipates and begins to manifest the presence of the lingusitic future in all its apparent novelty and unexpected turning. In language abides the key to creation—past, present and future. For the Word is the same yesterday, today and forever.

✠

God as eternal You is "panenthetic" to divine speech, be it of address or of creation. That is, God is both transcendent and immanent to the Word. Though participating in, God cannot be identified with that which God utters. The human person, however, is born in and through the Word of address. The person is therefore tied forever to the Word, to divine and subsequently to human language. For the being of the human person is directly consequent to the Word. The same cannot be said of the Person of God, however. The reality of the Speaker is prior to the Word. This engenders an eternal distinction between the divine and human persons, a chasm never to be crossed. The Word issues from the divine Person and forms the eternal basis of the human person. The human does not exist as person apart from the logos, from the

Word of creative address. The same cannot be said of the Source of the Word. The You of the Addresser can never be penetrated, nor the "inner life" comprehended. The Mystery ever abides, though the Presence ever pervades.

Yet behold, the human person was addressed as "You." In that address something unspeakable was passed, something conveyed by but not contained within the address itself. The "something more" of humanity is the You we share. It is not a possession of the I, but a kind of "divinity of addressability" constitutive of all persons. The human You, just as the divine is "panenthetic" to the Word, and to language itself. The human You, just as the divine, is to be addressed but not expressed.

✠

The word both denotes and connotes. Strictly speaking, the spirit is never the denotation but ever the connotation of the word. That is, the spirit is the common ground of speech, the joint context of meaning, the "Sitz im Leben" or setting-in-life of word. That which comes to be denoted of the spirit, comes to belong to the word itself. Hence, that of the spirit which comes into the word, into the denotative sphere of objective existence, in a real way ceases to be of the spirit. For the spirit abides free of the objectum of the word, free from the attention and constraints inherent in delimitation. The spirit is rather the not-yet-spoken but present—yesterday, today and tomorrow. And it is present not only consciously but unconsciously; thus, its presence may be discovered subsequent to the actual event of its life. The spirit of the word is the ground of the past, the life of the present and the promise of the future—all the while unspoken. The spirit, in brief, bestows life and meaning to persons and to the word, yet remains the unexpressed basis of both.

Love is a spirit. That means: love is the ultimate co-notation between persons, not the denotation. Whatever is lifted up into the word between the I and the You becomes the joint property of their relationship, their history, a kind of mutual objectum which may serve as the covenantal basis of their accountability. And though the spirit may continue to honor that of itself now objectified, the mutual objectum is no longer of the spirit. For the spirit is not a being of the past but of the future, the future present as unseen kingdom now.

The Grammar of Person

The essential triplicity of person is revealed by and one with the Word. Hence, the syntax of language manifests the "mutual arrangement" of persons. The etymology of the terms "grammar" and "syntax" is instructive here. Grammar comes from the Greek *gramma*, which means "something written, letter," and from *graphein*, meaning "to write." Syntax comes from the Greek *suntaxis*, meaning "to order together," and from *suntassein*, derived from *sun*, "together," and *tassein*, "to arrange," thus meaning "to arrange together."

The threefold "arrangement" of persons is carried over into the grammar of the Word itself. Or should we say that the grammar of the Word determines the "arrangement" of persons? In either event, the threefoldness of person appears in two grammatical contexts: the pronouns of I, You and We, and the first, second and third persons of speech. In the latter case, the first person represents the speaker, the second the addressed, and the third that which is spoken.

Yet behold, the threefoldness of persons is divided by an essential and in-built twofoldness: singular and plural. How is this to be reconciled with the triplicity of persons, human and divine? In the following way: human language is grounded on the twofold Word of creation and revelation, which gives rise to externality and internality respectively. Thus do the one and the many come into ontic and linguistic being, the either/or of existence—including the either/or of dialogue itself. *Human language comes into being in response to creation and to revelatory address.* It can say only what is implanted within it and subsequently emerges as response to those two Word-events. Creation is first the Word spoken by God: "Be"; and then, in the human situation, the Word spoken followed by the Word of address: "Be You." The external world was therein completed, as language attests: he, she, it, they, and You. The Word of revelation brought forth the internal "I am" of the first person singular, and, in keeping with the whole of the syntactical arrangement given from the very beginning, the first person plural.

The third Word-event, that of redemption, is yet to be spoken. Thus, *language cannot say what has not yet been spoken and revealed from above.* Language, which lives in response to the divine Word, cannot pre-empt God. Externality and internality are given unto it, but not mutuality. Hence, the either/or division of the singular and the plural may be clearly stated, but not yet the paradoxical both/and of true mutuality. Inasmuch as the whole is given from the beginning, however, mutuality is already built into language, though in a proleptic manner. For the logos has granted to human syntax a beginning recognition of mutuality through the pronoun We and the corresponding category of the first person plural.

The We is present in the human word. But the human mentality is still not sure what to do with it grammatically! For the We receives the same verb as the second and third persons plural, as if to say that all three belong to the same sphere of being, namely that of externality. And the verb is the action word! Hence, the We is judged to face and operate upon the world in the same way as the second and third plural persons. The We should indeed be in the plural category, for it involves more than one person or thing. Yet the We is both plural and singular; it is the plural-singular, the more-than-one one. Both the I and the You participate equally in the grammatical We, for it refers to the mutuality of the one with the other. And further, by the intent and action of the speaker, the We can be inclusive of all the other categories of person, singular and plural. One may state "We" with grammatical correctness regarding whatever one includes with one's personal being. Does grammatical legitimacy betoken ontological reality?

The either/or dialogic of language is yet to discern the both/and dialectic of the final upcoming Word-event, the "We Are" of redemption. And note carefully that I cannot even say the Word of redemption without using the "are," the general plural form of the verb to be! Hence, I cannot at present verbally impute to the We the unique status it deserves. In short and for now, language may create and reveal, but it is not yet empowered to save. It may bring healing to creation—our creation—through the right word of revelation and of love at the right time, but it is not yet prepared to bear the life of redemption.

Yet behold, to say "I love you" is to anticipate redemption. And how the spirit of language groans in travail to give birth to its final word!

✠

If one should ask here why the first person I, emerging from revelation, grammatically precedes the second and third persons, emerging from the prior creation, let this be said. It is only revelation which affords the apprehension of creation. That is, the knowledge of creation is given as a part of the revelation itself. Hence, the first person also represents the first awakening to the whole of reality.

✠

French has its "Tu," and German its "Du," but modern English has lost something precious and irreplaceable in the dropping of its distinctive second person singular pronoun "Thou." The one plural You, along with its plural verb forms, also serves for the second person singular. That I must address You as *You*, rather than as *Thou*, means that the language no longer recognizes a special relational state of affairs between me and Thee, as it were, no longer grants You a special mode of existence to me—as my Thou. It means I cannot actually bring to word your singleness and exclusiveness to me, your intimacy and inclusiveness with me.

What have we done here but relinquish back to the spirit, to "connotation," that which had already been attained by the word, by "denotation"? In saying You, I may intend and mean "Thou," but the word of address that I must use is nevertheless the plural form. And the verb form must also be plural: even your actions and being must be plural, O Thou of my life! Forgive me if I cannot say You, or grant You the special status You deserve. Our "co-notation" alone must suffice.

Along with the loss of the intimate Thou, English has also lost the associated verb forms. A special case is that of the verb "to be." To the "I am," the spirit of language responded with the second personal singular "Thou art." "Am" and "art" are etymologically related, as if the spirit of language were trying to hold the two realities together as special, and to distinguish them from the "is" and the "are" conjugations of the other persons of the present tense.

How did we come to this linguistic forshortening? What does it mean for the spirit of our common language? If the abandonment of the intimate form of address can be demonstrated to be associated with the rise of the modern state, with the English industrial revolution, thus with the birth of big business and factories, what would it portend to our civilization? That the individual Thou has given way to the group

You, that the I therefore must relate to all "Yous" alike, that private and intimate communion no longer has a linguistic acceptability? Is this not a primary example of the depersonalization that came in the wake of the birth of "industrial man"? The spirit of what we are doing to ourselves is manifested in our language. For language not only reveals who we are, but it also bespeaks our actions to and against each other.

✠

Word as Medium of Person

How, then, is a person revealed and communicated? Most intimately and profoundly through language and touch. The objective existence of a person as person abides in language and body, in word and substance. In a sense, word is the substance of meaning and personal being, just as body is the substance of matter and physical being. And just as our body puts us into the cosmos of time and space, so our language bespeaks our existence in the spiritual cosmos of meaning and person.

The word is the medium not only of the I and the You, but also of the We, the relationship as such. Language, spoken and written, constitutes a living and growing spiritual home for the human person, which houses our history, present being and destiny. Whether through personal letters or Holy Scriptures, the written word reveals and maintains an ongoing kind of presence of the life of the I, the You and the We. The written word, like the celluloid frame of the motion picture, captures something real and lasting of the life of concrete persons at specific points in their—and our— history. It holds something of the essence of our past and the promise of our future.

Yet the written word has no present life unless and until it becomes the medium of communication through being read. The author and the persons depicted can again come to life and again affect history via the entrance of the reader into the word. The word again gains presence, again becomes the ground of meeting and mutuality. Whether the author or the characters are alive or dead, the meeting can be real nonetheless—and in a way even reciprocal. It is reciprocal in terms of the seeming presence of the writer of the word to the reader, and in the former's clear anticipation of being read and therein encountered. Thus might one ponder, "She wrote this intending it to be read. Therefore she continues to exist and to exercise influence and presence in the world. As this word lives for me, just so does she live again to and for me."

Granted that the reciprocity cannot not be said to cross over the grave, as if the author were somehow transported to meet the reader as the reader is meeting the author. Granted that the sense of reciprocity emerges only from the side of the reader. Nevertheless, the mutuality is experienced as real *in the word itself,* like an unshakable awareness that "someone is talking to *me*!" Such is the power of the word: the sense of address abides, and with it the lingering intuition of the presence of the author.

The author continues to exist in the word. The person in their uniqueness and concreteness is captured and meetable in and through their words. And in the presence of the person in the word, the author's unexpressed but still present spirit is sensed as well, opening up ever new possibilities for meeting and insight. New horizons of meaning ever await discovery in the word; for the written word—and our relationship thereto—is greater than any one reading. And as we change, new meanings and shadings appear before us. Did then the author intend this new meaning all along, and was I just too blind to see it? What else awaits me in this word and from this author, which I am not yet ready to see?

I pick up and read one of my Mother's letters to me. And behold, though she is now dead she addresses me afresh; she lives again in her words. Further, *We* live again, and the memory of the meaning of our relationship surfaces and time is filled with her and Us, and the past opens again and mingles with the present. Though I have changed since last we met, she has not. She comes at me with the same old familiar patter of hope and good will, of idealistic longings and mundane doings. Yet as I read on in my changed mentality, I see her more clearly and from new vantage points. Hence, even in her death the relationship continues to evolve.

Death has no dominion after all. Through the word we can and do encounter the dead as among the living, and our relationships with them change as we ourselves age, as we ourselves draw ever nearer to their abode of the final relational summing up. And my Mother's letters constitute a testament, a witness of her and of Us, as well as a promise of a love not yet finished. Heaven is love's consummation. Nothing is really finished here and therefore nothing must be forgotten, for we do not yet see what has the greatest importance, nor do we know what we may need and when. Let us therefore be packrats of love, holding tightly to the memories of those moments of truth and beauty, of meaning and substance. Forget nothing; the truth is the whole; the story is the thing.

My Mother, though dead, lives on in her letters. She awaits me there, and at my convenience, for fresh encounters and new insights into her, myself—and Us. It will have to do until tomorrow brings whatever promises the heart cleaves to as its inmost secret, which may not be spoken in this life, but only believed—and lived.

Enter the Bible. Is it a dead or a living Book? Is it word or Word? It is both. Yet in and through it we may meet the Eternal You, I and We, as well as ourselves in our true nature. The Person of God lives therein, just as the human person lives in their written word. The written word can at any time and at any point become the vehicle for God's self-revelation; the written word can become the Word of divine address, the Word which seeks and finds and speaks to *me* here and now, right where I am, as if it were being spoken for the first time—which it is, for me at least.

Behold, I have heard the Voice of the Book. Now the We of the Bible includes me, and my story has become enmeshed in its unfolding drama. Its future is now my future. The whole of my existence is at stake in its vision and promise.

The Bible is sacred not because it tells us *about* God, but because it may at any time become for us the actual medium of the revelation *of* God; it may speak to You and to me as the Word meant for us, here and now, the Word of grace and truth, mercy and justice, healing and salvation. The Bible is the ever ready firewood for the revelation of the heat and the light of God's life among us. It is at one with the Spirit of God, just as it is one with the spirit of humanity.

THE PHYSICAL WE

Naming

In the beginning is the Word. That means: in the beginning is the Address. And that means: in the beginning is the *Naming*. For the address of God is a concrete act of naming, of intending, of designating and delineating. In divine intention, the name depicts the reality: the name or word is at one with the soul-life or psyche which the Word of address brings into existence. God's name in creation *is* the center and ground of the human I. The Word of creation for each individual human person is, "Be You ______." The name given therein by God is thus linked forever with the You of God's address. That is, to participate in the unique You of God, requires as well the designation of a *unique name* over and above the holy pronoun. For You are *You*, not just an instance of some universal and higher order "You-ness."

Personal being is that specific being named in a concrete act of creative address, which the name itself represents. Each person, precisely in their unique name—known only to God—, signifies an actual moment in the life of God, the event of that single address, of God speaking God's personal name to and for another. For God did not simply speak the name for humanity, and behold, we were. Rather, God addresses each human person individually in the event of their own specific creation. Being made in the image of God means being addressed in singularity.

The meaning of the call to be, the specific intention of the Eternal You who created us, resides within the name with which we were originally addressed. Personal being is named being. We are more than a mere "You" or an "I." I *am "Hal."* I am the *who* that I am. Being is named; naming is being. We are to be addressed not only by the generic pronoun, which though applying equally to all does not bespeak our singularity, our non-repeatable concreteness; we are to be addressed by our "proper" name. Granted, Hal is itself a generic or common proper name. Nevertheless, it represents both the *way* in which I may be addressed precisely in my singularity, and the *reality* of my unique personal being. The name attests to my individual sovereignty, to my identity and status as a irreplaceable whole number, as it were, my irreducible existence as a personal agent.

The fact of my personal existence as a named and non-repeatable individual, when juxtaposed with the same conditions of existence for every other person, undercuts the legitimacy of the purported universality of human "types" and "categories" as espoused by psychology and philosophy. The "meta-soul" and metaphysics of their vision is a conceptual fiction. In brief, *person transcends schematic representation; ultimate truth is the Who rather than the what, Person not principle.* Person is the seer rather than the seen, save in true relationships of mutual seeing.

✠

As the "physical We" stands as the actual basis of the physical existence of the person, who comes into being via a "unique union," so also the "psychical We" of the family constitutes the ground of the personal existence of the I. And where the monologic of law dictates the physical product of the former We, the dialogic of language affords the latter We the extraordinary freedom of establishing the context of meaning within which the child will grow and from which attain personal identity. The linguistic basis of the psychical We of the family is to be seen first of all through the process of naming. In being named, the child becomes intended by the family, and enters into an already prepared specific psychic place of meaning in the family structure. The giving of the name also signifies that the child is intended to exist fully in the family spirit. That means to be physically and linguistically present and available; it means to be open to and drawn out by and into the concrete language system of that family unit. The We of language seeks to bring the I of the named person into the "word-spirit" of their mutuality, there to be found and to find being.

Naming is therefore a coercive invitation to a sharing of life and identity in a unique family of origin. And to the intention of God in the creative address of naming must be added the human concomitant of family naming and intending. The two names and structures of intention are not the same. And the disparity between the divine and the human modes of address represents the tension between creation and history.

✠

Love of the Body

The love of the body begins with the love of the Mother's body, the flesh from which one issues. It begins as need for sustenance and nurture, for continued union and intimacy, for pure symbiosis. Absence from her and cyclical need fuel longing, and longing awakens self-awareness. Mother's nearness in its intense totality overwhelms the infant and bonds permanently the one to the other. Her voice, her arms and swaying motions, her breasts, her face ever changing and ever alive with response-eliciting expressions, calling, summoning her little one into the fullness of personal life— these are elements of the infant's need-filled vision of the nurturing other. It is the Yes of the Mother that initiates the Yes of the child to its own personal being in the world, the Yes to being flesh, finite and vulnerable, the Yes to belonging to nature before history. It is Mother's embracing body, her flesh itself, which establishes the context of the corporeal environment of the child, which grants the permission for the child to embrace its own body, to cherish and to trust and to accept its own flesh, its own personal material world.

The We of the Mother-child, their mutuality of the flesh, is the ground of all subsequent self-acceptance. For first the body must be accepted, then the soul, and then the spirit. First the *It* of me, my body is to be loved—by virtue of the You of the Mother, then the *I* of me, my soul, then the *You* of me, that is, who I am in my relationships with others. And in each case, the feelings and prejudices about the one transfer over to the other. So the Yes—or the No—to the body becomes the primal ground of the self-image. If my body has been rejected, I feel rejected as a person, as an I. And if I experience myself as a rejected person, I carry that inner vision of self into all my relationships; it colors all my perceptions of how others see me. It can effectively block my capacity to enter into true relationships, to be the You to another.

✠

I experience my body, an object among the world of objects. I am aware of its being, in terms of both its time/space orientation in the physical world, and the presence of its inner psychic life. From hunger to satiation, from pain to pleasure, I am awe-fully alive to its pulsing extremities and exigencies. I exist in consciousness of its life amidst all other life, of its mortal frailty and certain end along with all other perishables. My body belongs here, and here it shall remain through endless metamorphoses.

O body mine—you are not mine but only borrowed for a duration and a space,before you shall return to the soil, there to be divested of the organic unity I now love and totally rely upon second by second. In the earth of your origin you will slowly yet thoroughly—and with utter ruthlessness—be reabsorbed for new purposes I shall never know. And nothing will you lose of my earth, O earth! How I cherish you, O body mine!

O body mine—mine yet not mine, possessed yet shared, serving my will yet with a will of your own, a perfect servant yet absolute master, under yet beyond my control—O body mine! You listen to me, yet constantly seem to being trying to teach me to hear and understand you. O body mine—an unbending lawfulness exists in you, one not of my own creation or will, but one I must accommodate.

Your lawfulness speaks by presenting itself as it is, and without apology: feed me, rest me, work me, love me, accept me, don't fight me, don't overtax me, don't abuse or misuse me. In truth, my body addresses me with the same Word of law all other bodies pronounce in the actuality of their being. For the Word of the law is common to all. The Word of the body is ever a third person Word, be it singular or plural. It is no respecter of persons. The Word of the body is not language but life in concrete and differentiated facticity. It is a givenness which may be discerned but must be accommodated. For the body knows only monologue, and must be accepted on its own terms.

✠

Desire

In the beginning is the desire. We meet and I behold arousing mystery in You. In your eyes and motion near me, in your voice patterns and gestures of soft appeal, in your need leaning toward me and inviting me to be its end point of desire and fulfillment, in all that I see and sense in You, I am breathlessly pleased. Behold, in me is mirrored what I find in You, and in being shared is permitted to be. From whence originated that desire, from me or from You? Whose eyes first met those of the other? Who aroused whom in yet unspoken passion? The way in cannot be reconstructed, nor does it really matter once the sphere of desire has been entered.

Something now lives between us. We share something of great power over which we could lose control, even if only for a time and with the silent and releasing Yes of our wills. Desire is a dance between You and I; I watch it dance in You and You move to its rhythmic and passionate life. In my silent embodiedness, now blessed, I move with You; I enjoy You and in joy keep pace with the beat We share. The word of this dance, this eros: "Be together, join each other, know and share me. Fear me not, for I am life-bearing and gratifying. I am your release, the fulfillment of your being here." And its word is its law. It does what it is. It is the grand monologue of creation: "Be fruitful and multiply."

Eros, this daimon of passion and desire, both frees and enslaves us. It frees a life in us and even calls it into existence. Yet eros lays claim to that life, and would bind us to itself. Eros is thus the unifying drive of bios, of the relational life of the physical world. It summons forth the sexual being-together of the *physical We*.

The Common and the Unique

The common is the ground of the unique. The common is the background, the unseen, the presupposed, the passed over, the all too often neglected and undervalued. The common is the glue which holds the parts together, the life not grasped but grasping, not held but holding, not sustained but sustaining. And even if we were to lift up the common as our perceptual figure, yet another dimension of the common would either become or remain the unexamined ground upon which we rest. For the common is as the blood which quietly and unobtrusively feeds the whole in all the latter's multiplexity. It is as the air we breathe, which though unnoticed cannot be lived without, even for a brief period of time. The common for the spirit: love; for the soul: language; for the body: air, food, water and all that the physical world requires for our continuing participation in its We.

The physical world has been wonderfully designed as the place to meet and to share being. All true life is sharing; all true life is mutual and corporate. It is a being together in which individual life is loved in corporate reality. And the life of the corporate sustains and cherishes the individual lives within it. The life of the whole grants purpose to the individual life, and each gifts the other—like music wherein the whole gifts the parts and the parts enrich the whole. In music, each instrument and section exists for the sake of the whole, and for the life of the music as such. Yet the individual is not to be swallowed up by and into the whole, as if the music were to become only a single voice without essential differentiations. Rather, the specific instruments actually have their life *in* the whole, which needs, recognizes and affirms each piece and note for the sake of the completeness and consummation of its life, of its melody. The whole is one in the parts; the parts find their life and purpose and justification in the whole.

The biological structures of being exist for the sake of the whole. Function determines structure; structure manifests function. The part belongs to the whole; it receives its life from the whole, and has a specific function to perform for the life of the whole. If the part does not fulfill this function, the function will most likely not be carried out, and the being as a whole entity will suffer. The context of the uniqueness of the part is its place or role or function for the life of the whole, as determined by its nature. The ground and ultimate meaning of individual "essence" is to be found in the life of the whole.

Which then comes first, the structure or the function? They arise together for the life of the "common one," when it is the proper time or *kairos*. Law and implementation are one.

✠

Life only begins at the beginning. Each human person began as a single cell. From oneness and singularity emerged multiplexity and diversity; from the "common one" came forth multiple individuation and relational uniqueness. Cell division presupposes a common law or physico-linguistic material entity which both directs the process and remains intact in the newly emerging structures of being. The whole abides in the parts; the common determines the differentiations. This encoded agent of organic development represents a kind of "We" as regards the common "orders" of a single vision for the parts and organs composing the concrete individual body. The parts develop by virtue of the operative presence of the essence of the whole within it. From the one came the many; and the one remains undivided in and as gift to the many.

We think in terms of unique individuals. Yet in the biological sphere the uniqueness of the individual has its basis in the specific act of a physical We. And the sexual encounter, though repeatable as regards human need and capacity, cannot again replicate the exact same combination of chromosomes given by both participants in the one event. Thus, the biologically unique individual is determined by the biologically unique We of reproduction. In the beginning is the We.

✠

Exclusion and Inclusion

All relational events in the spheres of nature and humanity, of physis and psyche, are twofold in accordance with the twofoldness of the Word of creation. That is, creation is twofold: the spoken and the addressed, the It and the You. Hence, all relationships participate in one or the other mode of the logos, of language—and therefore of being itself. The same relational event can incorporate both dimensions of being-together, *but not at the same time.* The I cannot both address the other as You and speak the other as It in the same word-event. We are either object or subject to the other person or being, either an It or a You. And if the other is subject or You to me, then I am a subject or I to the other. For the I lives as I only in the word of address to the other as You; in the spoken world of It, the I exists, but only as an It among other objects, only within the monologue of nature. Apart from the You, the dialogue of the psyche has no present, thus no true existence. Speaker to speaker anticipates a linguistic person to person response; speaker to spoken can expect no linguistic reciprocity, but only biological continuance in the realm of objects. Person as person does not exist in the objective sphere of creation.

A true bifurcation exists here: the relationship is either one of *exclusion* or *inclusion,* of externality or internality. In the subject to object or *"I-It" relation,* the being of the participants is exclusive, external or extrinsic to each other—and to the relationship itself. In the subject to subject or *"I-You" relation,* however, the being of the participants is inclusive, internal or intrinsic to each other, and to the relationship itself. In the former, the being of the participants is "incidental," in the latter "coincidental"—that is, "co-insidental"—to the relationship itself.

The exclusion-inclusion bifurcation may be seen from three vantage points, namely from that of the two participants and from the relationship itself—from the I, the You and the We. Thus, the speaker can address the other as You and intend mutuality, or as It and intend exclusivity. And the addressed can hear the addresser as you or as it, that is, can either step into an inclusive relationship in response or exclude or deflect the address, and therein "mis-hear" the other as a kind of "speaking object," as a being continuous with the world of things. In the latter case, the one addressed in effect negates their own I by negating the You of address.

From the vantage point of the relationship itself, the participants are either inclusive or exclusive to each other, thus, either one in mutuality or two in externality. Even if one or the other of the partners seeks and opens to a relationship of inclusion, it cannot happen without the *will* of the other and the mysterious *grace* of the Spirit between them. The We of inclusivity is thus the We of Spirit, of mutuality and intersubjectivity, the We of being-together. The We of exclusivity is thus the We of being-apart. The latter is a relationship of We in that the participants are *mutually exclusive* to each other, as it were. Inclusivity requires *two* or more subjects in lived mutuality. Exclusivity means only *one* subject, be it that of the addresser or the addressed. For if the I shares inclusively with the You who does not hear, only one subject is relating. And then in effect the internal world of the person is thrown open to the external world, and back upon the one who sought to share as an object of rejection. Personal being offered but not heard or accepted in mutual sharing and subjectivity comes back upon the speaker as a rejected and now objective self. Refused as subject, the I returns as object, as before the me." And in the exclusive mode of existence, no bridge spans the gap between the internal and external worlds.

In the We of inclusion, the being of the participants is *between* them, intrinsic to the relationship itself. In the We of exclusion, the locus of being is not between but outside the relationship, either within the subject or apprehended as within the object—and possibly in an alternating manner. In the We of inclusion, the being of the persons actually lives within the relation, whereas in the We of exclusion, the personal being of the participants lives always on the outside of what is unfolding, be it as observer or as the object acted upon. In the case of exclusion, the person is "self-conscious" and/or "object-aware"; in the case of inclusion, however, the person is "You-aware," and is thus both lost to self and found by, in and with the other.

✠

Is there then a *"will to inclusivity"*? A will for mutuality and common life? Is there not an inner intention of the heart to love and to be loved? In that intention lies the will to inclusivity. The will precedes any action and is the directional guide for the stepping forth into the common life of the We. The will to include has the goal or *telos* of becoming more than singular, of broadening the base of one's being to include the personal being of another within the boundaries drawn by the spontaneous fingers of sharing and commonality. It means to desire living together in the common world *between* the partners. It is a *willingness* to live with and for the other.

If there is a will to inclusivity, there is a corresponding *"will to exclusivity."* It is the *willfulness* to live for the self. And the will for the life of the *We* is in conflict with the will for the life of the *me,* of self-serving. It must be emphasized that the latter is not to be identified with the "will for self-preservation," for that profound intent in creation is incorporated into the striving for both inclusivity and exclusivity, on the one hand, and may be abrogated by the sacrificial commitment to the life of another and their relationship.

"To be together or alone, that is the question! To find my life in something greater than myself, or within myself, to give or to take life." This is the fundamental issue upon which the whole of life hinges. Salvation or self-destruction depends directly upon the resolution of this great though internal battle of the will. The history of humanity is at stake in this, the deepest struggle of the heart.

✠

The We of Nature

The We, in all three of its spheres, the physical, the psychical and the spiritual, comes into being through the Word. That is: *the We emerges in and through address and response.* The We *is* the *mutuality* of address and response. Is it possible then for the human person to have a We relationship with another form of physical life? If so, in what sense and with which phyla? From the perspective of the human person, a We of nature can be very real indeed. The key to the relationship happening is the experience or sense of the *mutual movement of being toward inclusivity in the sphere of the between,* through the reciprocity of address and response.

This can involve the inorganic as well as the organic dimensions of nature. For I may experience in a powerful way the address of a mountain, for instance, and may respond directly to it with awe and the intake of air, as if to breathe in its grandeur. Yet is there an actual mutual movement of being in this human perception of address and response? Is there not a genuine kind of meeting of being, my person interfaced with the unyielding hardened height of the mountain on the path of my life? Though the mountain may become in this encounter a kind of You to me, in that my person both addresses and is addressed seemingly directly, I cannot likewise become a You to the mountain. Yet from my vantage point, the encounter was real and the effects on my person lasting. My personal being has been inclusive with that of the mountain. What else could this mean but that We have shared in the mystery of the one Word of creation?

In the organic dimension of nature, however, there may indeed be a mutual movement of being toward inclusion, toward a living We. I may address a tree or flower and sense responsiveness to my touch and even to my voice. The strain toward dialogue here is real, if unsuccessful. This is a dialogue of being, a mutuality of the language of God rather than of humanity proper. That is, it is a dialogue of Word but not yet of word, of creation unable to awaken to the revelation of what it is—just as we are to awaken to the revelation of who we are. For that awakening would signify the transformation of monologue into dialogue. And who knows but that that is our very mission to nature. We are to "name" nature; and to name means to invite into the reciprocity of the Word. For naming means addressing; and addressing calls forth response.

Hence, the human encounter with organic nature—to which the human also belongs through creation—is a dialogue of law with freedom, of the physical givenness with the psychical givingness. Novelty is the result, and a new kind of history emerges: that of our life with nature. And what hath humanity wrought!

✠

Is there not a dialogue of language as well as of being operative in the case of humanity and its "pets"? What about the We between us and those higher forms of life that have adopted us and been adopted by us for various purposes over the millennia? It is when we address a pet that the being of nature sits up and begs, as it were! The pet can understand some words and make some fundamental associations between words and events. And the pet can bark or purr in need and response—a kind of language, hence a kind of "person" moving toward a real mutuality of being. And a genuine love can exist between a person and their pet, with a history and learned set of mutual expectations.

How then is this We of nature to be explained? The We utilizes but cannot be identified with language. And the levels of understanding and of personhood between the human and the pet are dramatically different. The difference between the human person and the pet, yet at the same time the similarity between their We and that of God and humanity, can be seen thus: as God addressed us out of creation, granting us the status of person in and through that address of Word, so we have in turn—and in accordance with the image of God—addressed our biological friends into the linguistic orb of our personal life. It is thus not God who addressed the animal in creation; it is the human person—who lives in the paradox of speaking as God while also being as creature among other creatures. We have created the "pet"—and through the word. Therein is our common life together. And therein have we "redeemed" nature.

✠

A We of nature: my cat jumps on my lap, as he always does in the early morning, just when I want to read the paper. A Siamese, small in stature but beautiful in form and touch, and in demeanor gentle, playful and attentive to everything around him. Without words, he addresses me nonetheless, for I know what he seeks. I even feel his little body shaking for it with a delightful sensuousness: to be caressed and stroked and loved with my hands and voice and the nearness of my being. He responds to my action with purring, his low and firm roar bringing comfort and joy to my heart. And at times he puts his wet nose softly against my chin—sometimes getting carried away and nipping me in misguided passion. And his remarkable blue eyes! They actually seem to see me and with an earnestness, as if he were trying to understand me, and to let me know how very much this moment means to him, this time of intimacy. We stare at each other in mutual address and response. All is well, here at least.

I love this little being, this something who is a named "someone" to me. Is being a someone as strange to him as being a something is to me? Perhaps my own love is sufficient for the two of us; indeed, he relishes the attention it affords him. In truth he lives in my love and the word between us; our beings are inclusive in the encounters of physical love we share. He fills my world at those times; everything is for a time beyond clock time funneled through and colored by his being before me—and by *Us*. I do not sense or grasp this We at the time of its presence, when it unfolds to me as I unfold in it; then, there is but intimacy and sharing, even if only of the most concrete and physical variety. It is only in retrospect that I apprehend the powerful bond between us, the We that is common to us—though the We is assuredly not the same for him as for me. Still, there is mutuality.

This We of memory becomes the basis of the history of us, the traditions and expectations surrounding our meetings. Behold, a kind of covenant comes into being between us—and both of us seem to sense its lawfulness and when it is violated or broken. Hence, when I do not have the time to sit in my chair and read the morning paper, my cat follows me around crying out to me, as if to say, "This is our time, what are you doing? Where is my rubdown? I have been waiting for it. Please don't deny me my time with you and your attention!" I watch him in my hurry and try to apologize, but of course to no avail. For he cannot grasp my explanation, and the only acceptable response on my part would be the sharing itself. And so, empathizing with his need for loving attention, I pick him up and stroke him. I pet him vigorously for a moment, as if to say, "Here, this is all I can offer for now." He seems to grasp something of what I am saying, for when I put him back down, he goes on his way and continues with his morning activities. He chases the dog. But let it be said, he did not purr in my arms.

✠

In truth, this We of nature obtains in one guise or another throughout all the phyla of the physical world. What is not available in nature for sweet mutuality? What precludes inclusiveness with my being? All is of the Word; what then can stand apart from the Word? With what therefore can the human person not relate in the whole of creation? What attribute or dimension of being do I find outside which I do not also find inside myself in some way? I share with the mountain the awe-filling sense of inner spaciousness, with the tree rootedness and aging, with the thunderstorm power, with the sea unseen depth and life therein, with the pond silence and the brook laughter. True and concrete mutuality exists between us and the whole of nature through the primal Word of creation. At any time and at any point along our way, we may meet and share inclusive being with whatever addresses us. But it is for us to hear that address, to respond and to address with our being as well. The It of nature stands in need of becoming You to us.

The Eternal I

Revelation and the We of Humanity

THE REVELATION OF THE PERSON

The Threefold World of the Person

The world of the human person is threefold in accordance with the threefoldness of God: *I, You* and *We*. Every person participates in all three spheres of personal being. All three dimensions are real and irreducible, though at the same time constituting an unbreakable unity. Addressed into the image of God, the human person is also a "three-in-one," with the three personal pronouns symbolizing the linguistic and ontological reality of each sphere of being: I, You and We. The very purpose and destiny of humanity is at stake in the recognition of the threefoldness of personal reality. And as is the case with the unfolding history of the individual, so also with the history of the whole: first comes the recognition of the You, then of the I, and finally of the We proper. This evolutionary understanding of the person is in accordance with the serial threefoldness of the divine Word, and hence of the history of the divine-human relationship as such: creation, revelation and redemption. Creation is You-centered, revelation I-centered and redemption We-centered.

As a people, we have already passed through the You-centered period and are now nearing the end of the span of I-centeredness. The time is thus at hand to discover with ultimacy and finality the Kingdom between us, the reality of the We. Failure to discern the truth and holy ground of the We would eventuate in our utter self-destruction. For it would mean revelation without redemption, knowledge of the I apart from the corresponding awareness of true life in the spirit of the We. Revelation now therefore must center upon the discovery of the We, and of the meaning of the I and the You in the context of that primal ground of mutuality.

✠

The essential triplicity of God is repeated in the human person. The creedal formula of the Church for the Trinity applies equally to the human condition: "Three persons in one substance." That means: the I, You and the We in the one Word. To be human means to participate in the divine "three-in-one." The I is the *internal*, the You the *external*, and the We the *mutual* dimensions of the person. The I is also the *subjective*, the You the *objective* and the We the *inter-subjective* spheres of personal being. Thus the You and the We constitute the "social" aspects of the person. And where the I represents the *depth* dimension, the You is the *height* and the We the corresponding *breadth* dimension of the three dimensional universe of person.

The essential triplicity of God sets the pattern for the whole of reality. The *person, logos* and *relationship* of God are translated in some form into all that God utters. So also is the threefold schema of being through the Word: *externality, internality* and *mutuality*. From the Trinity springs forth the interwoven triune relationships of God to the world: *creation, revelation* and *redemption*. The divine threefoldness determines as well the branches of creation: *physis, psyche* and *pneuma*. And since the whole is repeated in the parts, each of these three spheres is in turn threefold. *Physis* consists of matter, time, and space. *Psyche* manifests the tri-unity of the You, the I, and the We. *Pneuma* operates in and through law, language and love. In their way each of these further demarcations of creation relate back to the threefold relationship of God to the world. Thus, matter, the You and law relate especially to creation; time, the I and language refer to revelation; and space, the We and love relate to redemption. And behold, the pattern continues still: time is of three dimensions, past, present and future.

Space consists of the three dimensions of height, depth and breadth. And matter breaks down into solid, liquid and gas. Matter may also be grasped in terms of animal, vegetable and mineral. In sum, the whole continues in the parts, and the parts have their life in the whole.

✠

The human person may be apprehended in terms of the unity of *soma, psyche* and *pneuma,* of body, soul and spirit. Together these constitute respectively the *external, internal* and *mutual* dimensions of the person. Body would here represent the *inter-species,* soul the *intra-personal* and spirit the *inter-personal* dimensions of human existence in creation. We are three-in-one: body, soul and spirit—all in the Word of creation. We share body with nature, soul with each other, and spirit with God. The body operates through law common to all its parts, as to the whole of nature; the soul operates through language common to all persons; the spirit works through love, common not only to persons but to the Ultimate Person. For love *is* the sphere of God. When we love we are in God and God in us. All three operating principles, law, language and love, come through the logos and are spirit, in that they constitute the *mutuality* of their respective spheres. Law could thus be called the "spirit of externality," language the "spirit of internality" and love the "spirit of mutuality" proper. For true mutuality of personal being is only of and in God.

In the very event of human speech, through the medium of the voice itself, we see both the distinctiveness and the essential unity of body, soul and spirit. For the voice event includes, first, the physical dynamics of sound production. Second, it necessarily involves the person who is actually speaking and is to be "heard" in the utterance. And third, the event contains a concrete meaning and context, a denotation and a host of connotations. Its setting in the life of the person is its spirit.

We are, then, three-in-one: soma, psyche and pneuma. The psyche as the I is also a three-in-one: *will, mind* and *emotion.* The human person shares volition, cognition and affection with the divine Person. Volition relates to the will of the Eternal Addresser, cognition to the mind of the eternally Addressed, and affection to the spirit of the Eternal Addressing. The foundation of cognition is thus the Word, of volition the will of the Creator, and of affection the Spirit. Just as with the divine Persons, all three aspects of the human person are one and take their life in the word, in language. That is, consciousness, will and feeling all have their source within the Word of creative address and the consequent word of response. Hence, to be human means to stand in the Word through our word, to depend upon incoming address and outgoing response for our existence.

To be human also means that knowledge of both the human and the divine Persons cannot be separated from the Word. This does not mean that God cannot be encountered apart from the Word—any more than one person could not encounter another person without the medium of language. But it does mean that *there can be no knowledge of God apart from the Word.* Thus the mystic can rightly claim to "know" God but not with knowledge, not in a way that could be objectified in any sense. What we cannot speak about, we must indeed pass over in silence. Yet the experience of God can be *"trans-logos"*; being may in Spirit meet Being. The agent of language may come face-to-face with the Agent of the Word. The agent is in but cannot be strictly identified with the word that is spoken. Person is "panenthetical" to the word, in but more than word. For the word does not speak itself, the person does. Something over and above word abides as the being of person, specifically a *someone* who though named cannot become word, but is ever the one who speaks and who listens. And persons may meet the Person in utter silence. More cannot be said or logicized.

✠

The I is threefold: emotions, mind and will. Feelings bring us into touch with the memories and meaning of the past and into connection with both our bodies and our relationship with nature. Feelings thus grant us the ground of meaning of the past which bears on the present, the heretofore summary and "in-force" determination of the significance of that which is present and incoming to the mind. The mind is the epicenter of the identity of the person as present member of and agent in the world. It is the person as agent of perception and reason, as the one who operates in the world. The conscious context of the mind is ever the here and the now. The will represents the "heart," the seat of the inner person, of intentionality and meaning, of desire and passion, of faith, hope and love, which though originating in the past as seed, is ever future-directed.

The will is thus the home of the spirit in humanity. The rebelliousness of the will therefore takes on great spiritual significance. It is first of all a *No* to the entrance of the divine will, a denial of the voice of love, and a repression of the inner law of the heart. This *No* then affects the mind and the feelings, for both seek to be in accord with the will. Basic attitudes and orientations are forged through the fundamental decisions of the will, the whole process and result being more unconscious than conscious. The intent of the will consequently directs the mind and the affections to follow its lead. And love is above all a matter of the will. It begins and has its ground in the "inspired" decision to enter into the life of We, into primal relationship. Everything is at stake in that decision. And all else follows suit.

✠

In the heart and the intentions thereof, the spirit abides. The Word of creative address landed in the heart, as it were, and from there the response began. God's law of personal being and the sacred intent for the human person reside in the depth of the heart. The heart is the seat of the will, of the imagination and of intentionality. The heart constitutes the inner person. As such, it is the first line of communication with God, the original home not only for the Word, but for the Spirit. It is the center for the intent of God in the creation of both humanity in general and the individual person so addressed. The intent of the will is of the Spirit because it comes from God in address and is therefore *mutual* between God and us. Further, it is the "mutual intent" between partners in dialogue which gives rise to the "co-notation" of the word. Behind the word being spoken lies the intention of the speaker. The purpose in speaking then spills out into the ground between the persons, where it is joined by the intention of the other person in listening. The intermingling of intentions gives rise to the human world as mutual and meant. Behold, history is the spilled ground between us.

In the intention of the heart is the mutuality of creation— and the motive power of revelation. From the intent of God in the creative address arises the *who* I am to become, God's will for me in my creation, the hidden answer to *why I am*— for being is always intended. From the heart issues forth the divine intention, which must be decisively lived out in order to be finally discerned. That is, the *what* I become precedes the answer to the *why* of my existence. And I must choose to become whom I am intended to be. That is my *destiny*. Not to choose, or to choose actively not to live in accordance with the inner law of being, would eventuate in *fate* rather than destiny. For God's intent in the heart provides an effective compass to direct us toward the end of the course set before us from above. Yet it is for us to listen to and believe in that inner pathfinder. Too few listen to the voice of the heart. Pity that it does not insist on its own way.

✠

The Incarnation

Not only is the essential triplicity of God repeated in the human person; so also is the threefold movement of the Word within God. Each movement of the logos within the life of God, when directed from God to humanity becomes the basis for a divine-human relationship. Hence, the divine address, when directed toward humanity constitutes *creation*. The divine response, when spoken to humanity becomes itself the *revelation*. And the divine mutuality, when It is finally uttered, shall be the very substance of *redemption*. The revelation event is therefore of the *I*, both human and divine, and takes place within the already established context of creation—that means, in the presence of the eternal You.

And the Word became flesh, and dwelt among us. Behold, God the Addressed was *spoken* to the world of humanity by God the Addresser. A second Word-event has taken place to and for the human world, a kind of repetition of the Word of the eternal response of God to God. The One addressed from before the foundations of the world was actually and for all time spoken to the world. This One became a person, a man, like one of us; this One participated fully in the spoken creation. In being spoken, the eternal One entered into the same process of creation as each one of us, therein purifying, sanctifying and redeeming each stage of human development in the world. The "pre-existent" One became incarnated into our flesh, our concrete and temporal existence, our specific historical here and now, our finiteness—so that the Way of true Person would become open for us. Through the Eternal I, we have been invited to enter into God's life, God's We, in and through this Person Who is ever addressed and ever responding.

Where creation is the *You-event,* in which the Eternal You addresses the human person into existence in and through the Word of You, revelation is the *I-event,* in which the person, by the power of the Word, hears and responds to the address with the self-revelatory "I am." The revelation of the I takes place in the Word and in response to the Word of address. The I of revelation arises through the joint empowerment of the inner intention of the Word and the presence of the You. The presence of the You is the given of creation; the inner intention of the Word for the I unfolds as the givingness of revelation, as manifested in the human dialogue of discovery and discernment.

The "incarnation" begins therefore with human creation itself, when the being who had been spoken in creation received as well the Word of address. The I was implanted from the very beginning in the one Word of address, as the inner *Torah* or "blueprint" of person written on the heart. The incarnation of the I eventuated in the human replication of the second divine Word, that is, the Word of God's own response to God's own address—for we are made in the image of God, and thus carry out the divine pattern of personhood. Hence, just as the eternally Addressed responds to the Holy Other with the "I Am" of divine Being, so also the human person responds to the address of creation with the perfect image or echo of the divine communication: "I am." The second Word therefore is in direct and dialogical response to the first Word. Indeed, the two Words are One, passed between and uniting the divine partners—as also the divine-human partners.

By itself, however, the human "I am" needs the confirmation and clarification that only the Progenitor of the Word can grant it. For, behold, we have forgotten the primal address, and are aware only of our response. Our response seems therefore to be only to ourselves, or to nature or to an "unknown God." No longer is it a response; now it has become a mere self-assertion. It is as if the initial address of creation had been a dream from which we awoke in and through the responsive outcry "I am!" We can almost remember the event, for it still reverberates in us, but we cannot bring it to conscious clarity. We were asleep, and undergoing a deep and disturbing dream, a kind of visitation of otherness, but we were able to break free in our fear and wake ourselves up by the power of the Word we knew inexplicably how to call upon. Yet in the word which awoke us the memory abides.

Only God's own proclamation of "I Am" in counter-response to the human utterance of personal being can resolve our profound quest to understand the nature and meaning of being a person. The answer cannot come from the physical and personless world; nor can the psyche truly comprehend itself on its own terms. By itself alone, the psyche becomes an absolute circle of self-centerdness. On our own, we become an endlessly inflatable tautology of being. Something or someone over against us must mediate personal knowledge to us. For personal knowledge is relational knowledge. Just as two points are needed in order to triangulate one's physical position in the world, so two poles of personal being are required to attain self-orientation and knowledge in the human world.

Is then the silent and ever present You of creation an I like us? Is there to be real mutuality—and salvation in that mutuality? Or are we only an inexplicable aberration of nature, a psychical biosphere which seems to promise in its own life something greater than it can deliver or justify, something eternal and divine—yet provable only by its hidden past and mysterious future? Only knowledge of where we came from and where we are going could offer adequate justification and a legitimating ground for being persons in a world which seems to seek from us rather than to grant to us personal status. Where is God's "I Am" to the human enigma of internality? Only the revelation of the divine I can grant us both self-knowledge and the knowledge of God. For revelation is at once of the Who over against us and of the I within and of the Spirit between us. The whole is revealed to the parts, and the parts to the whole.

Thus the Word of revelation, the second Word, is that of the *Incarnation* of the divine I into the fullness of the human person and condition. It is God's Word manifesting and confirming the divine "I Am," which corresponds to and finally answers the human echo of personal being, originating in response to God's first address. The second Word of revelation is addressed to humanity just as the first Word of creation. Where God spoke "You" to humanity in the first, here the Word is that of "I." Where the invitation in the first address was to participate in the reality of the you, her it is to attain the full stature of the I.

"And the Word became flesh and dwelt among us, full of grace and truth." The "I Am" was in the world, the light of our personal being, calling us unto God's Way and Truth and Life. That means: calling us unto the true and ultimate I of humanity.

✠

Consciousness

Consciousness is one yet threefold in accordance with the threefoldness of the human person. Consciousness consists of the interwoven awareness of *externality, internality* and *mutuality.* The consciousness of internality is that of the inner domain of the I. It is the awareness of being an inclusive world unto oneself. The consciousness of externality is bifurcated between the otherness of persons and of objects, that is, between the You and the It, between the subject and the object over against the I. It is thus the awareness of spheres of being exclusive to the I. The consciousness of mutuality is the most difficult of all to comprehend and to objectify. For strictly speaking, it concerns the ground rather than the figures of consciousness. The consciousness of mutuality is the awareness of inclusivity, of the both/and of shared being, of the common breath or reciprocal atmosphere of being-together, of the interpersonal space between persons.

The mode of consciousness through which the person attains awareness of mutuality is that of the *intuition.* Intuition is the unified apprehension of another person and the actual state of being together. Only the intuition may grasp mutuality. For intuition emerges from the relationship itself, from the sphere of the between, which means from the actual and active involvement of the person. It is the individual appropriation of an event of shared person. Apart from personal involvement, there can be no intuition—for there is nothing mutual to apprehend. In short, the intuition is the primal awareness of personal participation and reciprocity. Hence, it can never be "objective," nor yet simply "subjective." It is neither, but has elements of both. Intuition cannot be justified outside the event it grasps—from the fulness of person to the fulness of person.

Consciousness arose in and through the Word of creative address. Its primal nature is that of response to something—Someone—outside itself. Consciousness is thus a relational necessity and constant grounded in the Word and in the Spirit thereof. By and beyond itself, however, it cannot be explained or depicted. It is ever the given, the presupposed, the stood upon. It may be comprehended only through the "way of negation," the *via negativa,* in which we define it not through what it is but through what it is not. For emptied of all its contents, what may we term consciousness but *"self-aware no-thingness"*?

The consciousness of personal being is of the You, the I and the We. It arose *before* the capacity for and fact of objectification through the logic of language. That is, the consciousness of the threefoldness of personal being is an *a priori* to human existence in the world. Just as time and space are *a priori* dimensions of consciousness itself, rather than an awareness coming from the outside in, so also is the consciousness of the You, the I and the We built into the person from the very beginning, from the first moment of creative address. The whole is given in the beginning, even if in an embryonic form. The consciousness of personal being emerged with consciousness itself, not as something extrinsic but as intrinsic to the Word as such. The channels of personal being exist in the Word, and indeed permit the human word.

✠

The threefoldness of consciousness offers a reinterpretation of what has been called the "Id, the Ego and the Superego"— which is actually a wholly unjustified mistranslation of the German "Das Es, das Ich und das Uber-Ich," meaning the "It, the I and the Beyond-I." These terms can be retranslated into the physical, psychical and spiritual dimensions of the person, respectively. And the deepest motivational drive of each dimension represents one of the three forms of love: eros, philia and agape. Eros is the vital force of the biological life-form, and is communicated from the unconscious to consciousness as drive, as need and desire. The "It" is that which is not the I within the person, or at least that which has a powerful law of its own, one not necessarily responsive to or in accord with that of the I. The "I" is the soul proper, and its law of love, philia, is that of sharing and participation. Where the law of the It is monologic, the law of the I is dialogic. The

"Beyond-I" represents not only the locus of the "introjections" of norms, values and self-image from parents and society; it is also the locus of spirit, from which arises meaning and morality. It is the abode of the law of the heart, the law of God's love, agape. Thus, it is the sphere of the mutual, of that which is greater than the I.

The It is the ground of creation, the source of need and passion, drive and motivation in the world. The Beyond-I constitutes the ground of meaning and morality, the foundation of self-image and actualization. What then is the I, but the meeting place for the two dimensions of existence, the one from below and the other from above? The I serves as their wedding chamber, as it were, the place in which the two are to be united and through human effort, unified.

And in the current human condition, they stand in desperate need of each other. Passion needs morality and morality passion; desire without a vision of that which is highest in us leads to self-destruction, and a vision cut off from the desire to make it actual eventuates in a vapid perversion of form without substance. Apart from the integration of our threefold nature as persons, the human condition turns from a gift of grace into a tragedy of disintegration.

✠

A "collective unconscious"? *Was bedeutet das*? What does that mean? It means first of all the universal human memory of the primal Word of creative address. In that Word is contained the whole code of our existence past, present and future. Call it the nucleus of the soul, within which the totality of divine intention is recorded as an unfathomable constellation of archetypal message-elements, thought-action forms, idea-images of what has been, is and is to come. As such, the collective unconscious is the given, the skeletal framework of language and meaning which exists prior to the individual's conscious appropriation of any idea or image, and indeed makes possible the thought and action form itself. That is, it is the internal structure of the word which makes possible an organized and coherent world.

What has been called, then, the collective unconscious represents the innate *Weltanschauung* or "world-view," constitutive to all persons, which brings meaning and the capacity for meaning into all that is happening to the person, from incoming perceptions to upcoming feelings. God does not bring a person into the world as a "blank sheet," as it were, upon which life is to write whatever it will. Rather, the Word that is planted within us brings from the inside the linguistic-elements which correspond in some sense with the being-elements of the events from the outside, from the environment. Thus, for instance, the "innate You" of the collective unconscious makes possible the actual perception and apprehension of the You over against the I. The event occurring *between* the I and the world activates the inner and startlingly appropriate prior notion of the elements of being which are presented to the I.

Behold, then, the *internal* collective unconscious of the psyche is presupposed by and founded upon the *mutual Word between* the divine and the human persons. In the beginning is the relationship; mutuality gives rise to internality. The Word which is passed between us becomes the basis for the word which is within us. Thus, the collective unconscious is the linguistic record of primal relationality—not only between God and humanity, but also the events and idea-forms ever emerging between human persons in our ongoing and unfolding history. From where then does "an idea whose time has come," come? From the unconscious life of the Word deep within us, and at its appointed time. The whole is in the parts—and from the very beginning.

✠

Can we be conscious of consciousness? Can consciousness be the content of consciousness? Pure consciousness is not being but of being *with* being, not monological but dialogical in nature—for it arises in and through the word of creative address and is responsive in modality. That is, consciousness is not of itself as such, but of being in relationship, of being with. And there is great power in the pure consciousness of being with oneself, the world and God. To be conscious not of being as existing but with Being as vital presence, that is true consciousness, that is real life and mutuality. Indeed, the highest form of consciousness—in either normal or "altered" states—is that of consciousness with, rather than merely consciousness of, the Other. Consciousness turned upon itself is not consciousness but the emptying thereof; what abides is not consciousness but its absolute abnegation. For being and nothingness become virtually indistinguishable. Consciousness with another being, however, is filled by a lively reciprocity of otherness and sameness.

O pure Being, in consciousness with You I am conscious of myself; in waiting upon You, I attain the one true personal being—our being together.

THE WE OF HUMANITY

The Human We

In the beginning is the relation. All true life is mutual life. Individual being emerges in and through the shared context of relationship. This relational world of the person, human and divine, is an essential and inseparable tri-unity: I, You and We. And while the I and the You and the We arise together as the three-in-one relationship, the We has logical and ontological priority over the other two— at least from the human perspective. It is from the ground of the We that the figures of the I and the You first emerge and in which they continue to have their true life. It is the mutual life that underwrites and nourishes the life of the individuals. The We bestows meaning to the I and the You, and grants them the "place" to be in together, the common home in which their individual uniqueness is loved and affirmed and confirmed.

Though one, the human We is threefold in accordance with the threefoldness of the person in the world. That is, the human person has three different though interwoven spheres of mutuality: the We of nature, *physis,* of soul, *psyche,* and of spirit, *pneuma.* As humans, we participate in three relationships simultaneously: creation, revelation and redemption. In creation, we receive being in the We of nature; in revelation, we share the We of psyche; in redemption, we are gifted with the We of spirit. In our life with nature, we participate in its monologue of law; in our life with each other, we are share in the dialogue of language; in our life with spirit, we have our being in and through the dialectic of love.

It cannot be overemphasized that the We is one not three, and that it is just as real as the I and the You. The distinctions are drawn for the sake of clarifying the nature and scope of being a person. Thus must we distinguish these three ultimately indivisible dimensions of the We between the human I and You, namely that of law, of language and of love. The We of law is the We of body (soma), and from gentle nearness to sexual intimacy and passion, it is the most profound union of creation—by which creation is fulfilled and carried on. The We of language is the We of soul (psyche), and its intimacy that of the revelation of one person to another. The We of love is the We of spirit (pneuma), and its mutualness is not only that of person with person, but of person with God. Love is shared being itself, and its life is our redemption.

The We of the psyche is that of a "unity-in-difference." For as the dimension of internality, the mutuality of the psyche is that of a reciprocal "exclusive being," as it were, the sharing of otherness in and through the medium of language. The I and the You are mutually different; their dialogue reveals two distinct and irrreducible logoi, two personal agents interfacing. Hence, the mutuality emerges precisely in and as the abiding *"viva la difference"* between the partners.

We are different together. Our separate overagainstness establishes and is of the very essence of our relationship. Speech is your speech and my speech in our mutually exclusive mode of operation and creative utterance. Thank heavens You are You, different and other than me! I do not program what You say, any more than You determine the specifics of my input. Rather, I experience your speech-events as the unexpected, the novel, as the direct expression of your uniqueness, calling forth my own in response. The alone overagainst the alone, sharing in the exclusive nature of the soul. In sum, what is common is the distinct, the otherness, the *ganz andere,* the unique and irreducible—the persons. The holy rub of one being against the other, from which, behold, a spark may fly into the volatile ground between us, igniting the flame of love. And how very dry that ground is! And how little it takes to kindle love! If only we would meet and rub against each other in true dialogue more than we now do!

The We of spirit is that of shared being as such. Instead of a "unity-in-difference," the We of spirit represents a "difference-in-unity." At issue here is not your being over against mine, not the I and the You in mutual otherness, but the *one being we share, from which emerges the individual beings we are.* Here personal being is inclusive to the relationship, here the operating principle of spirit is that of dialectic rather than dialogue, the parts emerging from and having life within the whole between them. Love is the dialectic of spirit. It is the relationship itself, the beginning and the end, the height and the depth, the *telos* and *teleios,* or goal and perfection of the relationship between us. Behold, in love we have our common source, our life and our purpose. Love as spirit is the "ground of being" of the human soul, of the psyche itself.

Note carefully: in the meeting between the I and the You, these three dimensions of the We are not distinguishable. When we are present to each other and the spirit to us, law, language and love are one in the same way that the I, You and We are one. In the actual relationship of presence, nothing partial or detached obtains; the mutual holds everything together. Only in reflection and retrospect may we glean and separate elements from a unified and paradoxical mystery that can only be lived through, the unfathomable mystery of Us.

✠

Why have we not heretofore adequately apprehended or indeed even discovered the category of the We? We have focused for centuries on the ubiquitous *I,* on consciousness and internality. We have viewed the I as a *ding an sich,* as a thing in itself. And the world of persons seemed to consist only of a great number of individual "monads," only of specific instances or instantiations of a single archetypal I, only private islands in an unchartered sea. In this century, finally, have we begun to discern the reality of the I vis-a-vis the You, of the primal "I-You" relationship. And behold, now is the time to discern the context of the I-You relationship, the ground of mutuality, the We. Our history and future are at stake in this redemptive discovery.

Why, then, have we not seen the We before now? First, because it is not directly observable, as are the I and You. The We cannot be grasped apart from the relationship itself, and cannot be objectified save only in and through human covenant. And in our empirical worldview, that which cannot be quantified cannot be accepted as real. One need only look at the unresolved struggle within the science of psychology regarding what to do with the reality of human love, to grasp the problem of apprehending the We as We. Psychology cannot treat the inter-human as such, but only the individual in relation to others and society. Hence, psychology must reduce love to something either purely subjective or purely behavioral. In either case, the inter-human reality of love cannot be accepted and dealt with on its own level of being.

A second reason for the difficultly of apprehending the We concerns the nature of the meeting itself. In actual concrete meetings, even though being is shared, the focus is upon the participants rather than the relationship as such. The center of attention is the alternating giving and receiving, rather than on the mutual. As one telltale love song puts it, "I give to you and you give to me, true love, true love." Hence, if sharing is lifted up at all, it is usually within the context of what each of us can appropriate from the giving and receiving. It is in terms of You and I but not really *Us* . The common is ever divided by and into the parts, but not seen as a "whole number," as it were.

Yet behold, the We is that which is never truly appropriated into either or both of the partners. The We is that which abides for both as the relationship, the love itself. The We is the common, the *koinonia,* in which we have our being— together. The We lives in us as we live in it, but can never properly be called "yours" or "mine." Rather, it is "ours"— or to be more exact, *it is Us*. The We possesses You and I, if we are willing and obedient to its life which is our life. In the We, I do not even belong to myself; I belong to the relationship and to You, to whom I have pledged my being between Us.

✠

The event of the We: You and I step in relation. I experience You in your movement toward me, and I sense your experience of me. The movement toward relation is not the relation but the preparation for it, the initial context of meaning between us, the "first impression" or attitudinal stance taken with the intent to meet. We speak, and behold, something happens out of the ordinary flux of daily life. A "place" or personal "seam" suddenly opens up between us—not when we are looking for it—and we find ourselves present together in its ever fresh and vibrant atmosphere. A world has opened between us through will and grace, through freedom and mystery, a world in which everything is heightened and our internal being seems to have become inexplicably manifest and understood by each other. The sense of aloneness disappears, and You and our mutualness fill both the heavens and my heart. But now I no longer "experience" You as objectum, for nothing is partial or detached from the presence of the whole in and through which we find ourselves. Now the relational ground is one with the figures of You and me. I do not experience You, for in the meeting You and I are one, for the being within each of us has come to stand between us as something—or "someone"—shared. Knowing and being known are unified. I am known as I know—or so it seems, though without being realized at the time, for there is no uninvolved observer here, but only one whole person finding wholeness with another.

We speak together. I hear *You* as living soul, as unique center of meanings and creative life. I hear You with such grace-filled presence to You, that I actually seem to *share* in your meaning and life, to *participate* in your being—your being with me. Your world is no longer exclusively yours; no longer are You isolated in fact and in worldview. Behold, in the unseen sphere we have somehow entered between us, I am with You, I share your life. I speak in turn, but not to You across the impersonal distance of time and space, not through the mediation of nature and culture. I speak *with* You and even *in* You; that is, I share myself in the immediacy of your being—which is in our mutual presence at-one-with our being together.

We have shared who we are, and in so doing, we have become what we shared. While the meeting took place not without interruptions both within and without, not without pauses to catch our breath, as it were, and to reconnoiter what was happening, nevertheless as the meeting unfolded something else unfolded as well, something unpredictable in its living peculiarity and uniqueness, something beyond the control and programmatic needs and desires of the participants. Yet this something moved with us, it never got out of synch with our phasic movements to and away from each other. It was not like a river which keeps moving whether we are in it or not, so that we can never step in at the same point again. Rather, it evolved with us, ever picking us up where we left off.

From the beginning of the meeting, as the initially unseen ground of the relation, there slowly emerged the unity of our togetherness itself, not as a personification of an impersonal force or power or univocal meaning that was discovered and shared, but as the very basis for the persons-in-relationship. As You and I meet, the *We* of our relationship comes into being as well—and simultaneous with our history together. The We offers both continuity and newness, both substance and promise, and a meaning-filled present which spills over into both the past and the future. Each meeting builds on our history together, the unfolding story of our common life; each shared event is recorded in and between us and added to the whole, like beads on a necklace or links on a common chain of being. And behold, at some point in this process of meeting and gathering what arises between us, our very identity becomes merged with the *Us* of our history. I *am* who I have been with You; the We of our past has afforded me a continuity between yesterday and today, and a reason for tomorrow. I am a part of *Us*; who We are has granted meaning and substance and nourishment to who I am.

✠

We meet. Being is shared. But the intensity, the "glory" or weight of the sharing, necessitates a cyclical relational stance. I must come up for air, so to speak; I must at points return to the world of the ordinary, of clock time and the mundane. I must "check in" with the usual in order to sense once again where and who I am in the "real" world beyond the relationship. For in the sphere of meeting I am lost—and found—in You and in what we share, and indeed are, together. I meet You, and I pull back. I open and step into this being that I am with You, and then I step back to safety, to the world of objects and control, the world I understand and have mapped out. I cannot take too much of You and I together—at least not all at once. The climate is too rich with the oxygen of spirit; there are too many new and pregnant meanings at hand, like an overloaded fruit tree between us, begging to be picked and consumed. Every direction presents a new horizon, and an unexpected life of freedom comes forward in me and between us, one which I cannot rein in by my subsequent demands. The world between us is ever open-ended and expanding. And in it I hear echoing still the Word of the first creation: "Be You—together."

The We has weight and substance, but cannot be held or quantified. Nor can it be mapped out, as if it could hold still for my sketch of it, as if it were willing to allow me to gaze upon it from the outside and apart from the relation itself, in which my being is intimately and inseparably bound together with You. Rather than being able to view the We from the outside, it only permits apprehension from the "ourside," as it were, only from within. It cannot be grasped apart from the relationship. For the We is the being of mutuality, and has no presence apart from our presence to each other, no other reality than that of "Us." It exists only in and between us as the being we share.

How then can this We be quantified, how can it be brought across into the world of time and space, there to become an objectified reality of the world of things and daily affairs? Only through memory, language and covenant—mutual agreement, as it were. It is never an object independent of You and I, but comes to be that to which You and I are *committed*. Behold, that which is the ultimate determiner of persons and of our "personality" in and to the world, the world cannot see and control! How God works among us!

Our meeting leaves its stamp on my being but not on the world. Rather, it commissions You and I to go forth and make the world around Us its home, to bring all that We are and have and seek into its sphere of life. I am more because of Us; something has been added to my personal being—and to yours, so that when I look at You, I sense that it is present in and with You as well as in and with me.

✠

We meet, in phases and over time. A shared being between us comes to be explored through unpredictable relational stages. The soundings into our mutual being are mapped out in memory—a kind of common memory—and thereby indirectly apprehended and known with greater clarity. It is the being of *Us*, a constant yet an ever new, either waxing or waning but never staying the same. We find ourselves in an invisible home of our mutual spirit, grasped only by us, who live therein. This home of our common spirit has a growing number of rooms and even wings, each one built on a single foundation greater than us—from where did it come, this gift of solid ground?—each one constructed and furnished through our concrete meetings and the events we have shared and undergone together.

In time, the *We* comes to be seen clearly, not with the outer eyes, but with the inner eye of the heart. Its ongoing life comes to be identified as our life together. To be more precise: we cannot—or will not—separate any longer who We are together from who We are apart. *I am who I am with You; You are who You are with me.* Whether together or apart, I am still with Thee; Thou art ever with me. Whither Thou goest, I will go. Thus does the holy life of the We, which is in truth the life of love, come into being in and between us. From apparent happenchance and the freedom of meeting has grown a common something almost more real and significant than the persons by themselves. A whole greater than the sum of the parts has emerged, a love born not simply in but between—and as—Us. Love is the spirit we share.

The We defines itself like the path of the atom in a cloud chamber. The track is seen only after the being has already passed by. Like YHWH with Moses, we may see only the backside, only the afterglow of the holy. Yet the We weaves its path not only between us, but upon our souls, with the substantive touch of meaning, truth and direction. The We would have us hallow the past, which it redeems through its continuing presence in memory; the present, which it fills like the shekinah the sanctuary, and therefore sanctifies; and the future, which it has already made holy through its promised re-appearance, when it will consummate itself and the persons who find their life therein.

All of our life in the world is a preparation for new meetings, for the re-entrance of the We upon the stage of our present being. Our memory cannot nourish us long without new events of being together. And our memory is selective and forgetful; and it permits our desire to pre-shape and program the We, be it for idealization in need, or diminution in fear, of its power. The present is arid and empty and shallow without the sharing that bears both individual and common life. The future becomes something hellish and dark without the hope and promise of the renewal of the We, of our life together. The future must hold You and Us to have the power to draw us toward it open and joyful.

✠

In the relational event, there is a cyclical shift of being, from an inclusive mutuality to an exclusive one, from a going over into a common being to a coming back into a private one. The doors of my being open and I go forth unto You; I include You in my world and being, even as You include me in yours. But then through a primal force in me almost beyond my control, one which operates seemingly whether I am conscious of its action—or will to action—or not, I recede into myself again, like the tide responding to a pull greater than itself. And I take whatever will return with me from our common shore of meeting into the deeper and unfathomed waters of the self. Our meeting place is like an isthmus between the silent waters of the exclusive being of You and me. We flood it and mingle, and then we recede into our respective bodies of personal dwelling. I take my being back, as it were, into my own exclusive sovereignty.

From a mutual subjectivity, I am once again subject and You are once again object in my world, once more not unlike the other beings over against me. And though I impute to You the status of being a subject with your own world, it is one which is no longer shared, no longer ours, but yours. You are now a subject of faith to me, but not of knowledge. I may believe in You as regards our past history, and risk faith in terms of a possible future, but in the present, You are to be known like other persons, places and things in my world. That is: with a knowledge separate from my personal being.

That We should come to this, even for a time, may be regrettable, but it is necessary if we are to function in the spoken world of creation.

✠

The We cannot be seen. How then can one believe in its reality? In what sense is it real? It is real only in and between persons. Hence, in a sense, it must be *agreed* to be real—not unlike the agreement necessary for language and meaning—and therefore for the establishment of a common world. Our mutual affirmation and support are essential elements of the life of the We between us. Its reality is contingent upon our belief in it. Belief here means an openness and an invitation to the We to become real for us. And behold, the belief proves itself by the relational fruit it bears! The Yes to the We is not only an invitation for life; it belongs to the very substance of that life.

There is no proof of the We beyond the world of persons. For the We does not exist in the world of nature apart from persons, though we may attempt to extrapolate from the human "animal" and to impute such a state of mutuality upon some of the higher and related species. The We is not an object to be pointed at and examined or quantified; nor is it a "quality" among other qualities. The We is its own reality in, with and under other persons. And we are that reality; and we discern it, with a perceptual mechanism we have not yet begun to identify and to understand. For, as with love itself, the We brings its own discernment as gift. It enables its own consciousness as a dimension of itself—just as it engenders a new self-consciousness of the persons it brings into mutual existence.

✠

Some, no doubt, think of the We as the epiphenomenon of the I and the You. But perhaps the opposite is just as true. Perhaps the I and the You are the epiphenomena, the essential by-products of the We.

✠

The *substance* of the We cannot be separated from the substance of the persons participating in the mutuality. Hence, an examination of the reality of the We is at the same time an examination of the reality of the I and the You. And reflective knowledge of the We includes knowledge of the participants themselves in the depth of their respective personalities. Knowledge of the We as objectum is therefore at once both objective and subjective. It is objective in the sense that it is and has been shared between two persons; it is subjective in that it pervades and affects the participants in the totality of their personal and "private" lives.

The substance of the We is thus paradoxically both identifiable with the substance of the persons themselves, yet precisely in their mutuality, other than the two. That is, the We is both between and within them. The substance shared between the I and the You is the taproot of the peculiar soul-life constitutive to each person in their respective and unique being in the world.

The persons meet and for a time beyond time are "inclusive" with each other. But behold, they are at the same time granted their respective distinctness as a gift of the meeting itself. Their unity gives rise to their diversity. Did the distinctness exist prior to the meeting? As a God-given potential seeking affirmation and confirmation, no doubt. But mutuality is required for actualization. What I may be in myself needs You to make me happen, and happen between us. What I am comes back to me from You and from Us as gift to me—and to You as well. In giving ourselves to each other, we receive ourselves back from each other; we become whole together.

✠

The We is just as real as the I and the You. What then is the being or *ontos* of the I and the You? And in what does the permanency of the I and the You reside? In physical embodiment, and thus in a purely temporary state of being? In a genuine sense, the I and the You together constitute the body of the We, just as the We represents the soul and spirit of the partners. One ancient definition of friendship is that of two bodies (soma) with one soul (psyche). Is not the We then two souls with one spirit?

The We is the ground of the I. Relational being stands beneath individual being. The We is the soil within which the I is planted, takes root and nourishment, and grows. The primal foundation of the We is the intentional and connotative meaning of the Word of creative address: "Be You." For that really means "Be You for and with Me. . . . Let there be *Us*."

Beneath the I is the We. That means: underlying the mystery of the I is that of the We. And while the I can never be dissolved into the We, as if the latter were the only real being or entity, the former cannot find or attain true life apart from the full and complete participation in the We. The We is the life of the I. And that means: life and relationship are one.

✠

The We is as lawful—and as *logos*-ful—as the psyche and the body of the I and the You. Hence, the relational parameters of the We may be grasped in the same general way as that of the lawful parameters of the body and the psyche. Yet inasmuch as real mystery abides regarding the meaning and extent of those parameters—for the body and the psyche, as well as the We of spirit—the task of understanding is one with that of attaining of faith. Faith in the We precedes and undergirds understanding. And behold, as the body cannot grasp the psyche but the psyche the body, just so, the psyche cannot grasp the spirit but the spirit the psyche. Only in the world to come will we know as we are known. Let it be emphasized, however, that one need not fully understand something in order to apprehend its predictability and lawfulness. So be it with the We. And in truth, the We *is* the lawfulness of language and love.

The We cannot be separated from the I and the You, as if it could have a life of its own, independent of the latter. Yet behold, the I can have a life independent of meeting, a life of consciousness without subjectivity, a life of objectivity within a world of objects. This cannot obtain for the We, however, for it is the life and ground of the I and the You in their meeting and mutuality. The We lives between the I and the You, so that if they do not meet, the We has no life or present—and neither do the I and the You. This is of the greatest importance for religious life and indeed for human history: *the I and the You must will to meet in order for the We to exist in the world.* The will of the participants and the grace of the Spirit are required for "Us" to happen, and thus for a world to happen in which You and I can abide together whole and free.

As individuals, therefore, we have the extraordinary power to say Yes or No to the common life offered to us as our true life, and ultimately, as our redemption. Hence, "the Fall" must must be understood first of all in terms of the refusal of the I to step forth into sustained relationship with the divine You over against it. *The Fall is the breaking asunder of the We*—and that leads inevitably to the death of individual life as well. And the image of the divine You becomes only a dreamlike memory and a kind of restless possibility, fading away with the ebbing of the life of the I. For the life of the I and of the You is at one with the life of the We. And when our We dies, something of You and me must die as well, namely who we have become together.

The We of Humanity

✠

The *uniqueness* of the human We is founded upon the uniqueness of the divine We. The Eternal We is the ultimate "concrete universal," the endlessly peculiar otherness in which at once both our sameness and our privateness take their root. Yet the Eternal We is also the ever-present and available ground of all common life. Behold, both the unique and the common find their unity and origination in the We, human and divine.

You and I meet. In our individual lives, in the silent depths of our ever-springing souls, we are non-repeatable and stamped with a uniqueness and singularity beyond either our grasp or our redesigning. We meet, and the ground of the common emerges between us and We happen. An event real and unforgettable has transpired. For a time beyond time, You and I shared not only each other's lives, but we partook of a common meal from a strangely mutual life between us. This common life, on reflection, bears the seal of uniqueness, just as You and I do in our own humanity. And the uniqueness of this We, while built upon the merging of our personal peculiarities, is nevertheless a whole not only greater than but different from the sum of its parts. With us, as "Us," something new has emerged, something with its very own identity, something actually distinguishable, though certainly not separable, from our own respective individualities. And that identity opens us to—and is indeed in a manner beyond our vision consistent with—the identity of God.

The event of Us includes but is not reducible to our feelings, thoughts and perceptions. My feelings and thoughts, my memories and dreams, my perceptions and needs are not creative of but rather responsive to, the event of meeting. During our meeting, our respective personal reactions are not seen as constitutive to the event itself, but only as essential elements of the unfolding sharing. In the meeting, nothing partial takes over the whole, nothing issuing from either of us biases the common spirit between us, the spirit of truth, of life—and of fire. *Everything* that happens, both within and without, *everything* that is felt and thought, *everything* that emerges finds its life and meaning, its context and justification in the We itself. Every word that is shared, every mode of reaching out and touching, everything passes through and lives within the spirit of Us, of the We.

After You and I have met, however, both of us can—and will—begin the process of reconstruction, and, all too often, of control and ownership. Subsequent to our meeting, I may seek to claim a greater share of responsibility and ownership for what was shared. Mutuality and equality give way to the hierarchy of the Fall. The meeting was for *my* sake more than for yours; *my* concerns gain precedence and priority over yours. It is no longer really our relationship; it is now *my* relationship with You. It is *my* uniqueness over against yours.

✠

Paradox: acts of meeting, of inclusive mutuality, are distinct and different, numerically and temporally. Yet the We is integrative and life nourishing. Behold, the not constant is constant, the sometimes is also the for all times! All true life is meeting, yet meetings are not an unbroken fact of daily life. The We-experiences constitute the oases of life. And water that is absorbed must sustain us through the deserts that have to be traversed and conquered.

The life of this oasis-We may be entered into suddenly and irreversibly or in stages and with real or apparent reversals. We may discover each other with unexpected totality and intensity, or we may play hide-and-seek, as it were. We may come upon each other slowly, gradually building a common history, and through memory discerning piece by piece the reality and extent of our spiritual home. Or we may meet with such open abandon and power as to be swept along to some hitherto uncharted domain of both personal and corporate life, to a realm that may be entered only jointly. In the latter mode, we may therefore awaken to ourselves already in that common sphere long hoped for, having somehow said Yes even if we don't remember when and to a person we had just met. The *Yes* was and is our willingness for an inclusive life, our decision—whether conscious or not—to "follow Me," to go the way of true life. And what great risks in that decision! And how we may hide our decision even from ourselves, until the one comes along whose eyes capture us and whose offer of being summons us to step forth.

Whatever the course, it is the We which is the constant and the content, and the I and the You which are the variables and the forms. Behold, You and I are the forms of love; the We is the content.

The We is at once event and being. It is a mutuality of immediate personal life and of reciprocal presence, a concrete and inclusive wholeness. Of it and from it issues afresh the persons so joined. The very being of the self thus emerges as a *being-together. "Person" constitutes the objectum of the We.* In Latin, *objectum* means literally a "thing thrown before or presented to the mind or to thought." Meeting is thus the event of the movement of being to mutual opposition and lived apposition, wherein the partners become united in their being objects inclusive to each other and to the relational spirit in which they find themselves and one other. From the vantage point of the I and the You, this is a unity-in-difference; but from the perspective of the We, it is a difference-in-unity, a both/and rather than an either/or.

The being which is both shared and one with the event, this We of meeting, cannot strictly speaking be called "your" being or "my" being, or even "being itself." Rather, it must be termed "our" being, the unseen but living ground which has given rise to You and me together. We do not possess this being; we belong to it. As we take our stand, one to another, it draws us into the vastness between us, an event in which we are both active and passive—for it requires both will and grace. As we discover what lives between us, wherein and where from our true being summons us to meet and to embrace this shared life together, our response creatively furthers or hinders the growth of the spirit-being of Us. It is not for us to create but to fulfill the We of love.

Is then the We *objective* or *subjective*? Once again, it is both and neither. The being we share is not reducible to either person's subjectivity, though it permeates and affects—and is affected by—both centers of conscious life. That is, and here we must stretch the meanings of the words we use: what is shared is in its peculiarity, depth and truth, "objective to joint subjectivities." Inasmuch as the event of meeting is non-repeatable, not fully observable by anyone outside the relationship—nor by the participants themselves—and remains "private" or inclusive to the individuals involved, both during and after the meeting, the We must be termed "non-objective." Yet, inasmuch as it was experienced by more than one subject, indeed by both the participants as something shared and mutual and profoundly real—more real than the world surrounding its surrounding of us—the We must also be termed "non-subjective." Is not the We then the "jointly or intersubjective," the "personally objective," and the "privately public"? Is there not a "paradise" of Us, in the original meaning of that term, namely a "walled garden" of true life in the desert of alienation and privation?

In truth, the We is the ground or frame of reference for the meaning of both objectivity and subjectivity. As the basis of meaning and of language itself, the We is the common trough from which we must draw all distinctions and definitions. As such, the reality of the We is prior to the differentiation of objective from subjective.

✠

Does the We have its own consciousness? And in what sense? It may of course be said that the I has its consciousness, and that the You has its kind of consciousness, namely that of the I's consciousness of being a You to another. But what of the We? Is it the case that, as with the You, the I has a consciousness of being a participant in a mutuality, of being a part of a We? Hence, that all consciousness is really of the I proper, of the I aware of the additional modalities of being a person to and with another? The We does indeed enter into and affect the consciousness of the participants, not only in terms of its presence with power, but also as regards how they see themselves and each other. That is, the consciousness of the We directly affects self-image and the apprehension both within and without of meaning and purpose.

One may thus be conscious of the concrete presence of the We, as the orientative ground and lived through meaning of meeting. Further, one may intuitively grasp the "mentality" of the We, as it were, its *Zeitgeist,* its time-spirit, its voice in the mutual immediacy of being together. The life of the We directly affects both the *content* and the *context* of the consciousness of the participants. And just as there is an irreducible specificity and peculiarity to the consciousness of the I as an I, and of the I as a You to another, so also is there a consciousness of the I as a part of a We—but with this startling difference in comparison with the other two modes of awareness: *the I of both partners shares in the one We-consciousness.* That is, the consciousness of the We transcends individual awareness and is actually a *joint* consciousness. Yet behold, this fact of shared consciousness cannot be proven beyond the relationship. Rather, it authenticates and makes itself manifest to the participants. The common consciousness of the We is the ground of the individual consciousness and the psychic world of the I and the You. The We-awareness establishes the parameters and context of the I-awareness. Yet it is the last to be discerned.

Is then the We *transcendent* or *immanent* to the I and the You? It is both and neither. Between the I and the You, the We is the relational ground and the spiritual atmosphere in which and through which they meet and exist in mutuality. The We becomes the frame of reference for the determination of the height and the depth of the I and the You, of that which is within, beyond and at hand. The sphere of the between cuts through the categories of transcendence and immanence, participates in both and extends their meaning for concrete personal life. Due to and in the We, that which is transcendent draws near and makes itself known and present—even as emerging from within me, as well as coming to stand over against me. And that which is within me comes now to include that which is greater than me; it comes to include You and an actual and concrete context of sharing, where meaning weds place and time.

In the event of inclusiveness, a new world is entered, a world which reveals both that which is beyond and that which is within, a world of meeting and merging, a world of interfacing and interpenetrating, a world filled with new possibilities within and without, a world where at last the height and the depth have reached out and embraced each other. In the world between us, all that had heretofore been beyond or strictly within is now shared, is now included in the common life of Us.

It must be understood that the We is shared *person,* not some kind of shared entity or quantum. The We may be called "transpersonal," but only so long as this is not taken to mean "transcendent of persons"—for that immediately conjures up some sort of impersonal substance beyond and even greater than the persons themselves. Person is ultimate—namely Persons-in-relationship. The We is the reality of *shared person;* it is the life between You and me, the personal atmosphere we breathe, which nourishes and sustains our individual existence. And like the narrow band of physical life, that all too easily overlooked and dismissed biosphere in which this life takes place, so also is the We bounded by the immeasurably large and the immeasurably small, by the micro and macro forces of an otherwise non-accommodating cosmos. As a fragile way station between spheres of an apparently impersonal universe, the world of the We constitutes our one and only paradise of life and meaning and love.

✠

We step forward and meet: mutuality happens. Where and when do we meet? Does not all this take place in the world? Are we not earthbound, and must not our relationships therefore be bound here with us? Yet what objective points of reference can I use to map out where and when You and I happened, where and when We lived? For behold, we entered a world invisible to all but us and existing nowhere else than between us, at a point when time either stood still and yielded itself to a higher mode of duration, or continued as if apart from us in an unresponsive realm without the true presence of persons—at least of our persons. You and I have found each other and lived together in a world only between us, for a time not to be measured in length but in terms of life-altering presence and power. That world is now a memory and a hope, and also a subterranean source of support and sustenance for the *chronos* or clock time of today. What we shared was something over and above the inter-species world of time and space; it was the inter-personal world only between us, yet in and through which the whole of the cosmos gains its true and ultimate context of meaning: the context of creation, of the "Let Us make...." From the intra-divine ground of essential relationality sprang forth the creation in and of time and space.

Behold, the where and the when of our meeting is the tri-unity of persons, and *precisely in our communion we stand together in the image of the mutuality of God,* and thus in the mode of that Holy Sharing from which arose through the Word the objective world. That is—and so much is at stake for us in this realization!—we meet in the sphere of person, which is prior to and greater than that of the physical world. For the sphere of God *is* the sphere of Person. Hence, though time and space as mutual presence and duration exist in the relationship of persons, the relationship does not exist in the "ordinary" time and space of our life in the world. We happen in an "eternal now."

When therefore did we meet? Though we may circle a period of chronological time when the meeting took place, such a designation is only for convenience sake, and serves as an orientative point for memory and for witnessing to each other and to others about the fact of our world, of Us. For in truth, we transfigure time in that the present became at one with our presence to and with each other. Time became the now of You and me. Duration was the length of Us. We filled time, and in and through us, time attained its purpose and life.

Where and when, then, do we meet? In that sphere wherein time and space are inseparable from person and relationship, wherein the time-space matrix becomes *"aufgehoben,"* both cancelled and annulled yet retained and completed, in the eternal time-space matrix of persons, of love, and thus of the Spirit of God. For indeed, what we call the "time and space matrix," is a created image of what is between the eternal You and I of God, Their life and love, Their Holy We. God is the where and the when of Us.

Hence: where You and I meet *is* who We are; when You and I meet *is* what We are. We are not in the cosmos but the cosmos is in us, straining to be brought into our life together and redeemed by and with us.

Further, in the We-event the borders of the present are extended into the past and the future. In the We, the whole of time is gathered or summed up. In the eternal present of mutuality, the past is ever available and thus ever redeemable, and the future ever attainable. All possibilities, past, present and future arise within this ever new, ever renewing event which bears our life—between us. The Alpha and the Omega of human origin and destiny, the beginning and the end find their Source in the world between us, the sphere of the kingdom of Love. Behold, the kingdom of the We is the Kingdom of God.

✠

Yet how can one stake one's life on something that is not technically in the world, even if it gives meaning to all the enterprises that unfold within the world? The risks of staking my life on Us, on our We cannot be denied or diminished—nor can the rewards it offers of true life and meaning. What we give is what we get. And what We are is to determine our all. When You and I are apart, where do I take my stand, where do I live but in faith and hope grounded in memory, but with meaning borrowed from Us, spending our common treasure in the belief that our future meetings will engender more riches yet?

I believe that what happened between You and me in the past somehow sustains me now, even though I may not be able to see or to say exactly in what ways. What we shared is the context of my daily hope and the silent expectation toward which I move. Before our next meeting, I seek—if I am faithful—to make my world more open to and consistent with Us; I desire to place everything I am and do into the context of what lives between us. Though not physically present, You go with me as I go with You, for We abide in our love. You affect all my doings and happenings; I hold dialogue with You in the atmosphere of our mutualness. We give each other life; we have given each other Us. Our time and our place slowly invades the time and place of the world, and would transform the latter into a home fit for Us.

✠

The problem of listening: Your word comes to me. I am addressed: a message and a messenger seek me out, intending me—not only me, but a listening person who can hear and respond, who can join in a communicative arc of shared action. As I receive the word it evokes life in me, thoughts and feelings, memories and incitements to behavior. Too quickly perhaps, this incoming word is covered over by my own being-in-response. The center of attention too readily can become me and my reactions and sentiments. And the listening ceases save to myself, and true dialogue becomes an inner monologue in your presence—therefore not our presence. Truly, at the heart of the human dilemma lies the problem of listening. Do we then know how to listen to each other? To whom do You listen? Who really hears You? How serious is Jesus when He pleads: "You who have ears, listen"!

To listen to You is to become one with You. That Jesus was one with the Father meant, as He Himself said, that He listened with absolute openness and constant obedience and preparedness to the Voice of the One who was at the same time greater than He. For, as He said, "He who belongs to God hears what God says" (John 8:27); and "My sheep listen to my voice" (John 10:27).

Yet to listen to the self is not to become one with the self. Self-reflection, while necessary for understanding the meaning of being human, and greatly beneficial to life and to the preparation for meeting others, nevertheless all too easily results in division and distinction rather than unification and wholeness. Unity and wholeness come into being only in a relationship of true reciprocity and mutual inclusiveness.

The We becomes present not through self-reflection but only through other-apprehension. You and I gaze upon each other; You are my center of attention as I am yours. In listening to You. We happen; in responding to You, I come into present being—and with You, rather than as a being unto myself. The We happens only when You and I are not looking for it—as if it were a cargo ship that we in our hunger are straining to glimpse enters into the waters surrounding our individual islands! The We happens only when You and I abandon ourselves for the sake of the other. In listening to You, I hear myself as well; in addressing You, I become myself. For the We—that is, You and I—live in the fullness of the word between us. This word denotes You and I, but it connotes love, even if unspoken. Perhaps if we could live with love without calling undue attention to it, love could live with us in completeness and peace.

It is so difficult to meet! For we look but do not see, we hear but do not let in. The exigencies of our inner world, our prejudices and tunnel vision, our habitual mental sets all interfere with stepping forth and meeting afresh, all prevent Us from happening. When I see You I am in a "current" state of being: where am I going and coming from, what am I walking around with, what pains or burdens or concerns color my perceptions of You and of what You seek from me? What specific thing or things, what partially attracts my gaze, so that I distort or even miss You? If You smile at me, are You being friendly and sincere, or nervous and manipulative? If You scowl are You then mean and stand-offish, or only afraid and self-protective of my possible motives?

O the never-ending jockeying for relational position and advantage! O, how tempting though unfulfilling to reduce You to my object—which would make me your subject, the one in control of the relationship. We seek points of safety and thus elevation, of esteem and thus pride, hierarchies instead of the open plain of equality. Yet behold, the sphere between us is the vast plain of mutuality and communion. It knows or admits of neither pits nor peaks, but only the immeasurable breadth of its own realm. When and where we meet, when and where we happen is a holy and living ground, level and trustworthy, even though unseen. For we see only each other. We do not grasp that which grasps us as the sacred hands of our relationship. And how sure is that grasp!

✠

How fragile, how radically dependent upon each of us is this We of our common life! The life of the We between us hinges on our will to step forth and walk together, on our respective commitment to each other and to the relationship, on our daily desire to meet and to continue the growing of Us, as it were. If either of us should pull away, if either should determine to cut the common cords of our living connectedness, You and I will die as a We. And behold, it is a real death. The dying may be slow and almost unnoticeable, like a gradual flattening of affect, a fading first of passion then of substance. Or it may come with the sudden and searing torch of rejection.

Behold, what begins as spirit seems destined to end as flesh. The spirit of love leaves behind the skeletal remains of the "law." For relational legalism is a symptom of the dying of the We, and only serves to propel the relationship toward its final demise. The "shoulds" and the "should nots" are a poor covering over the absence of the *is* and the *is not*. When ritual enactment hides the loss of genuine desire and presence, the relationship is at best a memory and a hope, but no longer an actuality. And the divine Person is no more to be appeased by grand and glorious liturgy performed by persons whose hearts are far from God than the human person can long be wooed by poetry without presence.

When the words and actions of former love have no present life, they crucify rather than comfort. And for whose sake are these actions carried out, for the one no longer loved and sought after, or for the sake of the one performing the acts, as if to give assurance that all is well, and that the convenantal substance of the We, be it between God and humanity or person to person, is still intact and in force, and that therefore the world is yet whole and meaningful? Do we really want to see the cracks and the potholes, the walls and the voids that remain between us? Who could withstand seeing the actual state of the We in the world? It is in all truth the agony of God.

How much of our lives do we spend in an "as if" world, existing as if something which was real and meaningful once, is still thus, even when it is not? How many of us think we believe and live as if God were real, even though we stake nothing on God's Word, even though we do not risk the Kingdom, seeking and trusting only in the security that the world offers, only in money and the companionship of the lost? Behold, what are we but practical atheists?

Or how many live through a dead or seemingly always dying marriage, all the while denying this fact and living as if it were still somehow viable? How much of our precious time are we engaged in the futile attempt to deceive ourselves and others that things which are not are so?

In our deception and the will thereof, the evil among us takes its home and prospers. Where lies and illusion are sought, there darkness moves in and reigns. And do we love darkness rather than light after all? And do we prefer the hell of unknowing and unfulfillment to the illumination of the Truth, and to the offer of eternal communion?

Perhaps it is after all the We which is the constant, and You and I who are the dependent variables in the vast sphere between us. For it is You and I who discover or deny each other, who enter and exit from this unseen and unseeable world of being and life always available between us, like a pool of being we can always dive into and from which we can always retreat. The We is ever offered; it is You and I who must choose whether to step forth or not; it is You and I who must will to meet. But the ground of grace is ever present and ever possible. Woe to us that we so rarely choose to find ourselves and our life in the Kingdom between us! We blame love for its inconsistency and feebleness, all the while looking the other way regarding our own culpability and inability to maintain the unity of love together. Love is as powerful and life-sustaining as we allow it to be. When we do not believe in love, we really do not believe in ourselves in love.

Yes, the We among us is fragile indeed, yet its substance is that of life itself. Strange that true life is so readily losable, so seemingly weak and susceptible to both inside and outside influences! Nevertheless, our very future as individual persons and as a whole people rides on the establishment of the We upon the earth. The Kingdom of the We is the Kingdom of Heaven, and even though it has begun in the seemingly most inauspicious way, with the coming of a solitary figure long ago to a tiny and insignificant land, a short-lived prophet who was crucified in shame and absolute failure, it has arrived. And it shall prevail.

✠

Modes of the We

There is an *"intrapsychic We"* within each person. It is the innate archetype and germinal yeast for all relationships. It comes into being with the I itself as the unconscious yet ineradicable remembrance of the We of creation, of the primal relationship with God through the Word: "Be You." And in that Word is contained the hidden mandate and code for the "how to" and the "why to" of all subsequent relationships—with God, with humanity, and with nature. The intrapsychic We sets the context for and participates in the three spheres of spirit, soul and body. It is of the spirit in that it is the earliest record of divine-human spirituality, which though not spoken was and continues to be present to and in the individual as the Source-meaning of all that follows. It thus establishes the spiritual ground for every development of individual and communal life.

In being spoken through the command to "Be" common to all of creation, the intrapsychic We undergirds our life with nature. That is, through it we belong to the We of nature, to the physical world as animal, as a species of the whole. And in being addressed through the "You" common to all humanity, this innate We grafts us onto the wondrous vine of the soul. It thereby grants us a place among humanity and a position from which we may contribute to the unfolding dialogue of history.

The intrapsychic We is the remembrance of our "first love," our first command and our first word. The love of God, the Word of both the command and address of God are united in the event of our creation, and recorded in the innate We of the soul, the inner reality which makes possible all subsequent relationships, without which love, law and language would not exist. But then, neither would humanity! Love, law and language therefore find their interconnection and common source within the person precisely here, in the hidden relationship of the soul to its Creator.

By its very existence, the intrapsychic We engenders the possibility of the perversion of the mandate to relate to others, by the I relating to itself in lieu of and as if it were to another. Thus can be formed an *"ideational We,"* a fantasy relationship existing only within the person. For it is of the nature of the I to form relationships and to live always in the context of them. Where there has been no real and primary bonding between the I and a significant other, the I is forced, through need and the innate call to relationship, to form such a relationship with itself. Call it a "surrogate You." In an act of desperation, the I disassociates an imaged dimension of itself, and establishes a purely subjective We, a We without a corresponding You. The I relates only with itself, be it in isolation or with other persons actually present. In the latter situation, the I relates to itself through the other person as medium. The I does not really see the other as the You over against it, but rather its own projected self on the screen of the other's face.

The key to distinguishing between a real and an unreal We is the paradoxical presence of both genuine *otherness* and *mutualness* in the relationship. This also means that the participants manifest the capacity to *hear* each other in their otherness, to be open to the other and able to enter into real mutuality rather than only manipulation, freedom rather than controlled ritual. In a genuine We, the locus of being is between the participants; in the ideational We, the locus of being never leaves the individual I.

✠

In addition to the ideational We, the I is prone to generate an *"idealized We."* This happens when the I distorts the We of remembrance by its own desire and design for what it wants and needs the relationship to be. The idealized is not the same as the ideational We, in that the former is based upon a real relationship to a You, whereas the latter never transcends the arc of the I. To idealize means to lift something or someone out of its ordinary and genuine mode of being in order to make it appear greater than it is for the sake of its meeting—or failing to meet—some subjective and non-attainable need or standard. The energizing power of idealization is *desire*; and it is desire which spawns *maia*, illusion. Yet desire sees something of the truth it seeks, be it only as a feeling within or as an element of perception without, before it spins its web of illusion, before it announces "This is it!"

The idealized We is thus the We of experience refracted through the lens of desire, need and hope. It is memory blinded at the point of need. The I sees the You of memory now clothed in the garment of the longed for, the could be. Such idealizations can distort not only past meetings but future encounters as well, even to the point of the person closing off from and thus shutting down any real relationship. For the I may be responding not to the You present over against it, but to the You wrapped in the multicolored cloak its need has fashioned. Hence, the I might "miss" the You of the now for the sake of seeming intercourse with the You of the could be.

And behold, the danger of such an idealized perceptual constancy is that of idolatry itself. Can we then encounter what we worship? Or would our need-based images prevent us from waking up to the Real before us?

✠

Is there not also an *"illicit We,"* a We of unholy union or of "forbidden fruit"? This is the We of adultery, and is indeed one with the unclean spirit or We of idolatry. For both adultery and idolatry represent self-serving in opposition to the serving of the interests of the other and of the relationship. In both cases the I worships whatever will maximize personal gain—thus the I in reality worships itself. The We of fidelity is broken for the "me first" of egoism; the life between is given up for the sake of the inner life of pleasure and personal aggrandizement. The illicit We is not therefore a We at all, though it may give the appearance of one. At stake is not mutual being but mutual advantage, not a sharing of life but a covenant of exploitive power. The illicit We seeks temporal and temporary gain at the cost of true and eternal life. It is always only "for the time being"—i.e., "Eat, drink and be merry, for today we die."

Let it be emphasized that the whole being of the person can *never* enter into an illicit relation, if for no other reason than that the eternal in us would never give itself entirely to the temporal. And the spirit would die before it would give itself to evil. And many walk among us for whom the spirit is but a memory encountered only in their sleeping dreams.

The illicit We is the adulterous union. In marriage we become one spirit and one flesh. Every part of our being, the totality of our body, soul and spirit is married. Nothing single and uncovenanted abides. We do not belong to ourselves but to each other, and to the relationship, to "Us." Adultery, be it only of mind or also of body, is thus always preceded by an inner divorce, by a decision of the will that "I am my own—I can and will do as I please, for I belong to myself alone." This signifies a direct *No* to the priority of marriage and a corresponding *Yes* to the priority of the self, a No to the We and a Yes to the I. By its very nature therefore, the illicit We disunifies and breaks asunder the covenant of marriage—divine and human, as well as person to person. In place of the life of communion and covenant is the "no-life" of self-law and anarchy, the lawlessness of the will in rebellion, in freedom—or better, escape—from all responsibility to the other, to the marriage, and to God.

"I am answerable only to myself." That means: "I am my own god." What kind of a world would result if the majority of a people took that stand? Behold, we are now finding out, for that is indeed the current malaise of our culture. And a people cannot long survive when the very fabric of its common law and mutual consent is torn by and aflame with the self-destructive actions of the I without its You. Hence, are we not now witnessing the suicidal dance of the I apart from its We?

Yet the Word from above: "Thou shalt have no other gods before Me....Thou shalt have no strange god within thee." If God, the one and only God, who is the eternal You of our life, is not God to us, then only the I is left to plug the void that remains. Only the I abides and must project itself into an emptiness so vast that only the essential You of God could fill it. And behold, the god of the I's own projection cannot succor or save. The "strange god" then is the I apart from the You of true relationship. And that means the I in isolation not only from others—and the Other— but cut off from itself as well. For personal being is bestowed as gift only in true relationships, only in the partnership of the We.

The We of the Community

The Intensive and Extensive We

We enter into hallowed yet treacherous territory when we broach the subject of the We and its meaning for community. For we address our corporate world itself, the "public domain" we all share, that which all agree to be the "mutually objective," the "psychosphere" of common life and daily interchange. On the one hand, the "psychosphere" is a genuine corporate We of communal meeting and existing in a more or less unified and lawful world, in a land of common language, custom and history. On the other hand, however, this extensive We of community claims priority over and can even strive to preclude the intensive We of the I-You. Further, the corporate We can demand absolute dominion over the individual person, even to the extent of denying the right to and legitimacy of private existence, of any personal life hidden from its own coercive choreography. Such is the bane called "communism." And what a damnable surrogate is the We of the "state" for the We of You and me!

What then of the We of You and me? Is our mutuality a part of or apart from the We of community? Paradox: the mutuality of the We of the I-You relation interpenetrates both public and private domains yet cannot be identified with either. Is it not then a midway point, an irreplaceable bridge between the person and the community? So that the person lives in three intertwined spheres of that which is *private, public* and *mutual*? And does not the mutual ground the person in the community and the community in the person?

The *intensive* We of the I-You must be differentiated from the *extensive* We of all other human modes of relationality. To what shall I compare their relationship? A rock penetrates the silent stillness of a pond. The rock goes straight to the bottom in a vertical motion of power and singular determination. At the point of penetration a second and horizontal motion begins: a wavic action forms concentric circles. And as the circles emanate farther from the point of vertical ingress, they are both larger and less definable. A kind of *cross* is created by the two motions constitutive to the event itself. Behold, the vertical dimension represents the intensive We event, begun at the point of the creative address of God: "Be You." It sets in motion and determines the pattern of all other intensive and intimate We relationships. And the horizontal dimension signifies the extensive We, consisting of the ever-widening circles of family, religious group, neighborhood, community, state, and world.

The cross here demonstrates the three dimensions of personal life: the height, of God, the depth, of self, and the breadth, of the world of humanity. Note carefully that the intensive We is singular and discontinuous, whereas the extensive We is multiple and continuous. Yet the two are interrelated and ultimately inseparable dimensions of personal life.

The extensive We of community and the intensive We of the I-You relationship therefore can and must be supportive of each other. Both domains are essential for the full existence of the person. When they are not affirming of each other, however, a major crisis of identity ensues for the I: the private I is called upon to choose between the mutual and the public, the intensive and the extensive We. And most persons choose to live in the world, hence to honor Caesar and the "republic," in the original Latin and literal meaning of the latter term: "a thing or affair of the people." The loss of the pervasive acceptance and power of the mutual We leads to the rending of the world of the person into two now seemingly separate sectors, the private and the public, neither one being sufficient for personal existence.

Without the mediating intensive We, the I can no longer locate itself in the extensive We of the community, nor can the intimate We, which the I and the You nevertheless still experience between each other, find a fitting home within the community at large. Hence, the intensive We of the I and the You loses its connection to the community—and with that, both the I and the You suffer as well the loss of identity and communal confirmation. And the internal world is shoved into a deeper and terrifying privacy by the ever more daring incursions of the public We into the I severed from its You and the We of true mutuality.

What then obtains for the I when the intensive We is not permitted solid grounding in the extensive We of the community? Is the I to risk staying on the bridge of the mutual, exposed and vulnerable, and as a "martyr" witness to the possibility and power of the life of communion? Or is it to retreat back into itself, into the empty safety of privacy, the lonely security of unspokenness? Or is the I to cross over the bridge and make its grand entrance into the public domain of the communal and cosmetic I, of the chameleon self, ever changing and fading with every fad?

Where then is the I to locate its true identity, in the private or the mutual or the public sector? And how can it nestle into the intensive We if the latter is refused adequate mooring in the "psychosphere"? Would not the existence of the intimate We have been relegated to that of a kind of dirigible of the spirit, as it were, fine and enjoyable for an occasional "experience" but certainly not stable or safe for the substance of our daily life? Behold, when the intensive We of mutuality is not accorded sanctuary and value and even reverence by and in the extensive We of public life, the I loses as well the meaning and purpose of the other two sectors of personal existence. For without the go-between of the mutual We, the I is faced with a no-win choice between either the loss of the affirmation of privacy by a public sector seeking to absolutize its domain, or the loss of the affirmation of public participation and belonging in the community by a private sector in secret revolt. For the I cannot but rebel at the denial of the primacy of the mutual. Apart from its We, the I has no air to sustain its personal existence. For air is of the spirit, and the spirit is the breath of Us.

And behold, all the while the mass media of our culture gone public seek to create a materialistic I in its own image which can be fed and soothed and controlled. Such is the bane called "consumerism." And what an oppressive and suffocating surrogate for Us is this "have-it-all-now" We of public gluttony! Things, things, we are awash with things! The economic I—in *this* does our life consist?

What has been the traditional safeguard for individual life, and for the intensive and intimate We of the I and the You? *Religion*. In truth, the essential locus of being for the I is in the intensive We, and that means the We of covenant. And the two primary covenants of life are those of religion and marriage, with the former granting legitimating ground to the latter. Where the intensive mutuality of religion and marriage is honored by the public and private sectors of personal life, a cultural harmony exists, and individual and corporate life flourish side by side. But when one or the other—typically the latter—seeks to dominate the mutual sphere, to take it over, it is an immediate sign that the religious safeguard has broken down. And when religion loses its agreed-upon sovereignty over both the private and public sectors, the result is cultural and personal disintegration. Secularism eventuates in a hell of either privatism, and therefore lawlessness, or communalism, and therefore meaninglessness. Apart from religion, mutuality loses its secure paths of righteousness.

This is the precise situation the twentieth century has brought to a "critical mass." Neither religion nor marriage is truly honored and allowed reverent sanctuary. Hence, the glue of the mutual has lost its holding power. And there have been two primary attempts to grab the pieces and to replace the mutual, and through the mutual to gain control over the private sectors of personal life. They are the twin aberrations of the extensive We called *communism* and *consumerism*. Both are secular ideologies based on economics, and envision a purely material humanity. Communism is avowedly atheist—and must be so, for the meaning and spiritless "state" it has puffed up into existence is its god. Consumerism may maintain a facade of religiosity, but only for the sake of public consumption, as it were. For consumerism finds religion great for business, and would swallow any "other-worldliness" into its vision of the kingdom of the now, in which our future has been mortgaged to pay for its today.

Only a religious revival will stop the coming ignition of revolution and corporate dismemberment. Only a religious revival can reestablish and consecrate the holy dominion of the intensive We of the I and the You, and circumscribe the extensive We by and ultimately into the We of religious community. And only a reestablished We of the I-You relationship can reintegrate the I into the culture; only the intensive We can invite the I out of its anomic prison and into the world of community, safe and secure within its holy clothing. The intensive We is the living foundation and reservoir of spirit and love in the world . From it therefore shall spring forth the We of our redemption—not just as individuals but as a people.

✠

The We and the "crowd": sheer corporateness does not a We make. In the intensive We, the I and the You are discerned, determined and declared as true individuals in mutuality. The We is the home of the I and the You, the abode wherein the psyche has its original and legitimate dwelling place. In the We, knowing and being known are one, knowledge and person attain unity. In the extensive We of the crowd, however, it is the I which must discern the mood and social situation of the crowd and not vice-versa—for the crowd is blind save to itself alone. The crowd cannot see the individual, but only its own ethos, only its overriding purpose or reason for being. Yet the crowd can exercise a powerful presence to the I, and offer a persuasive kind of corporateness. The I experiences the *corporateness of the crowd* in *three interwoven aspects*: the sharing of *physical nearness* and identity, the *common consciousness* or "group psyche," the "us vs. them" mentality, and the spiritual sense of *common aim* or purpose—the "esprit de corps," as it were.

The crowd does not affirm the individual as such, but only its *image* of individual life within it. For the crowd is above all the *image maker* and *sustainer*. The crowd creates an image of the individual in accordance with its desire, and then constrains those who participate in its life to live out its models of being. And since the group defines the individual only in its own terms, it sees persons exclusively within the context of the models and roles it has delineated as acceptable. The crowd thus denies in practice the legitimacy of individual uniqueness, of that which it has not predetermined and approved of, of that which exists apart from its mere dream of "personality." The crowd is not creative of persons in their present actuality; rather it is conservative and coercive, limiting and suspicious, conditional and hence non-affirming. Like a bureaucracy, it justifies, affirms and feeds on itself alone.

In the corporate We of the crowd, then, the basis of being together actually *excludes* the I and the You. And it cannot be other, even if the crowd publicly lauds the value and existence of intensive We relationships in its own ranks. For such We encounters transcend the corporateness of the crowd and are ever a potential threat to group life and cohesiveness. And does not the shadow We of the crowd have every reason to fear the We which lives in the light?

✠

What are the *numerical limits* to the We of true presence and encounter? How many can experience the mutuality of shared being at the same time and place? Is it not open-ended, like the number of words in a sentence, or musicians in an orchestra? Yet, is it not the case that the greater the number of participants, the shallower the We, and the more impulsive and reactionary? Once again, we are faced with the question of the extensiveness over against the intensiveness of the experience of shared being. And there does seem to be an inverse relationship between the two: the more intensive the less extensive; the more extensive the less intensive.

Yet behold, the pressure toward conformity and conversion increases with the number of persons involved in an event of shared being. Religion is a central case in point. Enter the "Revival" meeting. Does not such a meeting seek to force the choice between heaven and hell upon the individual? Can a true inner conversion of heart and mind be pressured from the outside in? Note carefully that *the pressure toward is not the same as the power of conversion*—for what percentage of those "converted" in a large meeting are truly transformed in and by the meeting, rather than only moved toward transformation by the emotional pressure cooker of the crowd and the preacher and the sensed involvement of God? A genuine conversion at such a meeting would happen as much in spite of as because of the meeting itself. And indeed, God uses even the sweltering group to reach the I with the message of the love and the invitation into the We of eternal life.

The true and ultimate power of conversion comes in and through the most intimate and intensive We-event accorded to the person in this life: "co-union" or communion with God. Nothing in the world can begin to approximate the "new birth" event of the entrance of the I into the Holy We of God. This most intensive We upholds the We in all its extensiveness; in God the intensive and the extensive We are one; in God, the height and the depth of mutuality are not in opposition to the breadth. And the day is coming when the We of God shall attain such extension that God will truly be "all in all." In that day, the We of God shall have redeemed both the intensive and the extensive We of humanity.

✠

The relationship of the We of the I-You to the We of the face-to-face community, be it of church or social group, of the work place or the military unit, may be symbolized by the cross. The vertical beam represents the foundational I-You relationship, and the horizontal all other relationships of mutuality, each mode continuing to be dependent upon the vertical for support, for height and depth.

Language itself affords a more graphic representation of the two-foldness of the We relationship. For in its "spirituality," language offers through its own syntax both a manifestation of and a way to discern this division of intensive and extensive We relationships. Does not an ontological and relational state of affairs correspond to the differentiation of the second person singular from the second person plural? While in English the pronoun "Thou" is no longer used for the singular, the grammatical arrangement still recognizes the distinction between the two modes of persons. The singular and the plural You correspond to the two types of We relationships. And further, *it is a different I which addresses the singular as opposed the plural You.* The I cannot address the plural You with the fullness of being; the I cannot but address the singular You with the fullness of being. The I of the singular mode is the more "private," the I of the plural is the more "public" I, the I more readily identifiable and objectifiable as the person in the world, present to and impacting upon the community.

The greater the number of persons involved—up to a point yet to be determined—the greater the extenuating and flattening of the meaning and depth of being a person, and the more thematic and stereotypic become the participants to each other. In the group, "personality" is born. We become known and distinguished by certain physical, behavioral and characterological traits. In the spirit of the group, in its living ambience, the I cannot be apprehended in its wholeness and integrity. Nor can the I be responded to in its depth and with the mutuality of the I-You. Rather, though the mutuality of the community may be real and even profound, it can envelop the participants only in partiality and to the extent of their involvement.

Further, the We of the I-You relationship is different from the We of three or more. Yet it must be stressed that the We of spirit cannot be neatly "logicized" or experientially chopped up into discrete realities and sub-particles. It is not as if the We of the one-on-one intimacy could be grasped as discontinuous with the We of genuine community, or even with the "We-sense" of a whole people. Rather, the ultimate unity and oneness of God and of humanity in God require the overlapping and interweaving of all categories of human relationality. Distinctions must be drawn, but the underlying unity must nevertheless be held, even if only on faith, rather than on insight.

✠

When two become three: You and I meet. We encounter each other in sweet wholeness. In the mutuality between us, the We of spirit and love emerges and in its unseen presence exercises its will. It guides us as we are open and willing to respond to and move toward each other in and through its life between us. Another person enters our time and space, as it were. The relationship undergoes immediate transformation. The water of another presence, alien and unknowing of Us, hits the burning embers of our mutuality. The steam of closing communion fills the sphere between us. And the depth dimension, the vertical bond of being together, bridges out into the horizontal. The mystery of an eternal present evaporates and a "public world" happens.

No matter how seriously and openly You and I and this new other may strive to expand and continue unabated with our intimacy, the mutual privacy of personal being cannot be regained or recaptured. For either one observes the other two relating, or the three of us experience the simple corporateness of community. Behold, where more than two persons meet, *comparison* enters the perceptual sphere. The "Yous" over against the I are distinguished by the I; they are compared and evaluated in terms of such polarities as attractiveness-unattractiveness, accepting-rejecting, warm-cold and the like. The mysterious presence of the We of the I-You recedes to the background, from the once palpable to the only remembered. The mystery may still be present, and behold, it lingers long in the soul, but the partners do not experience its affirming and uplifting and easy life between them. Where three or more gather, custom and tradition is in their midst.

The We of the more than two in fact consists of more than one relationship. Each person can, at least in potential, be in relation to every other person in a one-to-one mode, even while the group as a whole is involved with a single center of attention. That is, community consists of a chain of I-You relationships, and its unity borders that of God. For God is the consummation of all relationships. And the We of community is greater than the sum of its parts, including both the participants and their relationships one to another. The We of community *is* a mutual being and spirit, and as such evidences wholeness and integrity—or the lack thereof—just as individual persons. Indeed, it arises as a mode of shared person, a mutuality of the many, rather than of the two. This mutuality cannot attain to the depth or have the impact of the singular We of the I-You communion, but it is a real and essential mutuality nonetheless.

It cannot be overemphasized, however, that *no other relationship can replace or include intact and unaffected the We of the I and the You.* And without the vertical relationship of depth, persons cannot attain to the height of potential being. And the beauty and necessity of the horizontal level of koinonia, of fellowship, would become a prison of truncated persons without the constant grounding in the Rock of the vertical We.

In sum, apart from the We of the I-You, there is no salvation. Yet, apart from the We of holy and covenantal community, there is no final healing of our long term social and personal dis-eases. Hence, the Cross of humanity and revelation includes both the vertical and the horizontal dimensions of relational existence.

✠

The We of Memory

The presence of the We is not "experienced" or attended to during the actual event of meeting and mutuality. It is only afterward, that through the intimacy of memory, the presence of the We, the wondrous event of Us, comes to be revealed— and as imprinted upon my soul henceforth. *We have been.* You were present to me in my own presence to You, though not in a way that can be demonstrated to someone else—maybe not even to ourselves! This presence was not in time, though time was in it. Nor did the laws of personal space seem to apply any longer, for I was not "in" me any more than You were "in" You. *We were together.* Time and space merged into Us, as We emerged from time and space. You and I were one in our holy occasion. *The presence of the We is our presence together.*

Now I hold Us in memory. And in that memory abides the hope and the need of future meetings, of more moments spent in the eternity of communion. The memory of Us is a blessing to carry me through the deserts of public isolation and non-recognition, across the dry and dusty plains of a world eroded by its endless denial of mutuality. That memory is a reservoir of personal meaning for my life. And I may use its water to relieve—but not quench!—not only my own thirst, but also that of others who share in my daily pilgrimage. Behold, You and I have become a source of life for others; what We have been together grants us not only meaning but also mission when we are apart.

I remember You. I remember our inclusiveness. You are in my memory. Yet I may diminish or idealize You; I may deny, cut, transform, pervert, seek to gain control over You—and what We were—in and through my memory. For is not my memory private and unaccountable to You or to anyone beyond myself? What else is truly mine but my memory? It is a memory, however, which You have invaded. For I do indeed have You in my memory. In what way? As being inseparable from Us. And I possess something of Us in memory. I may return to the scene of our encounter, and touch or re-touch You in my heart.

Memory is a necessary aid to new meetings between us, preparing me, teaching and admonishing me, clarifying who You are and what We have been—and not been—together. Through memory, I may gather myself and identify with the person You seemed to discover in and as me. The memory of Us may thereby facilitate the vital process of personal integration and individuation. I can identify with You and with Us, and in anticipation be even more open and ready for new meetings, more willing and able to give of myself, to hold nothing back from You and from Us, to know and to be known, to trust and to be trustworthy.

At the same time, however, memory can grant a false sense of self-sufficiency, and an illusory feeling that I know all I need or want to know about You. With that comes the gnawing belief that our relationship holds out no new promises, no adequate justification for future meetings and no hope for further ground breakings. Thus may I say, "That is enough! We have no future. So let us just be thankful for what we have shared and be done with it. Good-bye . . . the relationship is over. The memory will suffice, thank You."

Yet the memory will also deceive. For there abides more to You and to Us than I could ferret out in a thousand meetings. In every true meeting, in every event of shared being, there is newness and novelty and unexpected revelations of who We are together—and of who we are as individuals. In every We occurrence, love rewards us with a new visage and more of itself. And as love increases in us, we increase in love. Love's more means our more as well. Love never stays the same; it is either rising or dying. The love-spirit of the We is eternally fresh, perpetually open-ended.

The memory of Us can also interfere with new meetings. For now You and I have a set of mostly unexamined but nevertheless operative expectations about each other and Us. Our meetings have established precedents and implicit standards—a "canon" of Us, so to speak. And do We now feel less free simply to meet and explore rather than to act out of our past? Are we dispositionally consigned to attempt to repeat a past meaning rather than find a wholly—and therefore holy—new meaning in the present? You and I in our separate ways, and thus in our separation, may treat each other in accordance with our memories and the needs that have come to be associated with them. Yet what are these unmet needs of our private world but parasites to real meeting and mutuality, hands from behind which move to blindfold us to the truth, to seeing each other as we really are in the present? When we bring our needs to be met by the other— then that is what we meet—but not each other. Needs preclude presence; they only serve to cover today with the unresolved issues of yesterday.

What then are we to do about our needs for each other? Plant them with gentleness and love in the ground between us. Yield them to the wholeness of our presence together, for only in abandoning them there will we find fulfillment. Only when and as we let go of that which we so tightly clasp as the substance of our desire and open naked and empty to each other will that which We are together, our communion, fill and heal us of poverty and woundedness.

And what is our deepest need but to be whole together? Why then do we so easily deny this tender yearning at the base of our souls? Why do we spend our time on the lesser needs, on the things which do not make for life, our life together?

The solution to the problem of unmet needs is seen in the vanishing of the problem in the mutuality between us. Our needs must be immersed in the kingdom we share. Healing is wholeness. And from wholeness shall spring forth holiness. And holiness is the wholeness of God.

✠

I remember Momma. I remember my smallness enwrapped in her warm and perfumed flesh. I remember her curtain-parting smile and the beckoning light in her eyes. Hers was a face of glamor and largess. She was present everywhere; my world clung to her side with my body. She was the center of my needs and the gratification thereof; she offered me life and sustenance. She was the first You of my conscious life, and thus she set the mold, standard and pattern for all the significant others to come. I early learned to study her face for news of my state and hers. Was I then all right or hurt or bad or good or just fine? "Tell me who I am, Mother! My whole life is at stake in your actions: your acceptance or rejection, your love or indifference will be driven deep as piles upon which the whole of my life will be built."

I remember not only Momma. I remember Momma and me. The first and primal We of memory is that of parent-child. Here is the die cast for the whole of our relational life. The parent-child We begins with the You of the parent writ large upon the heavens of the world of the child. And that You summons forth the I of the child in response. Thus is born the most pervasive and enduring human relationship. The colors it introduces into the world of the child, the child shall use to color all other relationships.

With what colors then do we paint each other upon meeting? Are they bright and trusting or sullen and suspicious? Are they few or great in number? Are they stark and ever oppositional or are they arranged neatly in hues sensitive to the differing realities of You and me? Colors spring from the memory box of our primal parent-child We. And how difficult to put colors into the memory box later, when they were not already present as gift! How difficult to make up for lost coloration!

This parent-child We, the earliest We of conscious memory, is either in accordance with or at odds to, the hidden memory of the We of creation, the We of God's creative address. And if the latter We of God's loving and assuring *Yes* to us is offset by an unloving or rejecting *No* from the parental We, a profound inner conflict is born. For the child faces the seemingly impossible situation of trying to confirm an unshakable inner Yes from a forgotten relationship in a personal environment that has already said No to it. How can the child to do other than believe in the No of the parent-child relationship? It is a No which seems to dislodge it—as if it were a permanent blind spot branded onto the inner eye of the person, a blindness to the Yes of God, and hence to the Yes of humanity as well.

Behold, it takes an act of God to reach the person with a repetition of the Yes of creation. And that is precisely what God seeks to do in revelation. And that Yes shall be finally proven and carried through in redemption. Redemption is the consummation of the Yes to our personal being given by the deepest We of memory, our We with God.

✠

The We cannot be objectified save through covenant, which constitutes its being "legalized" or "logicized." Apart from actual meeting, however, the We lives on in memory. Memory is the present being of the psyche in its extension through time, not unlike the present being of the physical body in its extension through space. Memory mines the meaning of the past, so that nothing of value may be lost. Memory is thus not passive, like an ongoing tape recorder, but active, like a film editor who cuts and splices in accordance with an inner director. And what directs the memory but the will, the inner person?

Memory is the record keeper not only of temporal life, but of the eternal as well. If anything is of value, not only for the moment, but for the always of one's life, it must continue to live in some form. And for a time, it must live exclusively in memory. Hence, within memory dwells the eternal as well as the temporal, the divine as well as the earthly. As the repository of language and love, memory is not only of the psyche but of the spirit as well. And all three spheres of the human person participate in memory: the body keeps records, the soul remembers, and the spirit ever recollects.

So central to our identity and personal meaning is our memory, that its loss robs us of our future as well as our past. To die to my past is to become groundless, to lose the context of meaning of my life—and yet somehow to continue to live! To look at others looking at me with an understanding of me and of "Us" which I no longer have, to look at myself with an emptiness unable to grasp how empty it really is—is this amnesia not a nightmare of living death, a true zombie-like existence? Yet behold, how many walk among us with memories repressed, therefore with a shallow and tangential consciousness? How few of us honor memory, and see in it a treasure chest of meaning and purpose! God is at the depth of our memory, and so also is the basis of our past and the promise of our future.

O memory, never let us forget where we have been and where God has promised to lead us! Never let us forget who we were called to be today and what we are to become tomorrow.

IDENTITY AND BELONGING

The Life Cycle of the Person

The human life cycle is threefold in accordance with the threefoldness of the person: You, I and We. And just as the fetus has certain "critical periods" in the womb, during which the whole sweep of development is focused upon one or another aspect of the body, so also the psyche has certain critical periods in the larger womb of human relationships, during which the focus of psychic development is on one or another of these three dimensions of the person. The sequence of these three phases directly parallels the sequence of our threefold relationship with God: creation, revelation and redemption. Hence, as with creation, the first stage of development is *You-centered;* as with revelation, the second is I-centered; and as with redemption, the third is *We-centered.*

These three stages are, of course, not mutually exclusive, and they do at times run concurrently in our lives. Nevertheless, they are distinct and unfold in a definite sequence. As such, the initial focus is on externality, the subsequent on internality, and the final on mutuality. In other words, the first centers on "otherness," then on "ownness" and finally on "ourness," as it were. The essential movement is one of the recognition of that which is beyond or outside the I, to that which is within the I, and then to the relationship between the two. It bears similarity to the dialectical movement of thesis, antithesis and synthesis, or of positing, then of positioning in response to the positing, and finally of "disposing," in the sense of arranging or ordering the other two.

The three stages of psychic life also correspond in a real way to the threefold path of spiritual life: illumination, purgation and unification. In the beginning is the vision of truth as otherness, as the holy, wholly over against us. This establishes both an inner motion toward the revelation of the personal correspondence to and divergence from that truth, and a mandate to purge the self of everything not consistent with that which is revealed. All this is in silent preparation for the attainment of and the cleaving to that truth. All is for the sake of the final stage of spiritual and personal existence, the actual realization of an everlasting "co-union" and communion.

The You-centered relationship is that of creation, the I- centered is that of revelation, and the We-centered is that of redemption. The history of both the individual and the race can be traced in terms of the pilgrimage toward and wrestling with the attainment of being in these three relationships. In the end, the search for either the ultimate You or the ultimate I of our life eventuates in the discovery of the ultimate We. That is, the end of our quest for our true self and the God of our existence, will be the realization of both precisely in the mutual ground of Spirit, in the Eternal I-You, the Holy We.

In the You-centered relationship of creation, we must differentiate the You from the It, the Creator or parent from the cosmos of created objects. Likewise in the I-centered relationship of revelation, we must distinguish between the I and the "It" within, between the true self and the impersonal being of impulse and desire. In the We-centered relationship of redemption, however, our task is to unify rather than to divide the It from the I and the You, to turn the world of It into our home, to redeem the It as well as the I and the You. Hence, redemption signifies the consummation of creation by the entrance of the It into the world of persons through the We. Now we are in the world; one day, the world will be in Us.

✠

In the beginning is the relation. The primal relation, be it of infant or of humanity before God, is *You-centered.* The You is creative of the I through address. The world of the I is permeated by the sensed You of address. The presence of the You of the parent is encountered in, with and under everything which presents itself before the child: in toy or pet, in stranger or in the sensual sights and sounds of the playground. The waves of the parent-You seem to reach everywhere. If the child falls and hurts itself, the parent immediately appears and the ground of painful insensitivity is juxtaposed by the tender hands of the knowing human earth. The You of the parent is ever present in both the external and the internal world of the child. The parent is the object of fantasies, dreams and reveries. The You literally invades the psychic being of the child, calling forth need and person.

In this relationship, the child is at first seemingly passive and acted upon by the parent. For the child does not initially discern its own impact upon the You over against it. The parent-You is the active one, ever shaping the behavior and feelings, the inner and outer life of the one so helpless and needy. The parent-You is as the world to the child; in etching upon the being of the child the structure of the human world into which it has been born, the parent-You sets the guidelines and parameters of psychic and social existence. The You sets the agenda for the I, and charts the relational course between the Yes and the No to meeting and mutuality. The parent-You establishes the context of meaning in which the I of the child grows and takes its stand and finds its "estate" in the world. At stake here is the basic framework of *trust* or *mistrust* of the child toward the whole world of persons.

The second phase of personal life is entered into gradually, as the child comes to differentiate itself from the parent-You and to discover itself as a potent and mysterious center of life and attention. As seen clearly by the school years, the parent-child relationship—and indeed all relationships—have become *I-centered* for the child. Everything that happens must at some point be refracted through the I of self-awareness and image, the I of need and desire, the I sought for as ideal and the I dreaded as non-acceptable. The I must now establish its own existence both within and beyond the parent-child relationship. And how difficult if the You of the parent does not want to relinquish the center of the relationship!

The I-centered phase of personal life can continue almost unabated throughout the person's whole life. Many never get beyond the "me first" mentality. For the I seeking itself and infatuated with its own concerns and needs, life is an open-ended adventure, and almost limitless are the options for personal and professional experimentation. It is a time for dreaming and for participating in the dream of the generations for personal greatness and success. It is a time for heroes and models, for the fear-grounded fashions of "in" and "out" dress and behavior. During this intense period real *acceptance* or *rejection* by others—and therefore by oneself—hangs in the balance. "Is it good to be me, or must I reject myself and act like another? Am I adequate or inadequate? Can I accept myself?"

The third phase of personal life is in fact the hidden constant of the whole of one's life. And it incorporates both of the previous stages and places each in their true context. It is entered into through the peer relationships in which the I seeks to attain identity and esteem, the We of the group, as it were. Yet it comes into full flower only with the search for the "other," for the one who will complete my being, for my mate and partner, the one who will love and cherish me as none other. This moves us squarely into the *We-centered* stage of personal existence. It is also the time for the surfacing of the great question of meaning: "Why I am here, and what is the purpose of my life?" Hence, where trust or mistrust is at stake in the first stage, and acceptance or rejection in the second, the issue of the third is *meaning* or *meaningless*—that is, life or death.

Behold, the question of meaning is the question of Spirit, for Spirit *is* meaning. Spirit is our "ultimate concern," in terms of both the depth of our present existence, and horizon toward which we inexorably move. The striving to attain the meaning of life *is* the religious quest, and will be ended only in the holy We of God. For our hearts are indeed restless until they find rest in God. Our shared life in and with God *is* the fulfillment of the quest for meaning, purpose and truth.

In this phase, the I searches for the You of its life. That You is ultimately God, but another You must be found as well, namely the You of one's spouse. In finding that one, the I attains as well the fundamental We of life in the world. From that shared existence is to arise new life, children and history, meaning and memories. The cycle is thus completed: the We becomes the ground floor of the family-spirit, out of which children will spring forth and encounter their parent-You. We become to others what others have been to us.

The Quest for Identity

The life cycle of the person may also be viewed as an ongoing quest for identity. Every person has an intrinsic need to define oneself, to determine the meaning and purpose of one's own existence. "Who am I? What does it mean to be me, both in myself and in terms of my relationships with other people?" The "what" of my existence needs a solid "who" to chart the course and see the way clearly. Who I am determines what I do, and establishes the context of meaning for my daily life. The sense of self grants the sense of life itself.

As with the life cycle, so also is the quest for identity threefold in accordance with the threefoldness of the person. Indeed, the identity process closely parallels the life cycle itself. Hence, the You-centered phase constitutes the period of the *identity of intention*, the I-centered the *identity of retention*, and the We-centered the *identity of extension*. And while these phases are not mutually exclusive to each other, so that the person may be wrestling with more than one aspect at a time, there is nevertheless a definite sequence to the process. The phases can be summarized in terms of three successive and interlocked dimensions to the question of personal being: "Who are You, and who am I to You? Who am I in myself? Who are We and who am I with You?

The identity of intention begins with the will of the parent-You for the child. It arises with the "family of origin," and can be symbolized by the name the child is given. For the identity of intention is above all something the I *receives*. The parent-You says in effect, "This is who I am and who You are with me and with us. This is your name and the place of your belonging. We have birthed You, and we have intentions for your life, who You will be and what You will do. It is for us to raise You into that person. Receive from us our language, our law and our love." The I is thus permanently shaped by and into the family of origin; family intention for and response to the I grant the lens through which the I will henceforth see itself and the world. And how difficult to regrind those lenses once they are molded and set in place!

The identity of retention begins when the I actively introjects that which has been received during the initial period of identity. The "You are" directive from without becomes the "I am" imperative from within; and the external "You shall" of the law of being is replaced by an internalized "I must." The passively received identity of the intention of the parent You begins to be actively retained by and integrated into the I. The I now grabs hold of that which grabbed hold of it; it now shapes that which has shaped it. The roles and expectations of the parent-You and the family of origin are selectively appropriated by the I as its own self-definition. The I gathers together all that it sees and senses belongs to its nature, seeking both to grasp the whole picture of its being in the world, and by molding and remolding, accepting and rejecting, to become consistent with its own inner ideal self. The question at stake: "Who am I? Who am I, not only in response to You, but as a thing in myself? And who am I in social circumstances other than my family?"

The identity of extension begins with the quest for another to share one's existence, for the intimate other, the soul mate or spouse. And this quest is in turn a part of a larger search for the meaning and purpose of one's own existence. The I seeks to extend its being, to become inclusive with and included in something greater than itself, to dive whole and free into some dimly perceived stream of life for which it cannot but thirst. The question that must be resolved: "Who am I in my relationships with others? Who am I in relation to the world around me? Where do I belong and what is my role or mission? What do I have to give; what impact am I to have upon others? And who then are We?"

✠

The process of identification is one of either *inclusion* or *exclusion*. Something either is or is not a part of me and my life. There is a definite Yes and No to identity; it is me or not me. It has been said that a person's self is all they can call their own. As regards identity, that means I am all that I include within myself. The identity of inclusion, therefore, signifies not only the owning of personal attributes, but also the sharing in common attributes and characteristics with others. That is, to identify with others means that what they are, we are too. We bond our being with theirs; we become intentionally like them. Call it a "mutuality of personal characteristics," or a common "personality."

I am an American. That means, I include within my own self-definition certain characteristics—both good and bad!— purportedly common to us as a people. Thus, for instance, on the positive side, I am independent, practical, and optimistic; and on the negative, I am self-serving, prideful and brash. As a Christian, I identify with and strive to become like the person of Jesus Christ. I am called to participate in His image and likeness. And through his Spirit I am bonded to Him for all eternity, so that what He is, I shall be as well. Salvation means to be included in His soul and spirit and body. Salvation is the We of Christ.

✠

The most pervasive identity of inclusion: *my father, myself.* A bond of being and identity, a We of likeness. His vision of manhood becomes mine; I approach the world with his attitudinal framework. His battles within and without become my battles; his shortcomings are visited upon my face. His love lifts me up and sets me on my course; his will puts forward guidelines for my character and my walk.

I am your son, O my Father. And am I not your self-fulfilling prophesy? In your intention of me I come into self-consciousness. In my sense of inadequacy and incompleteness, I step forward and experience You with the totality of my being. With love and primal need, I memorize and model You in all your mannerisms. I breathe in your self-assured confidence of being and having that which I seek but am not and do not yet have. Your hope for me is my hope. You seem to include me in your extended being; hence, I include You in your inclusion of me. Behold, what is mutual here is your being, your person, and your intention for me. This is a We of primal bonding and extension—namely of your being into mine, so that what is shared is one being not two, a *unity-in-sameness.* Like Father, like son. We are like You, then, O my Father. But *We* are, nonetheless. For the whole of my life, who I am in the world will never be divorced from our mutualness, and from your gift of yourself to me and for me.

✠

The "end" of identity? Something beyond, though symbolized by, the "mid-life crisis"? The end of identity is a narrow door at the end of each of our paths. And as we approach the end, the way narrows and turns upward. And we cannot carry as much baggage as we once did on the plains of plenty and youth. For identity is a never-ending process of pruning as well as growing, paring down and letting go of, as well as reaching out and including. What then is the end of identity but death? What then can we take with us there which we call ourselves and our own here? We will of course finish knowing—then.

Behold, the quest for identity is the search for the truth and of ourselves in that truth. In this quest we are all pilgrims on the way to something greater than the mind can hold. Only the heart may apprehend it as its farthest dream. A holy city, an eternal community awaits us. And here we are ever on the way. And everything we identify with here is only for a time, save for love, and our identity in love. The end of the quest for identity is the discovery and attainment of who we are in the love of God. For only love can tell us who we are.

✠

The Family We

We enter the world not alone, but as a part of a family. The family is the basic cultural unit for corporate existence in the world. It is the earliest and most impactful, long-term and pervasive We experience of our lives. The family is the psycho-social sphere of "home," of being and belonging, the original and paradigmatic matrix of relationships in which persons have their roots and take their stand for the whole of their lives. "The life is in the blood"; and in the family, the commonality of genes and generations, of history and traditions, make for a commonality of psyche and spirit. Family is in truth a "unit of spirit," as it were, a We of identity and reference, a common "atmosphere" in, with and under the members, both seen and unseen—and just as real as the persons themselves. The spiritual atmosphere between the family members may be a haven or a Hades, a well oxygenated "psychosphere" of acceptance and communion, or a terrarium of fear, with only enough light and breath to survive each day— and one another. The greatest blessing or the most grievous curse, this is the family unit.

Is there not a kind of shared "personality" manifest in a family? That is, does not a family reveal a set of characteristic approaches to life and to other persons? Call it a "common stance" before the world. Yet the family spirit can also generate and support a mosaic of differing personal quirks. Like an accordion, the family can expand or contract in accordance with the nature and number of current membership.

The family intends and defines us, expects and rejects us, teaches and wounds us, nurtures and engenders life-long problems in us, sees and misinterprets us, affirms and reforms us, embraces and casts us out. The family is simply the "people place" where we live and move and have our being in the world. It is the spiritual abode where the deepest We-events of our lives are to happen and to have their sanctuary in the world, the We-relationships between parent and child, husband and wife, brother and sister. Behold, the human family is made in the image of the family of God, in the likeness of the eternal home of the I, the You and the We. Hence, when it is defaced and devalued, not only the family, but God suffers in the world. And how God is suffering today! How our culture is disintegrating! For as the family goes, so goes the nation.

✠

A child is born. So, therefore, is a parent-child We: You enter my world, my child, our child, and my world will never be the same again. You are the unique result of a unique physical union, the concrete fruit of a biological We. From the physical inclusivity of your Mother and me, You have wondrously emerged. You are living evidence of the awe-ful sanctity of the act which conceived You! Though new, You spring in part from my being; for the rest of my life, a responsibility will connect us. You and I, my child, are a mutuality from your birth. My love for You is immediate and beyond my understanding. But your very existence has opened up new meanings to the term "inclusivity." Henceforth, who You are and who I am are contingent upon each other.

In You, I have become generative. If nothing else, I will leave You behind as my living legacy. You are the future beyond my future here. In You, I have become something more, in both quantitative and qualitative ways. We share genes and physical characteristics; we are one through the act which conceived You. You are indeed the end of that act, its purpose and fruit. This mysterious bond between us has been called a "bond of blood," and on the biological level it is that indeed. Yet blood also has a symbolic meaning, namely of the common life we share in the family your very arrival has brought into being.

Belonging has physical, psychical and spiritual dimensions. All three dimensions are operative between You and I. Unto the end of our lives, You and I belong together. Who am I? Whoever I am, I am your Father. Who are You? Whoever You are, You are my son. We are one, O my child.

THE I ALONE

Individuation

The mandate at the depth of the human soul is to stand forth and proclaim the awe-ful "I am," in response to the Word of creative address. That means: from the beginning springs the urge to individuate. For in the address itself is the divine command to "become perfect, as your Father in heaven is perfect"(Matthew 5:48). And the term for "perfect" in the Greek text, *teleios,* means "fully grown, mature, whole, complete, undivided and thus perfect." Hence, in each of us exists a primal drive to become completely, to actualize fully the who God calls us to be in our creation. God intends the individual we are to be; the guidelines and the motive power are built into each of us—not unlike the compressed air in a deflated life raft. Both the air and the size and shape of the raft are predetermined by the creator. And once the seal is broken, the unstoppable force of the air is to fill every centimeter or bust! It will succeed or fail—but there is no going back! And the outcome will determine the life or death of the person who must inhabit that raft. Just so is the life of the person at stake in the success or failure of the individuation process.

We must then all become an individual, a "single one" before the face of the true Single One. That is, the goal or end—*telos,* in the Greek—of our individuation process, is the attainment of maturity or *teleios* in our relationship with God. Further, as single ones, we cannot reach full individuation save through the unfolding history of our primal relationships with one another. For maturation happens not in strict and simple accordance with some innate process alone, as if the I were a psychic embryo entire to itself, needing only time and impersonal nutrients to spring forth fully developed. The individual is not like a "monad" or a star igniting in space. Behold, something where there was nothing! A shining where there was darkness, a light apart, visible and giving, yet alone in the vastness. A space filled, nothing more.

Individuation is a relational reality. We are individuals only to and with each other. And we receive ourselves as gift from the spirit of mutuality between us. The I becomes from and in We relationships. "I am who I am"—in and by virtue of those past and current relationships in which I have found my being, a being shared with another, a being-with. Even the deepest intra-psychic acts of reflection and self-insight, of personal choice and decision, even these inner facts of freedom have beneath and behind them the mediation of what has been and is between myself and the "significant others" of my life. No person thinks in pure isolation, but as a member of a living network of those who share that language, of those who have granted specific meanings to specific words. Individuation, in brief, emerges from the ground between us in our mutuality, rather than from the being within us in our aloneness.

And the end of individuation and self-actualization? Call it a "consummated mutualization." The attainment of the fullness of the I is toward the end of and entrance into and the life of the Eternal We. Our entire existence here is a preparation for that union, a place to grow, through distancing and isolation as well as nearness and intimacy, and a time for becoming, through privation and denial as well as feasting and affirmation. The whole is required to make us whole, the agony as well as the ecstasy, the sorrow as well as the joy. To deny one aspect is to deny the whole. Would that we could refrain from judging God until we see the finished product of ourselves in God!

What then do we seek? Truth, knowledge, meaning and purpose? Do we daily and almost exclusively seek pleasure and the avoidance of pain, as some suppose? Or do we not seek above all a shared life of true communion and beauty, of knowing as we are known, of love and truth, of fidelity and peace? Behold, even the beast in us seeks that Holy Grail which would reconcile it to the lamb within, that they may at last lie down together. We are seekers after truth—even if we seem to be doing nothing to attain it. Still does the urge abide with every beat of our heart: "Know Me, know Me."

We seek truth. But truth as mere insight into a state of facts does not satisfy the drive to know if it does not bring with it new life—and a life which *includes an otherness*. At their basis, the desire to know and the urge to individuate are one and the same. Knowing and being attain at-one-ment in the beatific vision of the Truth. And the union of knowing and being happens in and by virtue of the mutuality with the Otherness over against us. That is, knowing and being become one at the point at which self-being signifies a being-with, and self-knowing a being known by the Other. For true knowing and being are mediated by the Otherness in and through which we find and attain our "owness." We are the mirrors for each other; we are therefore the images of one another. We are made in the image of God—and that means with the need for and capacity to mediate being and knowledge to each other. Hence, knowledge and being are between us before—and after—they are within us.

What, then, do we mediatate to God? What image do we reflect back as we stand before the Face? What possible being and knowledge could be at stake for God in the sphere between us? In the time to come, we shall know as we are known.

Personal Knowledge

Personal knowledge is bipolar. Self-knowledge is mediated by language, and language by dialogical speech-events. Knowledge of what is within me comes through reflection on that which has emerged between myself and another person, or through an interchange between myself and some element of my environment with which I stand in relationship. Even self-examination is in a real way bipolar, in that I am both the examined and the examiner, both the object and the subject. And what seems to be known only by myself cannot be fully integrated into my self-understanding until it has been worked through the crucible of dialogue with another. My sense of self is gained from my apprehension of your perception of me. Your feedback is translated into my self-perception.

The I who I am must be distinguished from the me of self-reflection. *This I is the speaking one,* the subject who speaks, the non-imaged agent who arises from the inner ground of mystery, the one who sees but is not seen. The foundation of the I is God and the relationship of creation, that primal linguistic event of divine address. The I is thus of the Word by nature; it has taken its stand in this Word, and has its life in and by virtue of this hidden but essential relationship with God.

The me that I know is an object to myself and to others, the one who I come to understand myself to be by a process of reflection and feedback. *This me is the spoken one,* the object before my inner eyes, the person of my imagery and dream life, my memory and covenants with others. This me is the one I envision myself to be in the world of persons, places and things around me. I am comfortable with this known and more or less predictable self, with certain needs well documented, and fears and hopes well circulated through my system—and that of others. The me that I am—or should I say that I have "accumulated"? —is the one, "Hal Green," the one who first came to self-consciousness as intended by parents and siblings, as already lodged in the womb of an established family-spirit.

✠

I do not experience my I, though I am somehow aware of being an I, as I unfold with You in Us. The inner person of my experience has no presence to me, but a past from which I may glimpse and cognitively grasp in retrospect this who that I am in the present. That is, the past is a mirror to the present—but without real presence, for that only happens when and as You and I meet. In meeting You, I meet myself— in and with You. But I can never see the You that I am to You; I may only infer it from the person I seem to see in your eyes and reactions. And even then, my profound and pervasive attitudes and prejudices about myself may at points effectively prohibit my seeing myself as You see me.

As with the I, so also with the We. I do not experience the We of You and I during our meeting. The We of experience emerges after the meeting, and is a being of memory and reflection. When We are together, we do not see the spirit that is between us; we just live and operate out of it. The spirit of Us is simply there between us, in the same way as the air we breathe is simply there around us. The We of experience, however, is paradoxically both living and present to me, yet abiding in the past, and from there calling me unto a future wherein You and I will meet again, and again share a common life. The We lives and is present precisely in its absence, as it were. And it ever addresses us, from both the present it fills as well as the present devoid of it.

Does not, then, this We of our experience call us together for the sake of its own disappearance into Us? For in the event of our mutuality, neither of us will experience but rather become one with this We of our life.

The knowledge of the We is also bipolar. For is it my relationship or your relationship? It is both and neither. Behold, it is *our* relationship; *it is Us*. Hence, the input of both of us is necessary for a more complete picture of the whole. And do we not need to hear what each of us has received from our communion? Do we not need to hear what this We means to each of us? Do we not need to confirm each other, to test out the love-ground we corporately stand upon? And this shared knowledge is one with the being that We are together, for it emerges between us, just as we ourselves arise in and from our sweet mutuality. Mutuality and the knowledge thereof are one. One does not exist without the other, even if we are aware of only one dimension at a time. You and I can know of Us only because We have become Us.

✠

Meaning and Truth

The meaning of something signifies its relational value. Meaning is relative to other meanings and mutual to other persons; it is common to a language and shared by a people. Meaning arises from and has its life in the We-dimension of the person, in the inter-personal sphere between us. If something has meaning, it can be said and shared. Hence, meaning is of language and participates in spirit. That which cannot be shared cannot be known. And that which cannot be known can have no meaning. The three dimensions of meaning, namely, intention, denotation and connotation, together constitute a matrix of interconnected relationships between persons, places, things and situations. Meaning is thus of the whole, by the whole and for the whole.

Meaning permeates the whole person, and involves volition, cognition and affection. As regards the will, the meaning of something represents its motivational potency and desirability. The cognitive meaning signifies something's position within a total worldview, and its capacity to explain and to direct, to grant insight and discernment. Meaning in terms of the emotions concerns the power of something to move the person to response and action, or to the pronounced prohibition thereof. The emotions are the depth reactions, and thus gage the weight of something for personal life. They bestow the "for me" meaning to all that happens and is the case.

There are three fundamental theories about the nature of meaning, as about the nature of truth itself. They are the the "coherence," the "correspondence," and the "pragmatic" theories of truth. All three have to do with our relationships to each other and to the world. And together they constitute interwoven spheres of concern for the mind, the will, and the feelings. Coherence has to do with how something fits with the whole. "Coherence" is derived from the verb "cohere," which comes from the Latin *cohaerere,* meaning literally "to stick together." Hence, the meaning of something has to do first of all with the way in which it logically adheres to or connects with other things. Meaning is how we find ourselves together.

The correspondence theory of meaning and truth concerns the manner in which something agrees or matches or communicates with other things. "Correspondence" is derived from the verb "correspond," which comes from the joining of the Latin prefix , "together," with *respondere,* meaning "to respond." To correspond, then, means to respond or relate together in a similar and analogous fashion. That is, it means to interface and to interrelate, thus to come together in a kind of reciprocal comparison, a kind of mutuality, a We. Meaning is thus not only how we fit together, but also how we correspond to and with each other.

The third dimension of meaning and truth is the pragmatic theory. "Pragmatic" comes from the Latin *pragmaticus*, meaning "skilled in business and law"; this is in turn derived from the Greek *pragmatikos* and *pragma*, meaning "deed, or business," based on the verb *prassein*, meaning "to do." Truth is thus simply what works and is practical; and meaning, therefore, has to do with the manifest consequences of some thought or action, and indeed represents their sum. Meaning here is just as relational as the other two theories above, for to be practical means to have an effective impact upon others and upon one's environment. Meaning, in short, is how we affect and are effected by each other.

All three views of the nature of meaning emerge from primal relationships, and concern the way we fit together, the way we respond to each other, and the way we affect one another. In the beginning of meaning stands the relationship.

✠

We humans require a meaning in order to live. And only a meaning greater than ourselves and our own lives will satisfy and fulfill the need for meaning. We must lose ourselves in some relationship of true significance in order to gain ourselves; only in giving ourselves away in love and for love will we receive ourselves back—along with the meaning of our life. Meaning is the ebb and flow of our lives together. Meaning is the current which is current between You and I. Behold, meaning is Us.

✠

Singularity of Being

Alone, the world of the individual *is* the world, and personal being but an uncharted dimension of conscious life. Motives, feelings, thoughts, and memories color the perceptions of what is seen as the life around the person. But these elements of the internal world go just as unnamed as the particularities which present themselves from the external world. Alone, the objective is at one with the subjective, the outer and the inner commingle, as two bodies of water without a dividing land between them—namely the dimension of the mutual. Hence, the world as it is and as the person intends cannot be separated. In truth, both objectivity and subjectivity require a mediating otherness and a mutuality.

The *singularity* of being emerges only in relationship, as the mutually found and "designated" persons we become together. Singularity comes into focus through the specificity of address and response, of concrete call and answer. A relationship of true reciprocity is required for us to come into the differentiated singularity potential in our personal being. The relationship acts as a prism through which the light of the self must pass if the colors of personal being are to be revealed and distinguished. Through our interaction we shape and mold who we are as persons together.

Behold, You address me as an I; it is I who am called to respond and to be in that response to You. Our interchanges of address and response cut a path between us, as real as any road in the physical world. Section by section, a connectional bridge is mutually constructed in the inter-personal space that has opened between us.

My singularity is therefore directly dependent upon your singularity, for We arise together as the poles of a relationship, not unlike the poles of a magnetic field. And what magnetism is present between us! We become singular and unique to and with each other—or not at all. Hence, *our respective singularity of being is not in but between us;* my distinct "me-ness" and your specific "You-ness" are shared by and contingent upon Us. "I am who I am"—because of and in relation to You; "You are who You are"—because of and in relation to me.

Singularity is an open channel between You and me, a river of language and love, discovery and dialogue, growth and fruition, differentiation and destiny. This river is both objective and subjective, both shared and private. Our mutual singularity is also like a rainbow: after our meeting and through the vision of reflection, we see its abiding life and wondrous coloration between us, but not its ends. Are we not its ends; do You and I not constitute the "pots of gold" at the bases of the rainbow? The ultimate treasure is nevertheless *between* us, and the rainbow serves as a sign of our life together, of our covenant of peace and harmony.

Solitude

Just as we need time together, so also do we need time apart. Mutuality requires respites of internality for its very perpetuation and life; intimacy is served and supported by regular periods of privacy. Primal relationship demands spaces of primal distancing. Who we are together needs to be integrated into who we are apart. The sharpening of the awe-full sense of who I am in my aloneness sharpens as well the experiencing of who You are in your singular humanity, and who We are in our holy mutuality. Relational intensity cannot be long maintained without relational "burnout" coming to pass; rest periods make relational periods new and meaningful—and restore passion.

Solitude represents an essential time for self-reflection, consolation and consolidation. It is a time to let go and let be, a time for detaching from the world of persons and things, a time for rest and self-appraisal. Just as the body requires substantial time daily for sleep, for that great physical solitude, so also does the psyche demand daily periods for both closing down its involvement in the world, and opening unto itself and its own state. Much of this, of course takes place during sleep, when through dreaming and unconscious thought we rehash and rehearse, build up and tear down, and in general, piece together and gain new perspective on the events of our daily life.

Solitude, then, is a time for solace and healing, as well as for facing— or being free of—the demons that drive and harass us. All this is in preparation for new meetings and intimacy, for new We-events and times of self and other discovery. Solitude allows for that in-gathering which prepares us for a renewed outpouring of ourselves in true communion.

Yet many fear time apart from one another, as if only constant attention will keep them together, as if a distancing of time and space will eventuate in the distancing of persons. Are not, however, the risks of relational breakdown just as great from the pressures of togetherness as from the pressures of aloneness? As time and space apart can indeed sever the connectional chords of mutuality, so also can dogged intimacy drain the power and ease from a relationship. And can we not become strangers together as well as apart? In truth, without grace-filled time apart from each other, the relationship, like a rope, will only tighten around the participants. Without solitude, the intimacy of love is doomed to suffocation.

✠

O my beloved! I need time away from You in order to better enjoy and appreciate my time with You. We must detach at frequent intervals, that we may have the joy of re-attachment. For our attachment requires both a "de" and a "re" to maintain itself, as it were. And sometimes I need to stretch our mutual being into the distance, so as to be able to turn toward You from that perspective and see You from afar as my beloved mountain, and with boldness to approach You with a new excitement and clarity of who You really are—and of what We are and have together.

✠

Loneliness

Where in solitude we have chosen to be with and filled by the self, in loneliness we are aware of the self in its isolation and emptiness. Loneliness comes to us all. An undulating sense of being in isolation, it sweeps across us in crowds as well as alone. "I am alone"—that means, I experience my center within myself, apart from other possible centers of being. I feel an inward still point of gravity, an inner void or vacuum with nothing there to fill it, an empty space where life is to be. Loneliness is a cry of incompleteness, of the searing recognition of solitary inadequacy. "I am alone"—that means, I bear the weight of an inner nothingness, a paradoxically heavy burden of the weightlessness of a life apart from others. This depressing burden signifies as well the absence of meaning in my life. I cannot live long without You—that there may be a meaning-bearing Us. We must be together, that I may receive afresh, in our mutuality, the breath of life.

I am lonely. "It is not good for man to be alone." I look within and sense myself awash with unmet needs and desires. In my yearning and despair, I become an unwanted object to myself. That which I reject becomes my shadow self—in two senses: first as ever following me, and second, as ever outside the light of my consciousness. My shadow self: a has been and could be, with a paucity of presentness. The shadow self—shall I accept him? Is this me that I have distanced in my loneliness friend or foe, child or beast, worthy or worthless? Loneliness pressures me toward either self-examination or a denial of my inner life. And how easily self-pity enters in, along with its ugly companions of anger, self-hatred and resentment. Behold, the irony: as I reject the loneliness, I reject the me that is lonely.

The resolution of the predicament of loneliness comes only through the entrance into and participation in the life of the We. Only the We can fill the void of the I, for that sensed emptiness is in fact the accurate awareness of the inner place where love is to come and set up its home—a home that will extend into the common sphere between us.

Loneliness, then, is a kind of separation, not only from others, but from ourselves as well. When I am alone, I am with myself as an I, but I am cut off from the You that I am and could be with others. I have only the remembrance of the You that I have been to sustain this sense of my relational self. In my aloneness, I seek to recoup my losses, to lick my wounds, to re-prioritize my life, and to gather myself together in preparation for stepping forth into life and mutuality, refreshed and reinvigorated. Yet apart from the currency—in terms of both time and value—of being a You, my life has no real meaning and purpose, and my present isolation is but a time-out for the sake of the revelation of who I have and have not been.

In my aloneness, I miss not only You, but being a You to You. To be lonely means not only to crave attention and being loved, but just as much the giving of attention and being loving. The deepest rewards of being a person spring from who we can be to and what we can do for others. Behold, to be a You means to participate in divinity, for God is the Eternal You. To step forth as a partner, to open and to receive, to address and to hear, to share and to grow therein and thereby, this is the way to God's own sweet and never-ending mutuality, this is heaven's path in the world.

I cannot see the You I am to another; I may only infer it from their reactions to me. and I must beware of idolatry here, of making an image of myself as a You and reverencing it, and treating it as if it were the truth of my being—and my share in divinity. For the other over against me is the only legitimate image of the You. We are not to make an image, not only of God, but of ourselves as well. Rather than image

You, I must step into relation with You—and therefore with myself as your You. Is not divinity then the mutuality of being You to each other?

✠

At the depth of aloneness, at the edge of non-being, comes the realization of the mutualness, the universality of being alone. This is the beginning of the primal movement toward the understanding of and paradoxical communion with others, precisely in our shared aloneness. And the way to true togetherness is not around but through the crucible of loneliness, through the awakened awareness of being a *Ding an sich,* a thing unto oneself. Even in our aloneness we are mutual; one mountain communes with another within the context of a whole range of mountains. Our identity in the "community of aloneness" is preparatory to and an essential dimension of our identity in the "community of togetherness."

Enter prayer, our community and communion with God. Prayer has been called "the flight of the alone to the Alone." The Lonely One seeks us in our aloneness, just as we seek God. The way to the Holy One is to enter with anticipation rather than fear into our isolation and being alone, and to wait upon God there.

Alone and lost within the forest of myself, I await being found by the Beloved of my soul. In the inner chamber of my heart, I long for the entrance of the One whom I love with a love hidden even from myself—until our union. Loneliness can be a preamble to glory, as need the qualifier for ecstasy.

THE BROKEN I

Grief

Grief is more than a subjective experience. It is a passage in and through the ontological death of shared being. It is the cross we bear of the death of inter-subjectivity. Grief is not only the woeful response to the death of a loved one; it is the slow death of the relationship, of the *We itself*, and of who We were in that relationship.

The moment of your death: suddenly and irreversibly our corporate world of being together disappears, and the solid ground of an instant ago gives way to a pit of isolation and aloneness. I am flowed with the sickening and unavoidable wrenching of the connecting bonds of shared spirit. There is slack where there had been tension, and silence where there had been intimacy. I am engulfed with shock: memories of You seem and seek to fill the present moment, to give orientation and assurance until the lie of your death is uncovered and You return to me, that We may continue. But there is no present presence of You and of Us; there is only a shaking past trying to swallow what had been greater than it, and a closed door where there had been an open future—open just a moment ago, yet now closed for all time, here.

You die and instantly I am left with a memory-bound We that can no longer sustain me in my present and future; I am stuck in the grip of a relationship suddenly become a weight I cannot carry alone. Not only have You died; your death has brought with it the death of *Us* as well. And in that death, who I was in our relationship must die as well. When a plane falls from heaven, all who are on board perish. We are fools to think that anyone can survive the crash of Us! As if one could simply go on to the next plane, the next relationship, unscathed and yet alive! As if there were any way out of the We-bond of spirit short of death and rebirth!

You are profoundly present to me in your absence. What a paradox, your visitation to me in the void! And no one can move in and fill your place, no surrogate can address me as You did, with Your voice, your spirit and understanding. No one can take over for You in "our history," so that the story could continue to unfold, and we could go on with our life, after but a small and highly unpleasant delay. Only memory now abides, and sealed within it is "our story." And now it is for me to clean up the mess within and without that your leaving has created.

Where are You, O my beloved one? And where am I without You? Who am I without You to see and know and share me? Who shall I become apart from Us, without the life of our We to sustain me? How could You leave me thus? And how is it that our meaning and life so full and profound could end so abruptly and absolutely, that We could be violated so thoroughly, as if We had never been, as if the now silenced significance we shared had never lived between us? How can love justify this end? How then can the will of God be explained and accepted? Tell me later—but not now!

More than never-to-be-repeated memories fill my consciousness, more than words which cannot be spoken to You cling to me, and plague me with their insistent demand to be released to one who can no longer hear them. More than all this, behold, I am awash with the spirit-breathed tokens of You and me, of Us. From your personal possessions to pictures of Us, from things which bless me still with the lingering presence of your smell, to the unfinished tasks that speak so loudly to me of who You really were, of your passion and non-repeatable life-form, all these things surround me, and in my stormy weakness, I do not know how I will survive You and Us—and when.

Need and resentment, anger and guilt, emptiness and despair, all these and more accompany my every turning. Whither shall I escape from this death of You and of Us—and of the me we shared? No matter what I do, You will not return. We are finished. You are gone. I am absolutely helpless to affect these undeniable and detestable facts. No matter what I do, the spirit of our relationship, the love we shared, the common life I took all too much for granted, now bleeds before my inner eyes, mortally wounded by your severing disappearance. There is naught that can be done to stop the bleeding, for a re-connection is not possible in this life. Each day I grow less, as the We continues to fade in a wrenching process beyond my control.

Who I was with You, that "Hal" You loved and addressed in your own inimitable way in our moments of inclusive being, died with You. Yet I am dying more slowly and painfully, and with the added weight of the remains of our life together. There is simply no going back to Us. We are now of the past. Yet behold, the past is now struggling to forge a promise of another day for us in another place. The past is desperately seeking a future that will justify and bring peace to the present.

✠

When grief has finished its appointed work, an invisible altar will have been built at the center of the spiritual home we shared, lighted in my heart by the will of remembrance, fueled by faith and hope in a time yet to come. Our love has created a seed within of a promise of something yet to be. Your death has added immensity and meaning to my farthest tomorrow. Though We are history, You are not. You are not behind but ahead of me. You belong to whatever is to come. With You, a new meeting awaits me, a new We. Only a chapter, but not the whole story of Us is over. Though We have died as a living being of the present, the We of history still lives in my heart, as do You. I will long remember You and Us; that which We were and shared together will continue to grant meaning and underlying purpose and continuity to all my todays.

Love never loses its own. Love never ends. It only deepens in us, even in its seeming absence. For the changes wrought by the grief prepare me for a new and greater stepping forth here, in this life. We have died, but I am being born anew as a fuller person, with a more mature apprehension of what it means to share being, to love and to be loved. My heart like a wine chalice is being deepened through grief, in order that more of love and life may fill me. And when the thirst of my longing is met by the wine of new love, then shall I understand thirst and its fulfillment, then shall I bless the thirst and the pain and the Bringer thereof. O Love, You are served in death as in life! We die only to be born again in more complete constancy with You.

✠

In truth, death comes to all relationships, just as to all persons. And though the relationship may die before the persons themselves, when the I or the You ceases to exist, so does the We. And the death of the We is just as real as that of the I or the You. Would that we recognized this as a people! But we have hardly begun to see the reality of the We between us. The loss of a loved one is still seen primarily in terms of the I of the survivor.

Yet as the redemption moves ever nearer, when the life of Spirit shall be revealed and consummated in our midst, and we in It, so also in us is awakening the true significance of the We, and of the loss thereof. And the "woes" of the realization of the meaning and the fallen state of the We are already upon us. And as the end approaches, the decay of mutuality intensifies along with the need and the cry for its redemption—and ours with and in it.

Who knows but that the purpose of death here is to awaken us to the meaning of the We of love and spirit! And when we awaken, let us turn and live!

✠

Divorce

Divorce is more than the "legal dissolution" of a marriage; it is the rending asunder of the We of covenantal union. Divorce is more than an issue of dividing lives and property, and going separate ways; it is a matter of life and death, of being quartered rather than merely splitting up. *Divorce is a jointly carried out murder-suicide*: we take the life of the spirit-We of our historical mutuality, and willingly die to being who we were to each other in the relationship. And we do so publicly and legally, with the ritualized traditions of priest-lawyers before the judgment seat of a god-judge.

For the psyche, divorce is equivalent to the death of a loved one. But in terms of the spirit, it is harder to bear and even more destructive of personal life. For death does not reject; but the rejection of divorce can kill the spirit. Further, in the case of the death of the spouse, we can appropriate the history of our marriage intact into memory, and make a shrine to our beloved in the heart. The memory can grant meaning and continuity to our present and hope for our future. In divorce, however, our former spouse lives on—*but the relationship does not.* Instead of the marriage having died a "natural" death along with our beloved, in the event of divorce we bear a responsibility in the "unnatural" and even murderous breakdown of the We which was. Where the death of our beloved blots out the future but not the past of Us, divorce nullifies not only our future but also our past. The former death does not make void the promise of our past, but only moves the possible future location of the fulfillment of the relationship to a point beyond the grave. The latter, however, cancels all promise of the relationship, past, present and future. And how slowly die the promises and vows upon which we once staked our lives!

What then are we to do with the memory of Us? Divorce makes difficult and painful the embracing of the memory of Us whole and unabridged—for our ship sank, for we failed, and our "lovely flame" died after all. Divorce creates a kind of "former life" in our consciousness, one from which we need to distance ourselves, and "re-record" over, like an old tape on which we must attempt ever so carefully to place new songs for a new life—or anything which would ease the burden of an untouched and now unrealizable memory! Yet we cannot succeed entirely; old songs and old memories can still be heard in the pauses of the tape.

Divorce is then a kind of living death. And You and I continue to be reminders of what was but is no more, of the permanent that became the temporary, of the vows of the heart annulled by the unexpected and unwelcomed. Yet does not who We were live on in our memory? And how difficult it is to kill the memory of Us! Even if we seem to succeed, it can always come back to life, and at times and places for which we are not always prepared. It is as if we are attempting to uproot the food-bearing plants of the former garden of our marriage, as it were, which have now been termed "weeds," publicly and legally. But alas, we cannot seem to pull out all the roots from the earth within and between us! So that during each season of remembrance, the plants begin to grow back. And do we dare to tend and to pick and eat of the fruit of our former garden this time? Or must we continue to throw them away unconsumed, and go on weeding once more? Behold, what goes to seed comes back to haunt us! Yet how different is the fruit of divorce from the fruit of marriage.

✠

Divorce: a *solemn decision* and a *death sentence*: who We were and vowed to be to each other, we can be no more. An operation is to be performed: two are to re-emerge from one. The spiritual artery of our marriage, which once fed us in our "one flesh," is to be severed and sutured back into singleness, so that, like Siamese twins of the heart, we can live henceforth independent of each other. The tragic takes place: in the severing of that which lived between us in our mutuality, our common lifeblood, we become self-destructive as well as relationally murderous. Behold, to divorce You, I must die to the me who lived in our We. I must divest myself of the me committed to You as my spouse, and find and extinguish any lingering flame of desire for You and hope for Us. And my self-image must be recast, right along with the painful defacing of your image within me. I must see myself as one apart from You and Us; I must abort irrevocably our bond—and no one else can do it for me.

My memory must be entered in a manner and deadly intent not previously authorized. And the word of this unholy incursion into the past still living in me: "make yesterday conformable to the reality of today." The new regime of singleness dictates the terms of the existence and nature of any traditions and meanings of the prior covenant. Nothing that was sacred is sacred any more; all is to be examined with the overriding purpose of justifying and supporting the dissolution, of proving beyond a reasonable doubt the rightness and righteousness of the sentence of death for the relationship. We need to find a meaning and purpose in the dissolution of Us—so that our lives may continue, and our past may maintain its connection to our future.

Into the treasure chamber of remembrance go I, on my "search and destroy" mission. O the pain and anger, the guilt and anxiety attendant upon this mission of "un-mercy"! Vexing questions replace what had served as the assumed solid ground of our life together: Did we ever really love each other? Did You truly love me, and how did You love me? Did I really love You, and was it an adequate and "right" kind of love? What is love after all? And how can real love die like this? Is love then—or at least our love—only a dream from which we have abruptly awakened? Did we merely dream of loving and sharing, only to awake and find ourselves empty and lonely strangers? And if so, could we ever go back to sleep, as it were, and dream again the dream of marriage?

Is love then a dream from which we are all destined to awake one day? Is it a web of illusion, which we place over ourselves and each other to cover the multitude of our sins, which we spin in order to justify our using each other as means for personal solace and gain, for purely selfish motives? Do we only play at mutuality, like children wearing adult clothes and mimicking grown-up mannerisms and situations, but without any real participation in or grasp of what is actually at stake in all our sayings and doings? Do we only pretend—even to ourselves—that we are engaged in dialogue, all the while missing each other in half-conscious dual monologues?

Behold, when the questions begin, like the plug being pulled from a bathtub, the whirlpool effect only builds unstoppably to the end, to the draining of all meaning and mutuality through the heart wrenching "never-to be-knowns" of a dead marriage. Such questions are a form of spiritual bleeding, and without the coagulants of faith and hope, the heart can bleed to death. It is not from a "broken heart" that some have perished, but from the heart finally giving up and out to the emptiness of its chambers, to the absence of the blood of mutuality and love.

✠

Divorce: a *failed relationship*. Whose fault is it, yours or mine? Though we may point fingers at each other, indicative of the "either/

or" thinking we are reduced to, the truth is almost always a "both/and." *We failed,* each in our own way, at persevering in the relationship, the spirit of Us. We failed ourselves and each other. And just as importantly, we failed *Us,* and the reality and promise of Us to which we had publicly committed ourselves.

How painful and angering and heavy is that sense of failure! It clings to me everywhere I turn; it returns to me no matter where I am and what I am doing. I failed, and just as importantly, We failed. Though pledged to each other for life, our actions could not make it true and lasting.

Divorce is a failure which must be seen and accepted as that, and not talked away or emotionally circumvented. No "extra credit" work can pull our relational life up to a passing grade, as it were. With divorce the semester ends, and we irrevocably fail the course. We may, of course, elect to take the course on "marriage" over again. But if we do, we need to work through a number of "prerequisites" first. We need to know where and why we failed; we must learn what went wrong, and what it takes to make Us work. And we need to be healed of the grief and woundedness of our relational abortion, before we can be readied to risk love and commitment again.

Woe to those who do not so prepare, only to fail the course yet again!

✠

It is not You or I, but "Us," our relationship itself, which is the center of attention in divorce. Here the relationship is seen most clearly, what it was and was not—therefore who we were and were not. The relationship is lifted up and publicly exposed in all its dying insufficiency, or even in its humiliating absence. Gone is love's essential privacy; vanished—or should I say "banished"—is the world we shared, the unseen glue of our personal lives. Now our relationship belongs to the world, to public sentiment and legality, to our "friends"—and to our enemies.

What now of those personal belongings that we called "ours"? Comes the division, comes the either/or. What was ours must now be split into either "yours" or "mine." Mutuality gives way to ownership, sharing to power plays and territorial imperatives. How vexing is the forced choice about things that were so clearly *ours*, that came into our possession by common consent, that came to represent and symbolize, our life-together, our marriage, our spirit-entity! And most painful of all: our children. They are the fruit of our biological and psycho-social union. They cannot be divided up. And in their precious facticity, they bespeak an ongoing reality of Us. They will keep us together in common need and concern. As long as they live, there will never be a final end to Us.

✠

Is there not a time when divorce is justified and needed? Is a bad marriage preferable to no marriage at all? Behold, the psyche is to be valued above the pneuma in the world; that is, the survival of the soul has a greater priority than the perpetuation of a dead relationship. Better that the marriage go under than the persons in it. Better that the We be sacrificed, so that the I and the You may live to love another day, as it were. For the We is of the future; it is our destiny, our redemption. We must not ever equate a We-relationship here with that which is to come, or feel bound into by law that which the spirit has already abandoned.

All human marriages end at the grave, legally but not spiritually. For love continues beyond the grave, and in heaven love finds ultimate fulfillment in our marriage with God. And in that coming marriage, we shall all be married to each other as well, all one in a covenant of pure Spirit. In the meantime, however, in our life in the world, even our relationship with God will have periods of separation and divorce—at least from one image of God or kind of relationship. But God divorces us only to remarry us in a greater union.

The I and the You are of the present, and must work out their salvation in fear and trembling. And when a We-spirit has reached the state at which one or both partners have passed the relational point of no return—and only they can determine when—, then divorce is going to become a fact of soul and spirit, if not of law. Let the law therefore follow the leading of the spirit, and not lay too heavy a burden of guilt or incrimination upon the soul. For marriage was not made for the law, but the law for marriage. Let the divorce therefore be finalized in the world. But let us be very careful that the point of no return has in fact been passed; let us endeavor to the fullness of reason and compassion to see if the marriage can yet be revived and redeemed. Let those of us who believe in marriage continue to believe in its rebirth where there is will and grace. But where there is not the will, let the fullness of the tragedy be realized, and the parting completed. And let the persons be forgiven and supported through what will be a death and rebirth experience. And let us be certain that they are brought into awareness beforehand of the enormous cost of spirit and soul, as well as of material and possessions. Let us also recognize our accountability before God, one another, and ourselves.

Let us, in sum, hate not only divorce, but a bad marriage as well. For a bad marriage is an even more punishing hell than a divorce. And God desires that we live in love not in hell. Hell is where love is not. And God is love; hence, whatever is of love must be of God. And love can end as well as begin relationships, though not without great sorrow.

✠

The Word from above: "I hate divorce!" What then is the unconscionably high divorce rate today but a pivotal and profound indication of the loss of the sense of the presence with power of God? It is not God who has "died"; it is our relationship with God, the divine-human We of Spirit and covenant, which has fallen prey to the "me first" spirit of the modern world. It is the decay in our covenant with God which stands behind the decay in our covenants with each other. Our fall from grace has led to our fall from mutuality; our inability to maintain life with God is manifest in our fickleness toward one other.

Hence, only a renewal in our covenant or "marriage" with God, can renew our commitment to the covenantal life of marriage as such. The current tragic divorce rate serves as a cry from below to above for the Word of redemption to finally be heard, the Word that "We Are," the Word of ultimate and eternal marriage, of the time and place in God and of God's own choosing, when we will be beyond divorce and relational severance, when we shall be together forever, in spirit and truth. Then worship and marriage will be one and the same.

✠

The Broken We

An ancient nightmare of the race has it that the souls of the dead wander the earth, restless and homeless yet earthbound. According to another image of great age, the departed enter into some kind of an abode in the bowels of the earth. Where then do the spirits of broken We relationships dwell? More even than the number of lost souls are the number of lost relationships! Greater than all the blood shed upon the sod of the embattled earth is the blood spilled between us in the severing of love. And if the blood of the body returns to the soil, where flows the blood of the spirit? Unto God? Is not God spirit and love? Whereto then but back to God would love rejected and scorned return, back to its Source and Sender? Behold, as the Word returns to its Source after having carried out its task, just so is love destined to return to its true home. For the earth is not yet the home but only the house of love. O God, Thou art the reservoir and redeemer of lost loves! Unto Thee returns all which comes from Thee.

Alas, not only unto God does the broken We return, but it also cleaves to us. Instead of being earthbound, the lost We is "soul-bound." Not cast loose into the world, where it never belonged, the We abides only in us, and in that heart of us which is of God and shall return to God. As we are freed by love in its liveliness, so we are bound in by its brokenness; as we are confirmed by love in its acceptance and release, so we are uprooted and disavowed by love in its jettisoning and abandonment. What was between us is now bound within us—and is present in the silent memory of God. And the pain of heaven at the breaking of the We, at the lessening of love in the world! How long will we continue to crucify the mutuality of the heart, the common life of love in our midst?

✠

Our relationship is broken. Now there is distance where there was intimacy, estrangement where there was ease, suspiciousness where there was trust. Yet when I look at You I still feel the existence of the We within me, entombed unmarked in my chest, dead while we live, we who must now bear what used to bear us. A former presence is now a past, available only in my mourning memory. What do you feel?

How long will this sense of the Us without a present persist? How long will my heart grieve this loss of You and of the life which nourished us? How much of our lives do we spend in secret grief, how much of our daily energy is consumed with mourning love lost?

✠

Depression

Depression: the carrying of the death of the We in the life of the soul. Depression: the weight of the body of spirit pressing down into the psyche. Depression is above all a matter of spirit, and of the sphere of the interhuman. The person bears the absence of spirit in the soul and body. And the weight of the loss of spirit is more than many can bear! It is the loss of the vision of one's life. For with the spirit is life and meaning, faith and hope. And in depression, it is as if the psyche were cradling the remains of spirit in its own grieving "soul-life." The psyche cannot long endure this heaviness without going under itself. For it is the spirit which is to carry the soul, not the soul the spirit. The I has not the strength to go on without the We nourishing and sustaining it. And how shall we measure the spiritual quantum or mass of the spirit borne by the I? By what scale shall we determine the gravity of our millstone of despair?

Depression thus signifies the going under of the We. It is therefore interpersonal before it is intrapsychic. It represents the loss of love and meaning, of faith and hope, of purpose and motivation, of trust and good will, of openness and mutuality. Paradoxically, that means the soul experiences not only the weight of the spirit, but also the void or vacuum of the latter's absence. Thus could the soul lament, "My weight is my emptiness; I am wasting away in an uncharted and seemingly boundless sea of nothingness."

Could we not also call this profound and pervasive void of the spirit in the soul a kind of *voicelessness*? For word and spirit are one. Therefore the loss of spirit signifies the loss of word as well—literally of breath and of word. As the spirit becomes bound and imprisoned within the soul, just so and to the same extent is the word circumscribed and encapsulated within the I. Depression is therefore the weight of the "non-word" in us. And what is not spoken cannot be lifted.

What is unvoiced also remains unknown. And in depression, we are ambivalent about knowing what it is that weighs heavy upon us. To know or not to know, to voice or not to voice— how vexing are these questions! What will the knowledge do, help or hinder, redeem or condemn? It could seemingly go either way! Such a risk the depressed person is either unwilling or unable to take. The motive and caring power left with the spirit.

✠

Depression is a dis-ease of time, affecting past, present and future. Its central focus is in the past, however, and the overriding sense is that of being locked into or imprisoned by some spiritless, inescapable and insurmountable set of circumstances. Looking back at our *past,* we experience only the periphery of suppressed but ever-present *anger* and *guilt, fear* and *grief.* Whatever we have done, whatever has been done to us, whatever we have lost, whatever has been taken from us, these elements have accumulated into a dammed up and poisonous reservoir of anger and guilt, poised precipitously over a deep and vulnerable valley of fear and grief. And how great is the amount of energy required daily to keep the waters of our despair from overwhelming us! Other feelings and ugly streams of the past make their presence known: bitterness, resentment, unforgiveness, hatred, and self-loathing. Yet, anger and guilt remain the predominant features of this inner landscape of darkness and dis-ease.

Looking to the *future,* we feel an acute sense of *hopelessness* and *despair, dread* and *anxiety.* We feel that nothing we can do will make any difference: what we are suffering through will be our ultimate undoing. Hence, we may well not want to face and voice what is causing us such pain and anguish. We may ask "What good will it do to talk about it? Talking about it will not change a thing." Yet all we can do is talk, that in becoming word the burden of spirit may be released and we may be freed.

In terms of the *present,* the predominant feelings are those of *helplessness* and *fatigue, confusion* and *ambivalence.* We seem to have no future and are consigned to an unresolvable past from which there is no escape. Caught in this time-prison, we have two minds about whether to come to terms with what is slowly destroying us. We seem caught—with our own grudging permission and even design—in a narrow vault between the unacceptable past and the much-dreaded future toward which we are inexorably marching.

In the midst of the quiet desperation of the vault of our present, we feel utterly alone and unreachable. The absence of mutuality is almost more than we can bear! Thus do we cry: "Who knows or cares that I have come to this? Who can find me where I am suffering and bring me help? Who will come forward and share my burden with me? Who will relieve me of it, and how? Help me—and do not wait till I ask, for I do not know how, and I cannot take the added weight of your saying no to my plea. Your rejection could be the one thing too many. I might fall—and right now I am just barely holding on."

✠

Depression: a daily, even hourly struggle to make it through the day without falling apart. You are wearied and shell-shocked, confused and anxious, yet somehow detached, as if You were really on the outside of your life looking in, and helplessly at that. You have so little energy available and so much to do and be in comparison. The demands of life push down on You seemingly without mercy or sensitivity to your state. All You can do is measure out your limited supply of strength and willpower with a teaspoon, while the recipe for daily life calls for cupfuls. Every day You feel You are going to come up short, but You cannot seem to help it, for You need most of your energy merely to keep afloat, merely to keep treading water. You have almost lost the capacity to swim, and fear You will never again move with facility through your life. It exhausts You even to think about the effort required to do so! How could life ever become easy again? There is so much now weighing down on You that relief and release seem beyond the realm of the possible.

Mere survival is the issue now at stake. And sometimes You wish it could simply all end, so that there would be no need to fight anymore, so that the pain would go away for good. Who can take pleasure in the face of such fatigue and anxiety? And what of meaning and purpose for your life? There is neither time nor energy to consider it. Your heart is too closed to life to be open to novelty, and too bitter to believe in the possibility of peace and healing.

In a depression things mean pretty much the same thing. Everything is homogenized to look and taste like the same gruel. From food to clothes, from simple decisions to life-altering ones, all come at us in a confusing totality we cannot separate or get on top of. Nothing sits up in us and says, "pick me." No option really appeals. Instead most options appall! Or worse yet, they do not matter at all.

Perhaps depression is nothing more or less than a denial of our existence, a deep and pervasive *No* to the whole of our hidden self. It is as if we say, "No, I really cannot or will not deal with that feeling; I will stonewall my problems and wait them out. Surely they will disappear in time, if I can just hold on." And so we often look the other way, hoping in our hopelessness that our inaction will lead to the eventual lifting of the weight and the ending of the pain. And so we stay on the surface of things, and never really get to the bottom of the problem. And staying on the surface only serves to increase our feeling that the depression is *bottomless*.

Even with "anti-depressant" drugs, the void remains in our life, though perhaps less noticed in our deadened consciousness. This void or emptiness is at the heart of our depression. So we try to fill it, usually with the advertised pleasures and values of our culture. During the times we feel enough energy and hope, we may seek diversions. But apart from a rebirth of the We, of love and mutuality— and ultimately of our relationship with God—no meaning, pleasure or purpose can satisfy or fill us. For the empty space we experience in depression is our own alienation or estrangement, our own inner space burning with a hellish fire fed not by oxygen but by emptiness. The fact of depression tells us that we are cut off from others, from life and purpose, from the things that make for joy and peace. We are lost in ourselves. Who will find us? Who will bring us new life?

O emptiness that saps my strength! O sea of meaninglessness that engulfs me whole! How do I find the shore? And even then, from where can I derive the strength and the will to walk once again upon the dry and solid land?

In truth, the healing of the inner being comes through mutual being. The lifting of the burden and the re-ignition of the light of the heart comes through the touch of You—in the sphere of Us. Where two find each other in mutuality, hope is reborn, and the black weight of depression, like coal, is kindled into a wondrous source of heat and life. Behold the miracle of God: night itself burns, as we dance before its day.

✠

Anxiety

Anxiety is the experience of groundlessness. And it is a groundlessness flooded with a vague yet foreboding sense of impending disaster, of grave personal threat. From whence will come the calamity, from within or from without, from the intrusion into consciousness of undesirable feelings, forbidden images and terrifying thoughts, all seeking to take over the I, or from some undetermined life-threatening force or person about to enter the field of view of the I? In anxiety, the inner and the outer merge in a continuous cacophonous rapids of unbounded danger. There is no safety, within or without. The I fears the danger within as much as any potential danger without. Hence, fear of self and fear of the world are one. The unknown as such becomes the enemy. And whatever has not been confirmed within the I through meeting with the You—that is, *grounded in mutuality*—the I cannot embrace as knowledge, cannot rely upon as known and predictable. And much lives within the I in the shadows of unvoiced presence. What is not yet word is not yet known, even if acutely sensed by the I. And in the state of anxiety, that which is unknown constitutes a real or imaged threat to the known self.

The beast is loosed, within and without. From where shall it attack the I, from what direction will this rejected being of uncovenanted power break through the integrity of the I? The perimeter of defense is weakened by the I's own ambivalence about what may live within it, wanting both to accept and integrate as well as to deny and cut off. At the point of this perimeter, along the edge of this inner conflict, emerges a feeling-state so powerful and terrifying as to present in itself an instrument sufficient for the disintegration of the I. From the center of the unnamed but present comes forth a sickening vortex, *anxiety,* which signals the presence of the enemy within, but either cannot or will not disclose its nature or whereabouts. The threat calls for immediate action—but without an image of the danger, no action seems possible, and no avenue of escape presents itself to the I. On and on the vortex whirls: at once a boundless void sucking the I out of itself and into it, and at the same time an internal sphere too small for the I, forcing the I into a black cell, inescapable and torturously tight. In both images, the key is the *disintegration of the I,* its possible death, condemnation, or loss of meaning. Without a ground to stand upon, where and how can the I affirm itself, how can it save its own life?

Anxiety evolves around three axes of threat, in accordance with the threefoldness of the person. To the *body,* it bespeaks the *threat of death;* to the *soul,* the *threat of condemnation;* to the *spirit,* the *threat of meaninglessness.* The I is thus intersected with three dagger-lines of concern, three spinning polarities pulling the person into panic: life vs. death, good vs. evil, and meaning vs. meaninglessness. Each polarity is decisive for the integrity of the I; the very future of the existence of the self is at stake—and *right now*! Am I to live or die; am I to be good or evil; am I to live in meaning or be cast into meaninglessness?

Behold, the major battleground of anxiety is internal. And the true enemy of the I is within. Anxiety bespeaks above all an inner conflict. For anxiety itself represents the vortex created by the vacillation between two options the I seems forced to take regarding itself, *either* of which could lead to the disintegration, the condemnation, and/or the loss of meaning of the I. The precise nature of this vortex concerns an inner conflict or experiential paradox between the *Yes,* to self over against the *No.* That is, anxiety is the stormy vacillation between the Yes and the No of the I to itself and its inner life, wherein the I is unable or unwilling to say either with finality and responsibility, unable either to affirm or to deny, to accept or to reject itself.

Anxiety is thus typically a conflict between creation and "normation," between the inner *is* of being vs. the *ought* of norms personally appropriated. Evaluation is in conflict with creation; a tension exists between who the I is and who the I should be. This vacillation gains power and intensity from the fact that the person does not really want to say either Yes or No to what lives within. The I experiences the mixed desire both to maintain the perimeters of defense and to tear them down and embrace the enemy. If the I said No to itself, that would eventuate in the loss of self, inner death, condemnation and meaninglessness. Yet, if the I said Yes to itself, that would also lead to the disintegration, condemnation and state of emptiness coming from the rejection of others.

This inner battle reveals the non-integration and non-acceptance of the I, as mediated by others in the course of the person's life. Hence, anxiety attests to the "groundlessness" of the I. And the only satisfactory ground possible is that of the sphere *between* the I and the You, the ground of open and unguarded affirmation and mutuality, the life-bearing foundation of the We. The resolution of anxiety comes through the voicing of the inner vortex, through the word living between the I and the You. For nothing heals like the word, the word spoken and heard, shared and mutual, the word in and through which the I is affirmed and confirmed in the peace-bringing commonness of essential relation.

✠

Anxiety is the experience of groundlessness. Without a ground, anxiety, like electricity, cannot pass through and out of the person, but becomes frozen in an inner arc of torment. The ground of being-together, the wondrous dissipator of anxiety, is *trust*. Trust is both the preparation for meeting and the concrete basis thereof. If the person in an anxiety state is unable to trust in another, or in anything, including themselves, that person will know no peace. Trust invites love, and serves as the inner host. Where trust guides, peace abides. Trust opens wide the world between us, and gifts us with the motive power to step forth to one another and to the mutuality that saves, that bears life and meaning and affirmation, the sharing that eradicates anxiety. Trust is the bridge between us, apart from which we remain islands of unrest unto ourselves. Trust is, in brief, the way into the promised land, the land of milk and honey, of mutual life and substance.

Salvation is the grounding of personal being in the Word, the Word of life and love, Spirit and healing. Only that which is greater than the I can integrate the I; only the love of creation can lead to the wholeness and holiness of the I in a rebirth of mutuality. And this cannot happen in isolation, but only through the mediation of the You, and only in the event of the We, of being known and knowing in pure simultaneity.

The resolution of anxiety signifies the transformation by love of the either/or of being or not being into a both/and, into a Yes and a No, the union of the good and not good, the peace-laden acceptance of personal paradox, held together and integrated not simply in the I, that is, the I in isolation and therefore estrangement, but the I-in-relationship, the I inclusive of the You in a genuine spirit-We. For personal integration requires both an otherness and a mutuality, a triplicity of I, You and We. And personal integrity comes into being and is sustained by the concrete oneness of all three in the ground of relationship.

That means anxiety is finally and absolutely resolved only in God, who is the true and ultimate ground of all relationships. In God, no fear of death, condemnation or meaninglessness can abide. God's love casts out all fear and anxiety. In God, I am accepted even and precisely in my non-acceptability. God's grace abounds, and unconditional love reaches out through the Cross to bring me, even me to the improbable consistency with the love with which I, even I am loved. In the ground of the holy mutuality between God and us, the holy highway, the lamb may lie down in safety with the lion; the parts of personal being may come together into the wholeness of God's love and light.

O my God, You have made possible the both/and of my being, out of the troubled ashes of my either/or!

THE FALLEN I

Rejection

Rejection: an act, an emotion, a state of being. To be rejected means literally to be thrown back upon or into oneself. For the word "reject" comes from the Latin *rejectus,* which is derived from the verb *reicere,* meaning "to throw or fling back" (*re-*, back + *jacere,* to throw). To be rejected, then, means to be denied a place of standing in a relationship, be it with an individual, a family, a peer group or a people. It means to be forced to exist on one's own resources, cut off from the nourishment and support of a We-spirit. Rejection therefore signifies the consignment into hell, into isolation and estrangement, into condemnation and a burning and non-quenchable emptiness.

Rejection: the cutting off of mutuality, the rending of the We. The We of spirit and presence is thus mortally wounded. What then of the I who participated in that We, the I who though spurned still seeks the You who has cast it aside? Does not the You leave the I there with the dying relationship, there to perish right along with the We? What greater guilt do we bear than for those times and instances when we have rejected another? When we have left another to die with the remains of "Us"? And what stands behind such "hardness of heart," but the rejected heart rejecting, but the heart closed to itself and thus to all others?

Rejection leads to anger, anger to resentment, resentment to despair, despair to bitterness, bitterness to hatred, and hatred to the wish for the death—at least in spirit and in the soul of the one who hates—of the one who rejected the person. And to harbor a death-wish for another carries with it a death-wish in kind for the self. To hate another means to hate ourselves as well—for in the silent depths of the soul lies the knowledge that we are just as guilty and reprehensible as the one we hate. For we have rejected them in their rejection of us; we have sinned in response to their sin against us. Not to forgive the other therefore means not to forgive ourselves.

Rejection: there is no more powerful an emotion or painful a state of being. What do we fear above rejection and the consequences thereof? To what lengths will we go to avoid being rejected? Yet the fear of rejection has rejection already within it! The fear of rejection brings rejection into the relationship, like a self-fulfilling prophesy. To fear rejection initiates the inner if hidden process of rejecting in return for the anticipation of being cast aside. To be rejected eventuates in rejecting, a sin against the I leads to a sin against the You in response: an eye for an eye, a No for a No. Which leads to which, the fear to the fact or the fact to the fear? It does not matter. The end is the same. Behold, the fear of rejection is a part of the spirit of rejection itself.

How many relationships have been broken, how many loved ones wounded or even slain in spirit because of the fear of rejection? How many "trigger-happy" persons have shot the innocent out of unwarranted fear? Why do we reject so quickly and accept so slowly? It is not rejection we should fear; it is the fear of rejection.

✠

Betrayal

Betrayal is interpersonal treason. And just as there is no higher crime against the nation, so there is no greater crime against love and the beloved than betrayal. Betrayal moves beyond rejection, though it contains the latter within itself. Where rejection is a casting out and away, betrayal signifies a murderous violation of personal trust and integrity. Where rejection throws the person back onto their own resources, betrayal hands them over to the will and power of the enemy. In its malevolence and calculated coldness, betrayal reveals something far more evil than mere rejection. Here there is an open intent to mock and vilify, to expose and shatter before uncaring or judgmental or condemnatory eyes that which was entrusted and held sacred; here the purportedly loved one is given over to the person or force in opposition to him or her—and to the relationship. Betrayal tortures the person in the relationship and torches the relationship in the person. Betrayal crucifies both the We of the spirit and the I of the soul. It is therefore to be feared above the crucifixion of the body.

Betrayal evidences not only a blindness to the other and to the love seemingly shared, but a deadness to the heart and the things of the heart. The betrayer is simply not there, that is, is not located in the relational sphere the one betrayed had assumed. Rather, the betrayer was also the grand deceiver, the liar, who masqueraded as one trustworthy only to use and abuse the trust given. Confidence was gained with the hidden intent to defile the person and the information for unholy purpose. Not only therefore was the person a mere means for the betrayer, but the person was to be spiritually sacrificed in the process.

The work of the betrayer is so insidious that it may result in the entrance into hell of not only the betrayer, but also the one betrayed. For in raping the love and the heart of trust, the betrayer may render the betrayed unable to believe in another, and thus unable to love again. And hell is the absence of love; hell is the endless suffering through of our lost ability to love. To lose the capacity to believe or trust in another means to be self-consigned to hell. And how the enemy utilizes betrayal to increase its ranks! For all too often, the betrayed becomes a betrayer—to themselves as well as to others.

✠

In the context of the divine-human relationship, betrayal is at the heart of what Jesus calls the "blaspheming of the Holy Spirit," the one unforgivable sin. It means to hand over to evil, and to renounce absolutely thereby, the Spirit of love in which we actually stand; it means to forever scorn the love with which we have been loved by actively seeking its extinguishing. To have a history of personal knowledge of God, yet consciously to betray the Holy Spirit of mutuality, to willingly turn one's back on the ultimacy of and identity with the Spirit once the deed is done, to knowingly sell out the boundless Yes of God for the sake of personal and thus idolatrous gain—for this there is no forgiveness. And for this God suffers long beyond our vision or grasp.

✠

Rape

Rape: a heinous crime of the spirit before it is a crime of the flesh; a vicious violation of the soul before it is of the body. Rape is a radical *inversion of mutuality*, carried out against the flesh; it is a sudden seizure repudiating sharing and giving, an event of perverse will and power warring against all freedom and sanctity. Rape is a desecration of the temple of the body, the integrity of the soul and the life of the spirit. The violence of rape thus cuts through all three dimensions of human existence in the world. In each dimension, it is the *me* of the rapist seeking to assert itself in its desire for power and the gratification of lust—all at the direct expense of the victim. The rapist says in effect, "It is *my* relationship on *my* terms; your body is for *me* to do with as I please; your soul is for feeling *my* existence and *my* wrath. You will do what *I* want. You will take what *I* have to give, and *I* will take what *I* want. You exist for *my* pleasure."

The rapist thus knows no both/and. For this depraved one, all relationships are either/or in nature: one is either on the top or the bottom, the user or the used, the master or the slave, the conqueror or the conquered. Here there is no respect for person or relationship; indeed, there is no understanding—from the inside—of what it means to participate in genuine mutuality. The rapist has never been bonded to another, and has therefore *no personal knowledge of the We*. Hence, the rapist knows little of the I and the You as well. That is, *because there has never been an Us, an "ours," the rapist does not really see the "yours" but only the "mine."* And the "mine" is one of emptiness and enmity, of an I existing in negation of itself and others. Behold, rape is not only a crime of violence and violation; it is a great crime of ignorance of the self, of others and of the meaning of true relationship, of being-together in love and communion. The rapist is unable to experience inclusion and mutuality with another. And in bitter blindness, the rapist would blind others.

Can we do other than to seek to make the world over into our image? Can we do other than to show by our actions against others how we see ourselves—and how others have seen us?

✠

Rape: the first and primal crime of man against woman and the heart. It is the nefarious act of sexual dominance and possession. Rape gave rise to the "oldest profession," prostitution. Prostitution is preceded by and is indeed a form of rape—only with the supposed consent and even active recruitment of the woman. But with her history of being used and abused, and with the consequential and seemingly irreparable loss of her sense of self-worth, what is the woman left to say No *with* and *for*? What force can she summon to say *No* to such a fate?

What stands behind such an utterly inexcusable and unconscionable deed? A kind of "original sin": the rapist has undergone in his own upbringing the inversion of mutuality; the rapist himself has been raped in spirit, if not in flesh. That is, rape is an unjustifiable paying back of the abuse and denial suffered during the vulnerable and dependent days of childhood. The male child never bonded with the female, never was embraced by woman in the essential covenant of flesh, never was affirmed in body and soul, never experienced the Mother-child We. He therefore seeks revenge against his mother's rejection of his body and its needs, against her denial of his power of presence and importance of person, her lack of love and sensitivity. Sin against leads to sin against—only the rapist intends to better the instruction. He will avenge himself on whatever woman he chooses in the capriciousness of his hatred. He will claim back, perhaps again and again, what he feels was denied him. He will imprint his body upon his surrogate Mother, because hers was not imprinted upon his. He will gratify his hunger for and hatred of woman; he will hurt and use as he has felt hurt and used; he will deny what has been denied him.

✠

What of the victim of rape? What of her rage and fear, grief and guilt? Nothing can undo the sacrilege perpetrated against her and her species through her. No human hands can restore the pearls of innocence and personal purity crushed by the felon of the body and the heart. Rape is an evil spirit that defiles the body, pollutes the soul and makes unclean the spirit. What is required therefore is the Holy Spirit to exorcise and free, to cleanse and forgive, to redeem and rebirth. Only the embracing waters from above can renew and reconsecrate the victim's sense of purity and wholeness. And that means, only a true mutuality with God can make possible a new life of and for the Spirit. In truth, there is no human condition heaven cannot heal. God well understands the meaning and anguish of desecration.

✠

Guilt

Guilt arises as the experience of the actual *breach of the We,* together with the weight of responsibility for the rupture. It refers to the state of a relationship before the state of the soul. That is, guilt *does* and *is* before guilt *feels;* guilt is an interpersonal state of transgression before it is a subjective sense of wrongdoing. We must therefore beware of reducing guilt to guilt feelings, the ontological state of transgression and fracture to the subjective concomitants thereof. We must focus first and above all on what has happened *between* us, rather than on what is going on *within* us, if we are to understand the nature and seriousness of guilt.

The feelings of guilt are not the cause but the effect of an event beyond feeling, the event of the violation of being-together. The feelings thus attest to, but are not constitutive of, the reality of the rupture of the We. Something has happened between us; something must therefore be healed between us, not merely within us. This is the case even if the only person who knows of the breach is the one who did the transgressing. Something unclean has nevertheless entered into the spirit or mutual atmosphere; a pollutant is present amidst the partners, and must be dealt with as something real between them.

Behold, part of our guilt is the awareness of the avoidance of the Word in us, the Word of the Spirit of truth, which seeks to tell us of our state, and illumine our culpability. And so, do we not seek to avoid our guilt, and thus avoid having to respond to what we have wrought? In the twisted logic of our half-conscious guilt, we may equate response with responsibility. Hence, our non-response would mean our non-responsibility. Yet our guilt abides in us, just as the "black box" abides in a commercial airplane, continuously recording the verbal transactions between the pilots and the ground, out of reach of any amending from the former.

So also does our guilt go on. We may try to talk it away, but we cannot eradicate its roots in our souls. It will always grow back, until such a time as we are willing to turn and address it in the only way that can lead to its resolution: through *self-examination, confession* and *repentance*. And our repentance must include redress and reconciliation. Further, it must incorporate forgiveness—of ourselves as well as others. For with forgiveness comes a release from the past, and thus a freedom from guilt. With forgiveness comes also the openness to a restoration of relationship—not of the relationship as it once was, but of a new kind of mutuality, be it fuller and more mature, or more distant and only as a renewed capacity to face each other free from guilt and resentment. At its bottom line, guilt seeks the re-establishment of relationship, and the cleansing of all involved.

✠

The lengths we go to avoid accepting and experiencing guilt! And the anger we feel when cornered! A vicious cycle ensues: we feel guilt, then anger against ourselves and also against the person who makes us feel guilty. And then we feel guilty about our anger, which is only widening the breach between us; and then we feel anger at our guilt about our anger. Behold, anger and guilt tend to come together, so that when one is at our side, the other is at our back. And so the cycle goes on and on, until it is faced and voiced, until confession breaks through our self-destructive gearing.

Not to be in touch with our guilt, however, means not to be in touch with the spirit—and that means not to be fully alive to ourselves and others. And so few around us are aware of the guilt which lives in them! The world is replete with zombies, who deny their guilt only to deny themselves, who say No to spirit and life in saying No to responsibility. Behold, in our avoidance of guilt lies our avoidance of redemption.

Sin

Sin is the willful transgression of the law of love. It means the falling short, by the conscious and voluntary act of omission or commission, of the mandate of spirit, of the way of mutuality. To sin means to do what we know to be wrong. True ignorance of sin *is* an excuse; if there is neither will nor awareness, let us call it error or mistake rather than sin—unless we wish to call ignorance itself sin. We know indeed when we sin, before, during and after, though we may attempt to block out the feelings of guilt and relational dismemberment attendant upon the event. That we have such knowledge but do nothing about it, that we know we have wronged but do not seek to make amends, is itself sin, grave and inexplicable.

Sin is threefold in accordance with the threefoldness of meaning: *sin is intention, denotation and connotation.* It is first of all an intention of the will, be it known or partly hidden to the person; then it is deed of denotation in the world, concrete and specific; finally it is something shared in the relationship which it transgressed, that is, it enters into the We-spirit, to be "co-noted" between the persons involved. All three dimensions must be held together if we are to grasp the full significance of sin in personal and interpersonal existence. It is within, beyond, and between us.

Sin is thus a *state* before and after it becomes a deed or event. It is sinfulness before any of its offspring are manifest. First it is an inner state of temptation, which immediately begins to affect the spirit of a relationship. Where there is inner impulse to sin, sin is already directly affecting not only the person but also the relationship as well—as Jesus so forcefully revealed to us. So, for instance, the impulse to lie itself distances the person from the other, even if the lie is not carried out. The inner state does not simply remain within us; its waves reach the other, and God. From this state comes forth the deed of the sin itself, which eventuates in the interpersonal state of disruption. This ontological state between persons in turn produces disruption in the psyche of both the sinner and the sinned against.

Sin thus involves a process with a definite sequence of events. It begins in the heart, in the center of the will, the source of imagination and the ideation. This is the mysterious moment of the initial "temptation," the turning of the attention upon something desirable yet "forbidden" and destructive to both person and relationship. From the heart, the temptation succeeds in gaining the attention of the conscious mind. It does so through the seductive use of imagery and imagination. We dream about what we desire; we carry out in our imagination what we are not yet willing and/or able to carry out in the flesh.

As the image unfolds and takes possession of more and more of the mind, a conflict ensues between the Yes and the No to actually doing the deed, between the gratification of the desire over against the voice of conscience and caution. If the Yes wins out, then we must create a climate of inner consonance, that is, we must seek to find some "socially redeeming value" to what it is we are about to do—or to not to do. For if we have a conscience, we also have a need to justify ourselves to it, and to resolve the conflict and the tension thereof, so as to regain our sense of consonancy in values. When that has happened—or when we have succeeded in merely suppressing the conflict—we are ready to act. And this whole proceeding might be accomplished in a few seconds—especially if we are well practiced in the ways of self-deception and relational intrigue. And so few of us ever realize just how devious we actually are! Yet who of us really wants to know?

Note that this whole process is worked by the I, for the I and of the I. It is selfish and self-centered from beginning to end. It is essentially an either/or situation, in which the I has chosen to serve itself rather than the You and the relationship, the We. At its base, therefore, *human sin represents our inability to maintain identity in and with the We.* Instead of *"We first,"* we seem ever to fall back on a *"me first"* mentality;

rather than living for each other, we want each other to live for us. The depth of our sinful nature bespeaks the fundamental tendency to reduce life-together to the needs and perspective of life-alone, the We-spirit to the I-soul. We thereby cut asunder unity and mutuality for the sake of personal primacy, the both/and of love to the either/or of power and possession. *My* needs and position come first; rather than I *and* You, our relationship becomes I *vs.* You.

Sin is anathema to the We. Its very presence dissolves the We into a number of I-worlds—and thus the I into a number of parts. That is, sin divides and "partializes"; it binds the whole in order to possess it as a series of parts. Sin cannot possess the whole in its integrity, be it of the I or of the We, but only the parts, only the whole in a state of brokenness and decay. Sin shatters the We and tosses the pieces back into the I, there to be used by the I—also in pieces—for those individual purposes at odds with common life. Sin is self-possession seeking world-possession, it is the striving for domination and power in order to obtain that which it can only achieve through self-abandonment, namely, self-fullness. And only in the We do self-fullness and self-abandonment come to be grasped in the grace of present being as one and the same.

Where does sin gain its foothold in the human heart? What is its starter-yeast? Behold the twins of *mistrust* and *disbelief*: we do not believe in the other and in the relationship, nor do we long trust and thus persevere in sustained intimacy. We do not really believe that the way to fulfillment is through and with each other, that the life of the We, of Us, is the one true life we are seeking. The lack of trust initiates a need to protect oneself, and to provide for oneself what might be denied from others. The mandate of sin: "Get it for yourself before others take it from You! Take care of Yourself, because no one else will." We thus seek to attain alone and for ourselves what can only come to us together, and for the sake of each other. It is only when we are not looking for it that meaning and fulfillment happen, only when we are gazing upon each other and giving as loving servants that true life is granted as gift of grace.

What greater sin than our inability to believe in love and in each other? What has it cost us, in personal and cultural terms? How many wars have been waged because of mistrust, how many private and public battlefields stain our history? Surely more than all the cemeteries that dot the land. Only here there are no honors or wreaths of memory. Better to believe and live, than to disbelieve and starve! For disbelief can only say No to love and life.

In leading to the dissolution of the We, sin eventuates in the spiritual death of the I. For sin strains mutuality out of meaning, and spirit out of daily life; it leaves us with only a shallow existence of immediate gratification and short-term gain. Fortunately—yet how unfortunately! —it also blinds us to the precipice towards which it inexorably leads us, to the long-term loss of life, eternal and substantial. Sin can only promise but never deliver fulfillment. And promise it ever does! Yet fulfillment *is* the life of mutuality.

✠

Sin precludes sharing and mutuality. It therefore perverts law, language and love, through the turning back upon itself, the "self-possession" or "self-serving" of what is meant to be shared. Through sin law becomes *autologos,* language and love *autoeros* or *autophilia.* The prefix comes from the Greek, and means "self, same, or automatic, e.g., by itself, himself or herself." In every case this perversion leads to the dissolution of relationship and the estrangement of the individual. The attempt to possess the common, to seek to refract the We through oneself, as if to become an androgynous and self-gratifying being, is really the desire to write one's I large upon the sky of the human world, and thus to become god. It is self-destructive as well as world-destructive. For the self-law of sin leads to *anarchy,* the self-language of sin's isolation to *autism,* and the self-love of sin's reactionary stance to *narcissism.* In seeking to possess all, all is eventually lost. The perversion of mutuality leads only to evil and death.

Sin is a violation of spirit before it is a transgression of law. For the law is but a shadow of the spirit; spirit is the substance of love and life, law is at best an essential blueprint. And behold, much that is "lawful" is nevertheless sinful; and much that seems "lawless" is of the spirit, thus of the higher law of love. Love is true to itself, whether the preestablished specifications of the law are prepared for its outbreak or not. Love fulfills its inner mandate, known only by itself and those blessed in the hearing and responding. Thus Jesus became law-breaker in order to become love-fulfiller. Better love without law, than law without love! "Lawful" love and piety without the spirit and spontaneity constitute abominations to the heart and to God; actions done in love and for love, thus in and for God, may break the law, yet remain true to the We, to true relationship.

Let us ever be true to the We! Whatsoever we do, if it be done in the name and substance of love, cannot be sin. Even if it end in error and distress, it is not sin but growth and maturity, planned from a time and place beyond our vision.

✠

The Seven Deadly Sins

The "seven deadly sins" are deadly indeed. *Pride, anger, lust, avarice, gluttony, jealousy* and *sloth,* are deadly to *relationships* before they are deadly to persons. And they are fatal to persons precisely because they are fatal to those relationships in which persons find their being and life. *Pride* lifts up the I to the exclusion of the You and the We, therein precluding equality and mutuality. *Anger* absolutizes the demands of the I, and can lead to violence against and even the death of, not only the We, but also the You. *Lust,* as a "strange god" within, drives the I out of the bonds and fidelity of the We, and into an unending search for a gratification of the body destructive to both soul and spirit. *Avarice* seduces the I into the delusion that its life consists in things, in having rather than in being-together, in the realm of the It rather than the We. *Gluttony* promises, but cannot deliver, the resolution of an unanswered need for love and nurture, for comfort and security, in its own We-less world of fullness and satiation. *Jealousy* veils love and the truth of the We with its mantle of heated fear and hatred, and, while claiming to represent the way to save love and the beloved from the embrace of another, it in fact seeks love's dismemberment, and the annihilation of the We. *Sloth* pulls the I into a state of inertia, and signifies the unwillingness of the I to share fully in the daily responsibility for the relationship—thus dooming the We.

These sins are relationally idolatrous in that they place the individual, the I, before the other, the You, *thereby precluding the We.* In the grip of one or more of these sins—each constituting a kind of spirit or daimon—the person loses the freedom to step forward and meet the other, to become a partner in a We. These sins harden the heart of the I and bind it into an inner darkness of emptiness and despair, need and restlessness.

The before, during and after taste of these sins is *bitterness, resentment* and *unforgiveness*—with an unsettling and ever-present sense of fear. This threesome of inner torture comes in the wake of relational events of trauma and sin, of rejection interchanged and grief buried. Yet these three poisons and the sins they fuel are in turn built upon a more primal twofold sin of the will: *unbelief* and *mistrust*. In the beginning is the *No*, the "I will not trust another; I will not believe in You." Whether justified or not on the basis of prior rejection and abuse, the I loses the capacity to believe in or fully trust the You as such. This is the *root sin* of the I. And this mistrust is the door through which evil of every sort may and does enter; this mistrust is the human ground in which and from which all sin takes root and grows—like weeds, so plenteous and resistant to extinction!

✠

The true ground of all human sin and all evil is the *No* to the You, human and divine, over against the I. And that means the *No* to relationship, to the *We* offered to the I as its true life and purpose—and salvation. This No prohibits openness and sharing; it creates the need for defensive walls and self-protection, for self-serving and self-preservation in the face of a human world the I cannot trust. The I turns back upon itself, and takes the life-force of its creation, intended to power it to the shores of the You and to beget primal relationships, and uses it to form a relationship-in-exile with itself. Instead of a true We, a false sense of mutuality is aroused by the I-in-self-defense, the I which comes to hold itself as an object ever before it, needing its protection and nourishment. The forces of evil and delusion are invited in by the will in order to support this untrue We, this self-kingdom, this world of the only-I, the I-in-relation-to-itself, self-focused and self-concerned, the I which sees itself as the only real person in its world, the only one who really matters.

Through this self-reflection and self-embracing, a "shadow self" emerges, namely the image of the I which either is not seen or is rejected by others. This imaged self is understood by the I to be the actual and underlying person, the person who the I must serve and gratify, protect and cherish, love and appease—for no one else will, or so the I believes. And the "mis-word" which is here active within the I: "Nobody loves me, and nobody is trustworthy; hence, I will love myself in place of others. I will create and provide the relationship I need from others, which I will never have with them. I will be my own You."

In the place of the You, the I lifts up the *"Me."* A "We of one" is thus established, a closed arc of the I-in-relation-to-itself, of an *"I-Me relationship"* instead of an I-You one. And once established, it is very difficult to break through, for the I does not *hear* as an I, but as a kind of We, as a closed society would hear a message from an outside world. It would first have to translate the message into its own language, and would require deliberation before being able to respond to the intrusion. So be it with the false We of the I and its imaged "Me"; spontaneity is replaced by a pseudo dialogue of mistrust and despair.

This I-Me relationship, the false We, is the ground of the seven deadly and idolatrous sins. For the No to the You also means the No to the We—which means to the life of the I. *Pride,* the first and cardinal sin, upon which all other sins take their stand, represents the puffing up of the Me by the I in defiant and mock esteem, a kind of self-creation by the I playing god with the Me. Pride signifies *exclusive self-love,* love which does not include the love of others or the love that others have for the I. This is in opposition to *inclusive self-love,* love which is built upon and includes the love of others and others' love of the I. Pride can allow others to enter the outer court or possibly the antechamber of the heart, but never the inner chamber. And it will allow others to enter only to praise and support the Me, the conscious ego. But the I will reject any criticism that calls its creation into question.

Pride is blind to the self; the inner chamber is never entered, even by the creator-I, but rather is feared. For the inner chamber cannot be entered alone but only in mutuality and communion. Indeed, it is the bridal chamber of the heart, the holy place for the consummation of the We, for intimacy and union. And the prideful Me dimly senses in its fear the underlying I who seeks its You, who stands yearning before the door to the inner chamber, waiting to be found and to find, to receive and to give. There the true I, living in hidden exile, awaits a mutuality beyond pride.

✠

Ambition

Ambition is the *eighth* deadly sin, and perhaps the motivating impulse for the other seven. What, for instance, is pride but a protective vestment for ambition? Ambition is a primal, if not the primal form of *desire,* and thus a matter of the will. And it is a twofold desire: first, to become like or to attain that which we want but do not have, and second, to become "better" than others in what we seek, once it is ours—even at the cost of relationships. For ambition places the I in direct opposition to the You, and reduces the sphere between the I and the You to an interpersonal battleground of "competition." And the *We of competition* is an I vs. You rather than an I and You, and either/or rather than a both/and. Mutuality is thus reduced to exclusivity, mine vs. yours. The true We of equality and mutual presence cannot long exist in a "psychosphere" polluted with ambition.

Even if the ambition of the I is sublimated into that of a group or "team," the oppressive spirit of the either/or, the "us vs. them," the "winners and the losers," abides. Reciprocity with the opponent can cost the person and the team the victory. The You becomes but one of "them," the opposition, and the We of "our team" exists for the common purpose of becoming "No. 1." A larger We of "the game," of opposition happens, a wrestling, an event of power-taking instead of power-granting. Both teams cannot win; and the winner takes all. There is no mutuality in victory, save within the team itself, and between those "fans" who seek to derive the benefits of participation in spirit with their "team," that is, who seek to attain through others the goal of their own ambition.

Yet even within the team itself, ambition permeates the interpersonal atmosphere. It can block genuine mutuality, for it pushes the members to judge and rank each other, and to jealously guard and always seek to advance their relative position in the team. Even the "esprit de corps" is not an end in itself, but for the sake of winning, of attaining the winning attitude and atmosphere. Thus, caring for one another has the backdrop of personal and team benefit. Everything is a means to the one end, the achievement of the team ambition.

Ambition drives us to use others as means to our own ends, rather than as ends in themselves, and our relationship as our shared end. Ambition places before the I its own goals, which can all too easily replace those of the You and the We. Yet the only goals that truly matter, that have enduring substance here and in what is to come, are those of mutuality and love, are those which are *ours,* rather than *yours vs. mine.* And what greater ambition than that life's tragic either/ors finally become love's wondrous both/ands?

The human person has an innate imperative from creation to individuate, to self-actualize. For we are commanded: "Be You"—that means, *become* all that it is in You to become. And that means, "Become perfect, as I Am perfect." But this does not mean to do so competitively, or in either/or terms. Rather than either/or, we are called to think and live in *both/and* terms. For ultimately, the "Be You" summons of our creation means "Be You *with* Me," it means a being together. Our ambition becomes sinful when and as it turns from the both/and of our creation into an either/or of self-will, when *apposition becomes opposition.* At the heart of human sin is the desire, not only to become like God, but to do so *at the cost of God's own sovereignty.* It is a power struggle for but one throne, at the cost of a divinely willed power sharing in a kingdom of Spirit. We can only lose this self-imposed war.

The goal of ambition, that of "reaching the top," actually contains a hidden death wish. For the higher we strive through our ambition, the greater is the fall which can be ours. If we would but renounce our ambition, for the sake of becoming all that it is in us to become, there would be no fall. And God would lift us up into the realm of mutual being and becoming. And what greater desire than to become one *with* God?

✠

The Shadow Self

Every I is "shadowed" by that which is of it, but not yet embraced by it. The shadow of the I is that dimension of the person which is yet to be incorporated into relationship, into the We. This signifies the "unknown self," which, not unlike the "unknown God," is sensed and effectual, yet whose motives are neither seen nor understood. The unincorporated can come to be seen as the evil within, as the uncommitted, the uncontrollable and the rebellious. The shadow self then haunts us with its presence, calling into question every relationship, every truth about us which does not take it into account. The shadow I can threaten to enter and plunder, to violate and despoil, any and all relationships into which it has not been invited, or from which it has been barred. This rejected or unwanted I carries with it the bitter venom of unwantedness. The unwanted self, who abides nonetheless and finds power from a mysterious inner center of energy, becomes the tempter and the scoffer, the enticer and the belittler. It becomes the one who in being unaccepted is mercilessly unaccepting. How this shadow I betters the instruction of the Me of the limelight!

The shadow self is that portion of the person which has not lived in the We; it is that being which remains unshared, and therefore essentially unknown—though present. As sensed but unspoken presence, this dimension of psyche can be taken to be spirit, something alien and dark. As such, it can be seen to be—and all too easily become, as a self-fulfilling prophesy—malevolent and unholy. Yet this "beast" belongs to that created and addressed I which God has already called *good.* Not integrated, it plagues the I, be it with unresolved fears or unmet needs, be it with hope and promise of something more to the I than the I yet knows of, or be it with woundedness and grief that threaten to overwhelm and crush an already fragile existence. Unknown and thus unloved, the shadow I rages in anger against the denial of, yet continues to yearn for, the light of affirmation.

Behold, much that we call evil is really that of the I which stands in desperate need of affirmation and integration into the known person. Whole and undivided, the I can neither sin nor be a partner in evil. In the light of unity and oneness, brought into being only through the confirming spirit of mutuality, of the We, no shadow self exists. The I is at-one-with its created being.

THE WHOLE I

Love

Love is threefold in accordance with the threefoldness of God. It is an essential triplicity of persons-in-relationship, a three-in-one. For every love relationship consists of the two persons—for love is fundamentally an I-You phenomenon—and the relationship between them. Hence, if the two persons were lifted out of the relationship, so to speak, something would be left over—namely the "spiritual quantum" of the love itself. The whole is indeed greater than the sum of the parts. The threefoldness of love extends into the psyche and includes the will to love, the feelings of love, and the thoughts, perceptions and imagery for love. But the love itself is the relationship, and these other dimensions are signs and concomitants of the interpersonal and intersubjective spirit between the participants.

Love is spirit, just as language. Thus, love is essentially an interhuman reality. The intra-psychic aspects arise in response to the presence of the mutual spirit and belong to its fruit. But these elements are not to be equated with the love itself. For to reduce love to a strictly subjective fact would be like reducing human conversation to an asynchronic interchange of two or more private languages. If mutual communication is not possible, neither is love—and vice-versa. Subjective elements of the spirit of love may lead to, signal the presence of, or flow as a direct result of love. But the love itself is the life of the persons together; it is creative of persons and is as personal as the persons themselves.

✠

The beginning of love: We meet. You touch something in me. I sense that I reach something in You. This mutual something does not yet have a name, yet it belongs or adheres to my very being. Are our souls then in some kind of connection? Whether consciously or unconsciously, this something you touched, and in touching opened, now lives in me and begins to unfold with a life of its own. Because of You, "something more" makes its presence known. I am therefore more as a person, and my worldview undergoes change. What You have opened up, though unnamed, is very real to me. When I see You, this something seems to apprehend You as well, and longs for itself in You and You in itself. It affects the very atmosphere between us, it interposes itself in our relationship, so that in looking at You, I sense it. In your presence, it is present. This something more in my being involves only You, though it comes to affect more and more of my daily life and activities.

Is this something only in me, or is it affecting You as well? At first a smiling question of simply being touched and seeking to know the full extent of the event, as this something more grows in me, my question comes to have life-giving or even life-threatening significance. For I come to realize that during all the times we met, whether in person or in my mind, awake or asleep, this something more in me has gained in being, power and expanse—how I do not know—so that I no longer can or will separate it from my soul itself. Now this something longs to speak to You through and even as my being itself. And at stake is its very life in me—and my life in it. For if it were to die, part of me would die with it—I know not how or why.

Comes then the question of my being. And at the point of needing to become word, this something more names itself: love. But now, as it gathers itself over against You, it needs to know whether its life is present within You, whether You feel as I do about its presence in and with and even as You, and whether therefore it may be given permission to come forward between us and fulfill itself and us in our relationship. Love not shared is love doomed.

All is preparatory to your response. If You say "yes," behold, a world is born between us. If You say "no," a life in me is condemned to feed only on itself until it expires unwanted and thus unattended. Love unattended is unfed, and will die the slow and painful death of unresponse.

"Yes, I love You, too!" Thus begins a new life, thus the something more within me finds release *between Us*—its proper abode. Thus may love finally caress You in the open, and unite with itself in You. Behold, where there were two there are now "three-in-one": You and I and Us.

Now we are "in love." A mutuality and an intimacy visit us, invading our presence together, abiding with us as promise and longing, as memory and ever-springing hope. Strangely, I long for You even when we are together. I long for those special moments of pure reciprocity. Our love comes to be grasped as the relationship itself, as our very life together, and as the ground of our life apart. The world beyond us must be seen from the living context of what we share, of our world. The new reality between us seeks to redeem all that is old, seeks to gather within itself all of our life, past, present and future, and to bless it with its own life, to bathe and cleanse and hallow all that we are and have been and shall be by and in its own life. The word of love: "Let the all live in me as its sea, let me pervade everything and bring it into my life, let me heal and resurrect and harmonize your all with my own life and being between and within You."

✠

A man and a woman fall in love. They seek to formalize their relationship by taking marriage vows. The love they have for each other, in the final analysis, did they *discover* or *create* it? Did they in their respective ways decide that they wanted to love each other, and so initiate the process, as if love were something under their control, coming and going at their bidding? As if love were like the electrical lights in a house, that they may turn on or off at their will? Or is love something that they came to be aware of as if beyond themselves, like a soft drum beating unseen but nearby and meant somehow for them, but which they could not hear until they embraced the silence between them? "How long has it been beating?" they ask. "Why have I not heard it until now?" each wonders.

Love is indeed something we discover living in and between us. We must, of course, decide what we wish to do about this new reality in our lives, whether we are free to say yes or prepared only to say no to it, whether we welcome or fear it in its motive power and life-altering potency. But we do not create love. What we can create is not love but our illusion of the fulfillment of our need thereof. And our illusions tell us not what we have but what we seek.

Comes the great question: the love that they discovered between them, in the final analysis, is it *one* love or *two*? Is it something objective and real and concrete between them, or are there really two different states of something only subjective within them? In truth, *the whole purpose of our history hinges on the answer to this question.* The love which they have is one love they share, one world between them, one corporate being-together, a kind of singularity, a unique spiritual entity inclusive of their personal being. Both persons have their own reactions and feelings toward each other and toward the love itself, but all these things belong within the context of what they share. The common is the ground of the private, the shared is the life of the personal.

Behold, the one love they discovered between them, while not created by them is creative of them. The "something more" which lived at first unnamed within them, then came forward as love between them, is in truth not only love but the self who loves. Love calls us into being; in our love, we see something in the other that no one else has seen. Of course not! For the love has called that one forth. The person who loves lives in the love, in the shared world into which they have been called and in which they have found themselves and each other—both at once. Love as relationship creates the persons who will live within it. Once known, it is up to the persons to commit themselves to this new creation of love and to the person who loves. It is for the partners to commit themselves to the love for the whole of their lives—for their very lives hang in the balance.

✠

I love you. The love is at once mine, adhering to the deepest identity I can consciously grasp, yet, it is I who belong to it. The love has a definite say in my comings and goings, in all that I do and think, in all that I feel and believe. The love has literally invaded me—and seemingly from the outside in rather than from the inside out. For inside is the need and capacity for love, for saying *Yes* with my life. And the more I cleave to the love which cleaves to me, the more it guides me, the more my role becomes one of thankful servant.

"I love You." That means: I cannot separate You from the love any more than I can separate myself from the love I bear for You—bearing it thankfully as my portion of, and task for, Us. Yet it bears me as I bear it, even as You bear me in your love, which in turn bears You in bearing me. I may distinguish but not divide our personal being from the being of love, or my person in general from the person who loves You. I am one with the love with which I love You. Our love is where and who we find ourselves to be; love is place and being in one; it is the ultimate meaning of the sphere between us, of inter-subjectivity. And the "inter" is as ontologically real as the "intra" subjective. The love creates and sustains us in itself, and reveals us to ourselves and to each other in the truth it has engendered. This love seeks to redeem us, to "buy us back" from the emptiness and oppression we had endured before the love walked in—perhaps through closed doors.

God is love and those who abide in love abide in God and God in them. The tracks of love lead from and to the ultimate love relationship, the Eternal I-You, the Holy We. And human love anticipates and actually participates in God's love, just as the river and the stream anticipate and participate in the sea toward which they flow, so as to yield back their existence to the depths from which they arose.

Behold, to say "I love You," is to anticipate the coming Word of redemption, God's final Word of Love and eternity now. For love does not yet fully belong here; it is of that holy life of the future, of the Spirit, which graces us with its humblest presence now, a presence which cannot yet proclaim itself in the manner of creation, with power and clear visibility, nor in the manner of revelation, with inner certitude and passion. Love only seems weak because it has not yet fully arrived. When it does, it will be to the glory of those who believed in and struggled for it while frail and downtrodden, and to the condemnation of those who disavowed it and sought its destruction.

The Cross is love's true revelation and symbol here, not its humiliation and defeat. And the glory of the Cross is sufficient for the day; and His Spirit is sufficient down payment for what Love is one day to bring forth.

✠

There is love between us. What matters any more is not so much *Me* as *Us*, not my life in itself but our life together, the life in which my true me is loved and hallowed—and saved. Our love has given me worth in the sheer grace of its presence. Our We offers me my me as a gift, not earned, yet requiring commitment and labor—on both of our parts—to be fully developed. This me that I am with You is like a vein of ore discovered in the common earth between us, and made precious by our shared life. And the ore of my being is something we must mine together. You help motivate the operation. Your affirming presence heightens faith, power and purpose for the exploration process; your commitment to me and to Us makes possible the long-term and delicate work of excavation and purification. In sharing the bounty of me discovered and found valuable between us, I joyfully yield myself up to You for the sake of Us—or shall I say to Us for the sake of You? Both are accurate. For when I say You, I mean Us; When I say Us, I mean You—and me.

✠

Only a loving *otherness* can confirm one's *ownness*—and as a part of an *ourness*.

✠

Love cannot be separated from the person who loves. The one who loves is *in* their love; love and personal being are one. Love is the ultimate *concrete universal*; it is the infinite wed to the finite, the absolute grounding the relative, the universal bestowing its own life on the particular. Love brings both concreteness and universality to the participants, the concreteness of shared individual life, named and confirmed, and the universality of ultimate purpose and life between those so joined.

Love is essentially personal. It creates and grounds personal life in itself. Law, however, is at its basis impersonal. And origin determines destiny. What begins as law cannot divest itself from law without a complete transformation. What begins as love cannot change its basis without a forced bondage leading to death. Determination breeds determination; freedom seeks to maintain itself for the sake of the life of love—which *is* freedom and grace.

We were not made for law, but law for us. Yet behold, love was not made for us, but we were made for love—and by love and of love, so that we cannot find fulfillment and true being apart from love. It is love which underwrites and legitimizes law and morality, and not the converse. Love *is* law, sufficient unto itself, understood only by itself. Love is greater than human law—religious as well as secular. Love has principles which morality knows not of. Thus did Jesus break the law in order to reveal and practice the higher law of love, of Spirit. How freeing and thus terrifying is this law of love, and yet how absolute are its demands, even if they be at right angles to the current laws and mores of a people. Loves calls for demonstration and promises no rewards other than itself. Love is the being of Spirit, the weight or glory of God. And love seeks to transform all of our laws as well as our very being into itself, that it may be all in all.

✠

Does love have a "will," one which may be distinguished from my own will and that of the person I love? If the answer is affirmative, then the psychological reduction of love to mere feeling or subjectivity, or as an epiphenomenon of individual response patterns falls by the wayside. *Does love speak itself* to those will listen and are involved with each other? And if so, does it speak with *one and the same voice* to both partners? Perhaps our very destiny is at stake in the answer to these questions. For if the true locus of love is between us rather than within us, then it is not we who are to judge love, but love which judges us; then it is not love which is under our control, but it is we who must yield to love's lordship. It is not we who may possess love; but love which may possess us, if and only if we are willing to say Yes to its call in the very freedom it grants us.
own state of being. Thus can we be diverted from the person we love, and from the possible presence of love between us. We may focus ex-

Love is as inseparable from word as connotation is from denotation. Where the latter pair coexist as interwoven dimensions of meaning itself, the former manifest the two interlocking dimensions of spirit in the world. While love as divine intent may in the incomprehensible mystery of God be prior to the Word, to the logos of address, be it of God to God or of God to us, it is nevertheless indivisible from the Word as the latter's true life and power. Love is the source and goal of the Word, the background of its first, and the farthest promise of its final, utterance. And behold, while love as Spirit, and thus as the unspoken Presence of our eternal future, may yet be beyond the Word, be it of creation or of revelation, it is itself to be the Word of redemption. That is, while love in a sense both precedes the Word and is subsequent to it as that which is present but not yet spoken, love is nevertheless the current and active power and ground of God's Word—and therefore of the human person in the event of their creative address. Love is the ground of the soul, of all that is our past, present and future. And love is the deepest stirring in us for speech; endless is its drive to become word and thus to become known; never does love cease striving to draw the word into and through itself. And how impatient is love for the final event of its becoming Word!

Is love then a "rational" or "irrational" presence among us? Many would say the latter. Yet behold, love is not irrational but little listened to, for its logic is not yet fully operational in humanity. If we would only openly and fully embrace love, we would discover that its logic not only sees the world aright, but is in itself the path of God among us. And what is love but the logic of God's will, implanted in our hearts as the ground of our very humanness? And love's "effectiveness" in the world, therefore, is ultimately one with that of God's. Behold, if love doesn't work, then God fails as well.

That love and "logic" seem to be more than distinguishable in this world is a tragic sign of the brokenness of the human condition. Their disunity is our disunity; their unification is our healing and wholeness. In truth, the logic of love is the logic of salvation.

✠

Love does not seek to be the center of attention. It would rather have the loved ones before each other's eyes, and self-giving be their focus. As perpetual servant, love prefers to be the mutual ground rather than one of the figures of perception. It would have us sing and dance and celebrate each other and our life together. Love seeks to be one with us and us to be one with it. We are to be its glory, for love would not be glorified or lifted up in a way that would make it appear to be something other than simple and pure, humble and gentle, gift and perpetual openness to the beloved. Love does not wish to have a glorified human "image" to live up to, one of glitter and pomp, romance and fantasy. To raise love out of quiet relationship and to crown it with worldly glory and fanfare would lead to its destruction. For such attention is not of love but of the self, and would lead not to the revelation of love's glory but to the glorification of the self. Behold, love's glory is its life; it accepts no substitutes or surrogates. And love accepts no external honors or badges of merit; love accepts only its acceptance. It seeks but to do its work.

Only as unseen may love be truly present and pervasively active. Only when we are looking to each other and not to it or to ourselves may love do its transforming and empowering work. And when love is lifted up and looked into, its presence soon evaporates. For love does not stay around for our examination! Such an investigation must be conducted therefore either in the past or future tense, and involve either memory or hope. We may see but our own longings and desire, our own expectations for and anticipations of love, but not love itself. Love in its presentness, in its intimate call to be received and shared and given away may be accepted but not objectified.

✠

Strange, but our need for love can blind us to its very presence and reality. The need can draw us into ourselves, there to reflect on our of the one loved. Unconditional love is non-reflective, self-giving love, love which does not count the cost or seek rewards beyond itself. It is a love without pre or post-conditions, without "If...then" contingencies. It is a love without strings attached, without any quid pro quo. It is the highest love, the love of God from above and the love for God in response from below.

✠

clusively on what we seek but do not have, and on our emotional reactions to this bleak inner vision. And even when we are together, we may secretly be looking not to our partner in love, but to an image of ourself in need. In so doing, we and our needs can become the center of the relationship—not our beloved, and certainly not the love we might really be sharing beneath all of our images. We may speak words of love and give gestures thereof, but the inner concern we have is selfish: we need the other to love us and to fill the void in our heart.

Behold, the void in our heart remains, no matter what our beloved does to fill it. It abides through the thick and thin of embrace and endearments, the void, the hideous cavity of feeling unloved—and therefore unlovable—at the base of our being. From whence came that seemingly insatiable need, that black hole of churning hunger? From early rejection and lack of affirming love. To have been (or to believe oneself to have been) unloved eventuates in feeling unlovable. Hence the void remains because no matter what love may be offered to us, the absence of our *belief* in love and in ourselves as lovable—and the two are the same thing—actively prevents the life of love from filling our void. For love must be believed in to be truly encountered. Belief carries life or death consequences.

The need for love when thwarted, can set in motion both an insatiable desire for love, and a desire for power to control love and those who might love us—for both protection and revenge. The offer of love thereby receives the response of manipulation. We need what we fear, and we do not want to be hurt again. So we must say No to it, all the while begging at its gates. And if we are still wounded and festering from past hurts, we cannot but say Yes to hurting those we love in return for what we have suffered. Any possible love relationship would therefore be turned into a prison and a daily nightmare. We might destroy what we need and love—and ourselves in the process.

✠

We cannot find fulfillment apart from self-giving. The deepest need of our heart is for the total affirmative response of love to the address of love from God. We are designed to give of ourselves in love. To what then shall I give myself? To You, O my beloved? Do I then yield to your needs, your will, your vision of my role in your life? To give myself to anyone or anything other than God is idolatry. And to give myself to any person other than God can lead to a less than fully human servitude, to my essential unfreedom, to the abandonment of my created being for that of a humanly designed one—which means the abdication of destiny.

Are we then to give ourselves to one another, or to love? Only love can contain us. And behold, to give oneself to love is to give oneself to God. For You are love, O God of my life! Thus to abandon myself to love here in the world means to surrender myself to You. By abandoning myself for love, I receive myself back from and in You.

Love, both coming to and from me is my freedom and my life. And to give myself to love means to invite love to become my center, to dwell in me as I abide in it. O love, into thy hands I commend my spirit!

✠

Unconditional love is the love of the beloved for the beloved's own sake, not for the sake of the one who loves. It is the love of being as an end in itself, apart from any possible means. But God is being itself and the end of all being. Therefore love of being is in truth love of God. To love another unconditionally is to love God, in and with God, the Unconditioned.

Only God is unconditioned; therefore only God can love unconditionally. Hence, only through participation in God may I love as God loves. As a conditioned being, I can love only as I have been loved. Only by being loved unconditionally by God may I attain the capability to love as God loves. And only in God can I ever love with God's own love. God is love; thus God is in God's own love. Therefore, to love with God's love means to dwell in God.

What is unconditional love? It is the will, the decision to love from eternity. It is a free gift without regard to the merit of the one so loved. It is not due to any attribute or sum of attributes or to the personality

And what is love's end or aim? The goal or *telos* of love abides only within love itself, and may not be uttered or grasped outside its own life. Love seeks nothing external or extracurricular to itself, save only to bring such otherness within its life, to redeem and make the all consistent with itself. Love is at once both way and end, means and final objective.

Freedom and Anarchy

Freedom can exist only within a relational structure. For freedom is always relative, relative to time, place, person and situation. Freedom is relative also in the sense of being *from* something and *for* something else. Thus, for instance, freedom from the fear of want means at the same time freedom for the peace of material ease. Or freedom from the necessity of toiling long hours also signifies a freedom for new forms of leisure. In these and all other instances, something must grant, contain and secure the freedom. And it is always an underlying lawfulness which affords freedom as a direct consequence of its operative presence and guidance.

In personal terms, freedom means the capacity to choose and subsequently to carry out that choice in action. It is inseparable from the power necessary to act on and implement our choices. Without power, freedom becomes empty and despair producing; without freedom, power becomes demagogic and demonic. Freedom lives happily within the lawful limits of its created context of life. And that context is a mutually agreed upon way of being together. Freedom is the capacity to choose within the context our mutuality allows. Freedom is thus of us, by us and for us.

Freedom without limits or context of mutuality is not freedom but anarchy. Freedom like water requires directional and limiting banks, that it may finally reach the sea of destiny. But anarchy refuses to live within those banks. Anarchy would rather overflow them; it is thus a flood upon the cultivated land of civilization. Anarchy is not freedom, but a demand for freedom's absolutizing—and at the cost of all lawfulness itself. The call of anarchy for autonomy or "self-law" is not lawful but spiteful, not supportive of but destructive to individual existence. For anarchy is antithetical to any *logos*-structure of common meaning and purpose. It is founded instead upon the rejection of mutual law as such, which it seeks to replace with its own law of immediate willfulness, of pure self-justification beyond any other recognized authority. The "law" of anarchy is nothing more or less than the direct opposition to the law and Word of God, the *logos*. Anarchy seeks to destroy the logos, just as anti-matter would have to destroy matter—and be itself destroyed in the process.

There is no freedom in anarchy, but only the slavery to the univocal *No* of its nature, its *No* to the logos, to the order and law of creation. For anarchy is first and above all a frontal attack upon God, upon the logos, in an effort to replace and thereby to become a god unto itself. Thus the meaning of the term "anarchy" in Greek: literally "against the rulers, against authority, against rule" itself. And the *No* to all rule is not freedom but slavery and absolute conformity to a rebellion that can end only in annihilation.

True freedom means the capacity to say *Yes* as well as *No*, in mutuality as well as singularity. And that which underwrites freedom must itself be free. Love is the ground of all true freedom; and love is ever free and grace-full, ever offering itself as gift and as gift-bearing. True freedom is grounded in and granted by love; it is the freedom of the We. The I and the You affirm and confirm each other's freedom in the We of reciprocity.

And anarchy, in sum, is a radical *No* to love, to there ever being an *Us*.

✠

Love, Law and Legalism

Love bears its own law, in freedom and in truth, with grace and with clarity. As spirit, thus as divine "wind" or *pneuma*, love moves where it wills, and without stopping to explain or to justify itself. Love is what love does; love knows what and why it is, and what it is about. And that consciousness enters into those who welcome and embrace that which embraces them. Love guides those who are willing to listen and do, rather than willfully to use and abuse love—which is always the result when love is not heard. Love seeks but to fulfill itself, and us in itself. How shallow and external are the demands of law in comparison with those of love! *Love demands all that we are to live in all that it is.*

Love *is* divine ethos and ethics, righteousness and morality. As such, it cannot be understood outside itself. Where love is present, there is the kingdom of heaven, there the law of God is effectual, there person and spirit abide in unity. Love does not require explanations or regulations to live by; it asks to be lived out as spirit between and within us. Rather than seeking that we carve out statues and statutes in its name, and thus to bind it to our images, love calls us to abandon imagery for the sake of immediacy, talking about for the sake of living in and through, law-making for the sake of love-making.

The "legalization" or "legalism" of love, be it between human partners or between God and humanity, develops only in the gap created by the loss of the immediacy, the presence —with power and authority—, of love itself. Where love does not rule, law must—and with good reason. But law must not be paraded as love, or as a satisfactory surrogate for love, for that would be a mockery and perversion of that which is the highest! Rather than a substitute, law is an interim governess, needed for guidance and safety only until love returns to claim that which is truly its own. Law must continue to be called law, and we must accept its essential, though stop-gap role, namely, that of helping to slow down and reverse the distancing and estrangement already underway.

Law is necessary but not sufficient for the establishment, perpetuation and reconstitution of love. Behold an analogy: electricity is to wiring as love is to law. Electricity, that great mysterious energy-force so vital to our civilization, cannot be equated with the wiring that is necessary for its useful flow in our lives. Without satisfactory wiring, electricity cannot work for us; with wiring, electricity becomes possible. All we need to do then is to attach the wiring to an outside energy source.

So is it with love and law. Love, like electricity, flows in and through its own relational lawfulness or "wiring." But when a relationship breaks down, the flow stops—and the light goes out, as it were. Now the law takes over: the wiring must be repaired, that the light of love may shine again. The law is necessary, but not sufficient for the attainment of this goal.

In addition to the law, to the "what" and the "how to" of rebuilding the relationship, two other ingredients are absolutely required: *will and grace*. The will of both the partners must be present and active, and in a persevering way. And the grace of the true Author of love must underwrite the whole venture. God is the one and ever-present power Source for love. And through the combination of law and will, the preparations can be completed, so that through grace, the love can flow again. And flow again it will indeed, for love can be reignited! Love is not like the nerves of the body, which once dead cannot live again; rather, like electricity, love can ever be regenerated. All it takes is law, will and grace. And also, alas, time.

It is thus simpler to rekindle love than we want to believe. For believing in its impossibility keeps us free of the responsibility of trying—and possibly failing. The problem is not with love or with law or with grace; the problem is with the will, specifically, the will to believe or not to believe. The whole of our life and love hinges on how we answer that question of faith in love—and with our lives rather than with our mouths only.

✠

The outright conversion or reduction of love into law, spirit into the letter thereof, represents a doomed attempt to put back the pieces after the gift-laden mosaic of union and communion has broken apart. *"Legalism"* begins with a denial of the loss of the love-spirit, and an implicit claim that in carrying out the letter of love's apparent intent, as gleaned from the study of the history and "sacred texts and traditions" of the covenant, the relationship will go on as before. It is like a love relationship where one of the partners has left, but the other refuses to see and accept this, and so must continue with the relationship *as if the other were still present* and supportive of the now merely ritual behavior of the remaining partner. Legalism is thus a monologue masquerading as a dialogue.

The mentality of legalism is to gather up all the invisible light-flecks of love, once shared and lived through together, thus now "sacred tradition," and to have these memories of actual and mutual presentness become the "norms" of behavior and belief, to be trusted and acted out for its own sake—and in order to gain some sense of assurance and comfort that the relationship or covenant is still in force. Yet in both religious and psychological terms, such a mentality is a sign of the decay and absence, rather than the promotion and presence of the relationship.

Instead of helping to mend the relationship, legalism only serves to intensify the process of relational disintegration. First of all, its very presence reveals the absence of that which it purports to serve—for love and legalism cannot coexist! Secondly, it seeks to bridge the gap between the partners with external and lifeless, unfree and unspontaneous replicas of that which came into being as gift and grace, freedom and fire. Instead of the persons simply desiring each other in the freedom and ease of their present beings, and the We signifying that pure mutuality which both participants move into and out of openly and without restraint, the relationship now has the added heavy weight of "accountability" to and "responsibility" for the past and the promises thereof. Now the law of yesterday's being has interposed itself between the partners and blocked off both the freedom and the vision of present being. In seeking to preserve the past, due to its absence in the present, legalism has effectively prohibited a new meeting in the present. It can thereby destroy what is claims to preserve.

Instead of bearing us out of the world and into its wondrous sphere of mutuality, legalism would have us treat the relationship as something to be borne in the world. Death is at work here! The normative gains ascendancy over the descriptive; the ethical "ought" flowers ubiquitously between the partners. What was a world shared, wide and starry as the heavens, free and embracing as the wind, now has become a prison and a sentence, a cell and a period of unfree time to be locked into it—and with a sham You with no presence and power. In its fear of losing itself, legalism allows only limited, specified and closed-in relational receptacles for the persons it rules over, spheres too small for love and grace, for the open-ended wonder of the eternal now of Us. What is left of You and I, of Us, becomes under its hand a hardened hull, a death trap, an empty relational cubicle, frozen unchanging by the cold wind of lawful strictures. Legalism is love's prison warden.

Legalism would replace and therein seemingly equate spirit with law. Law is of spirit; and spirit is lawful. But the spirit of the law is not contained in the law, but the law in the spirit. This relationship with spirit constitutes the glory of law. But for law to try to find spirit in itself, or to create spirit by its own machinations, would be like ice trying to generate heat by closing in on itself, rather than by seeking the heat of an outside source. Something beyond itself is necessary for the heating of ice. Just so, something beyond legalism is necessary for the regeneration of love and spirit.

That regeneration can come about only through a new meeting. The You and the I must "rub together" for the sparks of spirit to reignite the heat and light of love. Yet for that to happen, legalism must be willing to melt away.

✠

Romanticism

Romanticism represents an idealization of love. And love idealized is love in decay. Romanticism is in fact a non-loving response to the desire for love; it is an infatuation with the possibility of being smitten, an adoration of what one is feeling, rather than of the *person* one purportedly loves. "In love with love," as it were,—this one can do in isolation, this can be lived through best from afar, without the interference of daily sharing with the person one is so enamored of. Romanticism is thus a hidden denial of love, of the real love of mutuality and common constancy, one with another. It all too easily would betray love for the sake of its image, and for the sufficiency of its feelings.

Romanticism needs not the other but the image for its life; therefore it is a danger and an alien to love. It is strangely ignorant of the rigors of day-by-day existence, of the ordinary and essential acts of love, of the carrying out of a living relationship—like the mostly unseen and profoundly unappreciated work of a mother for her children. The romantic would prefer the uncluttered love of gestures and moods, of a love ever conscious of and reveling in itself, of a love that counts the cost and celebrates its every expenditure. And woe to this love if the return is not adequate for the giving, if the applause is too weak and short-lived! Comes the pouting, the self-pity, comes the end of the game!

Romanticism does not relate to genuine love precisely in this: it is at best a partial love of a partial humanity. It chooses not to see the whole of the person; it accepts only that dimension of the person which seems to be amenable to its dream world. In not loving the whole person in the fullness of humanity, romanticism is actually misanthropic in nature. Further, it evidences prejudice against the common and the typical in humanity, looking instead for the admirable and the exceptional, for the quality which would fuel its fantasy life. In short, romanticism is a "high" in constant search for another fix; it is an imaginary mountain of a magical love, disdainful of the valley and the plain, where love's fruit grows and must be harvested.

Let us not, then, romanticize love. For love is ordinary and quiet, gentle and rough, certain of itself and slow to progress. Love brings life, but only on its terms and with its own pace. Love creates persons, but only into its own likeness. And love's creation is not in the likeness of the romantic, of the idealist who seeks to carve the real into the image of the ideal, who accepts the real only as it serves the ideal. In truth, love is an ever-wakeful servant, not a dreamer—save only for the dream of its consummation, given to love as mandate and promise at its birth.

To believe in love, therefore, does not mean to be a romantic; to apprehend the glory of love does not mean to be an idealist. All too often the person we call a "realist" is actually the one who does not believe in and thus cannot see love. And "falling in love" has great beauty and power, and can include moments of ecstasy and flights of joy beyond the ordinary course of the workaday world. This is a part of love, especially in its early days of youth and gaiety. Behold, the truth of love is greater than the ideal; love is the "concrete universal," the real beyond the dream, which, when we are dreaming, we cannot see. And which, upon awakening, may seem at first to be less than the ideal. Genuine love is more and less than the romanticized version: it is substance rather than show, life-bearing rather than life-flirting. What is lost is not even worth comparing with what is gained.

The difference between the romanticist and the lover in full stride lies in the presence or absence of mutuality and communion. Does the person seek the other above all and yearn for times of meeting and union? And is the lover ever surprised, on meeting, by the radiance of the beloved and by the breath of the We-spirit present between them—as if the memory could not contain an adequate or accurate image of the beloved and the relationship, as if the lover had once again forgotten the truth that abides amidst them? Or does the person find again and again that, on meeting, the reality of the "beloved" falls short in comparison with the image created and cherished in times of distance and reflection? Does the unwelcomed yet anticipated sense of disappointment sweep across the consciousness of the person in the face-to-face nearness of concrete relationship? Is then the love greater together or apart? For the true lover, the answer is emphatically together; for the romantic, it is, regrettably apart.

✠

Covenant

You and I meet. Our meetings form a history of Us, a living record mutually remembered of who we are and have been to each other, a set of expectations regarding each other's personality and behavior. These expectations, even if never verbalized, constitute an interpersonal "understanding" of the nature and boundaries of Us. Call it an informal and unspoken *logos* or "law" between us, close to and consistent with our meetings and mutuality. It represents our way of being together, as it were, the recognized channels of our common moments. Not discussed but lived through together, this "understanding" or relational ethos, remains open-ended and susceptible to the changes that emerge between us. That is, our understanding is not fixed law but language unfolding and spirit inbreaking, and we must commit ourselves to continuing to listen to the "message of Us," just as to each other.

Though not formalized, what is our commitment to each other and to Us? The spirit is ever open-ended, but as created persons, we are not able to live easily and simply in the spirit! The flesh requires blood, and the soul word; we need law and dialogue, visibility and knowledge of who and where we are together. Over the course of our meetings, and by mutual recognition, a need to formalize the relationship emerges. A We of spirit exists between us, and the desire crystalizes to bring it into the world of humanity, and therein to pronounce its presence and our commitment to it. It is of love's nature, once sufficient intensity is attained, to declare itself in a public way. For love seeks to build its home not only in the heart but also in the world.

It is the destiny of mutuality to give way to *covenant*. The dialectic of love leads inevitably into and through the solemnizing vows of recognition and commitment. The ultimate end of the We is marriage, be it between man and woman, or the soul and God. And marriage *is* covenant. And nothing less than marriage is required to build a world of common purpose and commitment. Both the intensive We of the I-You relationship, and the extensive We of community and beyond, must have a solid and secure *form*, that the *content* thereof, namely the persons involved, may live in peace and in the assurance of continuity.

Covenant, then, is the formalization of the We. It is the temporal structure subsequent to and built upon the We, the objective bonds of agreement and law, rights and expectations, vows and promises, commitment to and perseverance in the relationship. The overriding function of covenant is to carry out the lived mandate of the We-spirit between the I and the You, to both bring the relationship into the world and to bear it safely through the world. It is the hull but not the substance of the relationship. Yet, is the hull or "chrysalis" formed by and hence continuous with the We of spirit, or is it constructed by the hands of the world, for the purposes of society? Perhaps both. So long as the covering honors the We, and does not confuse itself with or take itself to be the We—as if the robe would take itself to be the King!—so long as the outer garment remains in touch with what it represents, submitting as subject to the We and not pushing the We to conform to it, only that long will the We of love and mutuality, of presence and power, permit the hull to symbolize itself. Only that long will the We inhabit the garment. Only as long as the covenant remains true to the meeting of the I and the You, will the covenant continue to have and be in spiritual force. If and when the covenant becomes the surrogate for the We, or absolutizes itself above the We, the spirit will seek a new meeting—even a "lawless" one—and, behold, a new We will one day emerge. But will this new We have the same or different partners? The spirit is willing, but is the body and soul? Will those accept the new wine who have been reared on the old?

✠

Covenant is a sign of commitment to and ownership in the We. It is a commitment to live out of a concrete mutuality, a declared willingness to be built into and grow from, to be loyal to each other and to the

We, to the sphere of meeting between us. Yet, behold, covenants, like religion itself, *bind* those who commit their lives thereto. A central root of the word "religion" has real significance here. One of the the Latin words from which "religion" is derived is *religare*, which means "to bind back," from *re*, "back," and *ligare*, "to bind." Hence, the covenant of religion binds us into its history and traditions, into that past which it proclaims as the meaning of its present and the promise of its tomorrow. Yet the We happens only in the now of meeting and mutual being, only in the freedom of the union of spirit and psyche at the altar of the physical world. The We affirms what covenant seeks to confirm in the longitudinal movement of commitment. But confirmation can all too easily become an occasion for judgment, for conformity to and thus confinement in the modes of past meetings—or the current *interpretations* of covenant of the past. Hence, an intrinsic tension exists between the freedom of the We-spirit and the canon of the Us-covenant.

Covenants are means for the perpetuation and glorification of the We. They can, however, become tyrannical if they come to be seen as ends in themselves. As Jesus warns us, "The Sabbath was made for man, not man for the Sabbath." Covenants are necessary in the world just as language and law are necessary to give guidance and direction, to offer the consistent cords of love, the lead strings to eternity, to grant wisdom and to mark out the way we are to go. But the way is not the end. The end is the We of eternal life. The end is the return to Spirit of that spirit which gave rise to covenant.

At best, *covenant is the shadow of the We itself*. But the shadow is neither the light nor in the light. Yet, if it is true to the meeting, it sketches for us not the light but where we are to stand, that we may be in the light. It is a refraction of that mutuality which has been lived through and can still become life again—for that is the promise inherent in covenant itself. The shadow offers us the "last known whereabouts" of the other, be it the human or divine partner; hence, it represents the place to begin our search for meeting the You, for a renewed event of Us. That is, it tells us where the light of love has shown before, and by implication represents the jumping off point, the place we are to go if we are to find ourselves, each other—and God—in mutuality. But once there, we must turn, not to the shadow, but to the light itself, to the holy We. We must lean full into the future breaking in upon us, rather than stay clothed in the past. The job of the past is done when it has made us current with its currents, as it were, when it has led us to its ending, which is our beginning.

The We is never seen; *the We is imageless. Covenant is therefore the image of the We*; it is the very image and likeness of relationship. *But it is not the relationship*. It is rather a representation for the partners and the world, a mirror of and a way into that which abides unseen. Covenant must never be taken to be the relationship, to constitute the unseen, or to have captured the Unseen within its own confines or structures of meaning and purpose. For that would be both untrue to and idolatrous of the relationship—just as *Torah* and *Christ* can become idolatrous, if and as their image is taken to be the One they represent. The Word must never be worshiped, but only the Holy Speaker. To worship the Word would preclude communication and communion. Just so, covenants are not to be worshiped but reverenced, and to serve as the ground for new meetings.

✠

The Greek word for covenant, *diatheke*, has a most significant etymology. The prefix, *dia*, meant "through or across," as well as "by means of." The term *theke* originally signified a "tomb or vault." Hence, the term *diatheke* meant literally "across a dead space," or "by means of a dead space." How in keeping with the spiritual reality of covenant is this word! For a covenant happens by virtue of the meeting of two or more persons in and through the sphere between them. Yet covenants are always formed *after* the fact of meeting. Hence, they are in a genuine sense a "dead issue," an after-the-event formalization, which though necessary, can kill the spontaneity of the spirit. Further, a tomb or vault represents the place of the remains of a loved one. Again the word is true to the spirit, for the place between us is where we met—and lost—our loved one, and where we can go to meet them again, if only in our memory. It is thus our legacy. And it is also the place of promise for yet another meeting.

✠

There are two fundamental types of covenants in the world of persons. The first type is *created* by human consent in order to establish, structure and perpetuate human relationships. It corresponds to and images the "extensive We" of family, community and state. It covers all forms of mutuality and intercourse in the world. It is creative of *relationships*, determining their nature and limitations, and choreographing their roles and expectations. Born into it, persons receive and must accept the covenant as their yoke of belonging and responsibility in the world.

The second type is *discovered* by an I and You, and emerges with the persons themselves from the very ground of the meeting. It corresponds to and images the "intensive We" of mutuality and communion, of marriage, and ultimately, of prayer. It is not in the world, but constitutes the intimate sphere between two persons. It is creative of *persons*, of those partners who have found their being and life in the font of mutuality. The covenant of discovery can and must be formalized in the world. The persons need at some point to commit themselves to each other, and to what has been and is being shared between them. Without the commitment, the discovery of mutuality will never be brought into full actuality. Nor will love impact the world.

The primal instance of the first type of covenant is *government*; the primal instance of the second is *marriage*. The created covenant consists of common *law*, the discovered of common *vows*. Yet both are united within a common culture, and are interconnected through the mores and customs, the practices and understandings of a historical people. And the culture, in turn, is grounded on a specific religion, on a concrete divine-human context of meaning. The divine-human covenant, the relationship between the eternal and the temporal, determines the self-understanding of a whole people, and cuts across both types of covenants, bestowing meaning and legitimacy on both the extensive and intensive We, on both government and marriage.

The discovered covenant is a bond of grace, emerging as gift. The created covenant is a bond of law, accepted as given. At the heart of the latter is the determining intention of the creators; at the core of the former is the hidden intention of love. The created requires the life of the participants to sustain it; the discovered covenant grants life to the participants, and seeks their mutual presence to each other in order to freely receive, share and give of its own life. The law of love arises with and is internal to it; the law of government is external to the persons and is laid upon them. Yet, both types of covenant require the commitment of all the persons involved in order to be held intact. Without commitment, neither law nor grace, neither freedom nor a common world abides.

✠

What is the relation of the written to the spoken language? That is the relation of covenant to the We, respectively. The We lives ever in the *now,* in the dialectic of presence and mutuality; covenant is the record, the "dogma," the testimony and testament of the We event. Just so, the written word is the documented canon or standard of usage and meaning for both the past and the present spoken word, but not its future. Hence, the written is teacher and guide, but not master of the spoken word. For the living word of dialogue and reciprocity is ever creative of new meanings and modes of expression, new words and phrases, new memories of speech-events in need of being carefully recorded and brought into common use.

A "dead language," such as Latin, signifies one that is no longer spoken, no longer susceptible to the dialectic of the spirit and the dialogic of speech events. Yet the spirit abides in the word, so that if the word comes to be spoken again in the fullness of humanity, comes to be readopted as the language of a people, the spirit can return and the linguistic covenant move forward into newness of life. One need only look at modern Israel and Hebrew to witness the miracle of the simultaneous and profoundly interconnected resurrection of a people and their language. Can a resurrection of their religion be far behind?

As with a language, so with a covenant. What is dead can come back to life; the spirit of mutuality can return where there is the will of the persons and the grace of God. A We-spirit remains dead only by virtue of the lived-out decision never to meet again, never to "speak" each other, as it were. And how many dead languages exist between us? How many of us refuse to speak to each other? And if we would only do so, would a renewal in the spirit of covenant be far behind?

✠

The Eternal We

Redemption and the Divine-Human We

GOD AND THE DIVINE-HUMAN RELATIONSHIP

God and Redemption

G*od is the fulfillment of all relationships.* All moments of true meeting and every precious history of each We-spirit of love and communion have their source and destiny in the ultimate Spirit, the Ground between us. Every thread of mutual life has come from and leads to the one holy spool. Every We-event of our common lives abides in the eternal We hidden in our midst. The realm between us is the Kingdom of God. God is indeed the "ground of being"—but of our *being-together,* as the foundation of our being alone, as the before and after of our being apart. For God is between us as well as within and before us. God lives within relationships as within persons—and even more powerfully so, for relationships anticipate redemption, the consummation of all union and communion. God is not only absolute singularity; God is the ultimate mutuality. God is One-in-three and three-in-one; God is threefold Person: You, I and We. The three primal pronouns of person correspond to the three irreducible dimensions of the One God.

In the beginning is the Word. And in the end shall be the Word. From the You of God came forth the Word of creation; from the I of

God was uttered the Word of revelation; from the We of God is to be pronounced the Word of redemption. Yet the Word is one, as God is One. Hence all three Word-events spring from and manifest the unity and relational reality of the One God. The Word of creation is the "givenness" of the body and substance of the past; the Word of revelation is the "givingness" of the soul and person of the present; the Word of redemption is the "giftedness" of the spirit and divinity of the future. Monologue, dialogue and dialectic, these are the three modes of the Word, the logos, in the respective divine Word-events. The respective mutual context of meaning of the Word-events is law, liberty and love. And the motivating power or "love-energy" associated with each Word: eros, philia and agape, or desire, friendship and self-giving love.

As in the beginning, so in the end: God. Creation completed, the dialogue of revelation carried out, the moment dawns for the final creation, the fulfillment of speech, the unification of God, humanity and nature, the "eternalization" of the human person with God and in some imperishable "home," the secret place of the heart and the substance of faith. Redemption will be the final act of God in history, the Word-event which will consume the secular; it will be the summing up and consummation of that which belongs to God, and the actual moment of its transformation into God. Redemption will be life with God, in God and of God. It will be complete and eternal participation in the Trinity. And our "place," the eternal home of our souls, will be that of the "second Person," the Eternal I, who lives ever with the Eternal You, in and through their Eternal We. Redemption *is* the life of the Eternal We.

✠

Is then God somehow involved in a "process," in an ongoing evolution or development? Behold, it is not God who is becoming; it is the human person in relation to and in relationship with God. For God is not "changing"; we are changing in our relationship to God, as we grow into the fullness and perfection of the original intention of our creation, namely into the Eternal I of Christ.

Yet, a paradox unfolds here: while God is beyond change in relation to us, nevertheless in relationship with us divine truth undergoes a kind of metamorphosis. As we awaken to God's presence and life in and between us, new dimensions of the One God make themselves manifest. Hence, while the Persons of God are not in process, but are—before the foundations of the world—perfect, whole and complete, our relationship with God is in fact in process. Only to us does God appear to change as the relationship evolves, just as the shape and substance of a mountain appear to change as we draw near to it.

The process, however, is not only in us, but somehow between us and God. And inasmuch as God is the We of relationship as well as the Eternal Persons of the You and the I, and since relationships never stay the same, but move ever and always as the wind between us, do we therefore participate in what could be called the "process of God"? Note carefully that the *process of God* is the *movement of perfection,* whereas the relational *process of humanity with God* is the *movement toward perfection.* Behold the great Mystery, the Paradox beyond that which even the logos can contain: the Being of God is one with the Becoming of God, as the Speaker is one with the Speech. In God the End and the Beginning, the Alpha and the Omega are one and the same. Yet nothing of God changes or is gained or is lost. Only in relation to us is there personal and relational gain: the accretion of our personal presence to and love of God.

The human "process," therefore, is the love story of God and humanity, unfolding in, with and under the setting of nature and history. And only when we are beyond the temporal process of nature—which is not God—and the historical process of the soul toward the spirit—which is of but not God—will we discover the unfathomable paradox of the life of God, wherein neither change nor unchange abide, but only love in the moving stillness of its yearning fullness, singing its silent song of mutual aloneness in the oneness of distance with intimacy, in the mutuality of the One who is Three, God.

✠

God as Trinity

In the beginning is the Word. That means: in the beginning is the relationship. And the relationship of the Word is intrinsically threefold;

in the speech-event there comes to stand a Speaker, a Spoken to, and a Spoken, or, an Addresser, Addressed and Addressing. Behold, the threefoldness of God is revealed in and through the Word. In terms of Christian dogma, God as Trinity is "three Persons in one substance." The "substance" is the Word, the logos, and the "Persons" are the You, the I and the We. The Persons live in and by virtue of the relationship of Word; the Word is the ground of both the unity and the distinctiveness of the participants. In the Word, God is the Eternal You of address, the Eternal I of response and the Eternal We of mutual address and response. In the Word, God is threefold difference-in-unity.

It is of the utmost importance to understand the meaning of the original Greek and subsequent Latin terms used in the creedal formula of the Church for the Trinity. "Three Persons in one substance" can be deceiving without clear reference to what "person" and "substance" meant in the initial formulation. In the Greek, the terms are "three *hypostases* in one *ousia*." "*Hypostasis*" meant literally, that which stands under something, that which supports or is the foundation of something, its substantial nature. It is the final distinctive "sediment" of personality, as it were; it is what constitutes or distinguishes a person as a person, not in terms of attributes but of personal being and irreducible substance. "*Ousia*" signifies that which is one's own substance or property, the stable and immutable reality of something or someone, the primarily real, the substratum underlying all change and process. And in the Latin, based upon the Greek, the terms are "three *persona* in one *substantia*." "*Persona*" comes from the theatre, and represents a mask, used by actors in the depiction of their characters. It thus signified the irreducible and distinguishing characteristic of something or someone, the actual being or personage—at least for the course of the drama, as it were. "*Substantia*" meant that of which something consists, its essence or being, its contents, material or substance. In philosophy, it meant that which subsists by itself, and which underlies phenomena, the permanent substratum of things, that which receives modifications and attributes but is not itself a mode or an attribute.

This formula, then, in both the Greek and the Latin, well attests to the reality of the Trinity, to the threefold Person of God in the relationship of the Word. For God, so to speak, comes to stand eternally in the Word as underlying ground of relationship. In the one Word—and for the duration of the Word, like that of the drama—God is Eternal You, I and We, eternal difference-in-unity.

✠

In the beginning is the Word. And the Word is threefold in accordance with the threefoldness of God. Three primal Words denote three primal dimensions of relationship, both within God, and between God and humanity. The Word lives between God and God, and is one with the We-Spirit between the divine I and You. The Word between God and God is the eternal ground of the Word between God and humanity. The three primal Word-events are "You Are," "I Am" and "We Are." *"You Are"* is the *Word of Address,* and subsequently, as the command "Be You," the Word of creation. It was uttered first by God to God, then by God to humanity. Finally, it was repeated by humanity to the Creator, as the Eternal You. This Word posits otherness and externality, the first dimension of true relationship.

"I Am" is the *Word of Response,* and subsequently, the Word of revelation. It was uttered first by God to God, then by humanity to God as creation-inspired affirmation, and finally by God to humanity, as the confirmation of revelation—all as enabled by the Word of Address. This Word posits identity and internality, the second dimension of true relationship.

"We Are" is the *Word of Mutuality,* and subsequently, when finally spoken by God, will signify the Word of redemption. It was uttered *jointly* by God to God before creation, and will in the end be *jointly* spoken by God and humanity. For now, it has been promised by God and is of the essence of the human cry to God, of our need seeking confirmation and consummation. This Word, though now present only as anticipation in the other two Word-events, will posit commonness and mutuality, the third dimension of true relationship.

✠

God has been called the "Eternal You." Yet if God is to be the Eternal You, there must be an eternal Other to whom God is ever the You. That is, there must be an "Eternal I" addressing and being addressed by the You. Hence, there must be an "Eternal I-You." The eternal life of God is an eternal I-You relationship, that is, an "Eternal We."

The I, You and We of the Trinity constitute the ultimate Source and meaning, the end and actualization of the threefold world of the human person. In the I of Christ, the human I attains ultimate realization and legitimation. In the You of "the Father"—who is just as much "the Mother," that is, the eternal Parent—the human You finds ultimate form and direction. In the We of the Holy Spirit, the human We gains ultimate life and meaning. The Trinity not only reveals the nature of persons and relationships, but also grants them ultimacy and final security. The I is vouchsafed by the I of Christ, the You rests upon the rock of God, and the We is justified and contextualized by the Holy Spirit.

The Parent is the Eternal You, Christ the Eternal I, and the Holy Spirit the Eternal We. Knowledge of the I of the Parent, of the "inner life" of the Holy One, as it were, will never be attained. We may learn only of the I of Christ—for "knowledge of the Father comes only through the Son." But we can never cross over or extrapolate from the You to the I of the Holy One. Between the two spheres of being exists an unbridgeable ontological gap, namely that of the Creator over against the creation, the Addresser over against the Addressed. Yet in the extraordinary I of Jesus stands revealed a wondrous image and likeness (*homoiousia*) of the You of God, and by powerful implication, of the I of God the Creator as well. And in the relation of "the Father and the Son," in the revelation of the Eternal I-You between Jesus and God, the Holy We of their love, Christ and God are one (*homoousia*). They are one in Word and Spirit. Yet the mystery of the I of God the Creator abides forever.

✠

In the ancient world, the Greek birthplace of Western philosophy and mentality, God came to be identified as the union of the *good*, the *true* and the *beautiful*. How correct was this "natural" revelation given to their reason! How profound was their hidden knowledge of God, though they could not know what they knew—for apart from the direct encounter with God, no confirmation is possible. Though beyond all categories of the human mind and condition, God is nevertheless the Source and Endpoint of the good, the true and the beautiful. *The good*: God constitutes the ultimate ground of all law and morality, apart from whose absoluteness neither can attain an unshakable legitimating foundation. *The true*: God *is* the ultimate truth, which is *Person*, a *Who* rather than a *What*. Person is ultimate substance, Person-in-relationship. Hence, the Ultimate is essentially non-quantifiable and unknowable apart from direct person-to-Person relationship. *The beautiful*: all beauty tends toward the revelation of God, who as the Holy *is* the Beauty around which the whole of creation revolves in adoration and contemplation. The heavens declare the glory and the birds sing the praise of God; all of the beauty of nature is but an image, a "re-presenting" of God's creative touch and continuing Presence. Beauty is the signature of the Artist.

These three attributes united in God speak to the respective Persons of God in essential tri-unity. Thus the good points toward God the Creator, the Eternal You; the true bespeaks God the Responder, the Eternal I; and the beautiful attests to God the Relationship, God as Love, as the Eternal We. Each attribute builds upon and is inseparable from the others. From the will of God the You comes forth the creation, which God has called "good." From God the I comes forth the Word of truth, truth as Person and Relationship: "You shall know the truth, and the truth will set You free." And from God the We will come forth the beauty of the world to come, of the fulfillment of love.

For the present, it is the Spirit which inspires us with the promise and inner knowledge of the good, the true and the beautiful. And how beautiful is that promise of truth and goodness!

✠

It has been said that the human person has a threefold religious need: *transcendence, immanence* or *interiority*, and *belonging*. We seek that which is beyond us, that which is our inner life and substance, and that to which we belong. The first need is for the revelation of the Eternal You, and emerges with the primal question of philosophy: "What is ultimate Reality?" This is the question of overagainstness. The second calls for the revelation of the Eternal I, and arises with the primal question of psychology: "Who am I?" This is the question of identity. The third strains toward the revelation of the Eternal We, and is one with the question of life and meaning: "What is meaning? In what does my life consist?" This is the question of mutuality.

Truth, identity and life, these are the fundamental concerns of human existence. And they relate to the threefoldness of God. For in God alone abides the resolution to the human predicament. In the triune God alone is the need for the beyond, the within and the between fulfilled. For behold, these needs come from God, and bespeak the eternal relationship from which we were issued and towards which we are journeying as pilgrims.

✠

Image of God

> Then God said, 'Let us make man in our image, after our likeness; . . . .' So God created man in his own image, in the image of God he created him; male and female he created them. (Genesis 1:26a, 27)

We are made in the image of God: that means, in accordance with the above depiction, that we are made in the *image of mutuality and relationality*. The image of God is not in our solitary being or I-ness but in our simultaneous I, You and We-ness, not in our objective status as created beings among other beings, but in our subjective and intersubjective status as addressed persons among the divine Persons. Through the creative address, "Be You," we are stamped with the threefold *image* of the divine Persons; through our response, we enter as participants in the divine relational *likeness*. That is, the address incarnates the logos-structure of the I, the You and the We realities of God in and as our very personhood; and our response, carried out through the one logos-structure we have received, implements and manifests our likeness to the divine life of Persons-in-relationship. Together, our receiving and responding through the Word constitutes and concretizes our reality in the I, You and We of the divine Persons.

Personal being is thus received and acted upon through the Word as inner mandate. Hence, being and act, image and likeness, are one. Who we are determines what we do; what we do reveals who we are.

We are made in and for eternal relationship; we are called to image God back to God, returning our personal being to the Person to whom it belongs, in glory and praise, in love and awe. We are addressed to reflect back, to mirror the Eternal You, sharing in the mystery of the divine I in and with the Eternal We.

Hence, it is not as if the being of the Person of God—and of humanity—were primary and the relationship followed in consequence. Rather, the relationship is just as primary and eternal as the "being" or essence of the person of God, and therefore, of humanity. *God is relationship as well as being. God is Person-in-relationship.* Thus, we image God not only in our individual being, but essentially and primarily in our being-together. Being made in the image of God means, therefore, being made in, of and for relationship.

The image of God, in sum, is not of singularity as such, but of singularity within mutuality, not of being-in-isolation, but of being-together, of reciprocity and endless relationship. The image of God consists inseparably and irreducibly of the I, the You and the We. They must ever be held together. Their disjunction in us constitutes the estrangement of our "essence" from our "existence"; the rending asunder of mutuality signifies the fall of humanity from its true nature and destiny. The loss of the We eventuates in the loss of both the I and the You; the loss of the life and likeness of God leads to the darkening of the image of God within and behind an imaged I, now become a world unto itself, a *ding an sich*.

✠

A second profound aspect of the above Genesis depiction of the creation of humanity in the image of God concerns the *male and female* dimensions of *both* the divine and the human persons. "In the image of God he created him; male and female he created them." Behold, male and female emerged together—and at the same time—as simultaneous and mutual manifestations of God's own life and Persons. God is both/and rather than either/or: God is male and female, I and You, a holy and eternal difference-in-unity. *Viva la differance*, for the sake of God's own life! And also for the sake of human existence!

In the second chapter of Genesis, the meaning of the male and female dimensions of the image of God is expanded to include their spirit and mutuality. That is, just as the I and the You of God live in and by virtue of their We-Spirit, so also do the male and female dimensions of the human persons live in and by virtue of their unity. For when Adam meets Eve— made from his rib, and thus of his same age and continuous with the first creation—what he says to her constitutes a revelation of the utmost importance for the whole of human existence, past, present and future. At that primordial meeting, total and open, unexpected yet intended, at the very moment in which the archetypal human We happened—and not as a parent-child, but as a man-woman meeting—Adam spoke the truth of mutual being, and to the life-bearing one before him: "'This at last is bone of my bones and flesh of my flesh....' Therefore a man leaves his father and his mother and cleaves to his wife, and they become one flesh" (Genesis 2: 23,24).

The first utterance of the man is that of recognition and praise of the partnership and mutuality of the You over against him. And behold, the very first word issued from the mouth of the woman, as recorded in the next chapter of Genesis, is "We." In the beginning is the word. And the word is of and in relationship; the word is of the spirit, of the We. The word happens in the context of primal relationship, in which the word—and the persons who speak it—ever have their life and meaning.

The "We" of Eve is in fact the initial instance of the "pronoun of mutuality" in the Bible. And it is stated to the Tempter, as Eve in innocence begins to explain the divinely commanded conditions of human existence in the Garden. Her "We" speaks not only to the unity between her and the man, but to the oneness of their common life of obedient harmony within God's ordered world. As seen in the context of the "Fall" that follows, however, this We between the man and the woman—and also between the human and the divine partners—is the first to be lost, and indeed, will be the last to be restored. The "We" is not again uttered in the creation narrative.

The loss of the We signifies above all the loss of the image of God-in-relationship. And that eventuates in the loss of the image of the We itself, the rending asunder of mutuality in the world. Without the We, humanity is left with only the You and the I, the primal personal elements in search of their original setting-in-life, of their We.

✠

The image of God is thus a three-in-one: *male and female*. And the *"and"* has the same status and significance as the *male* and *female*. Does that not mean that the male and female in isolation are only part of the image of God, incomplete without the other and indeed the relationship itself? How then can the I be whole without its beloved You, living together in their We of communion?

The Genesis creation narrative lifts up one human "three in one" relationship as the image of God's own interpersonal life, as it were. That is *marriage. Marriage is the proper analogy of the divine We*. In our married existence, we anticipate our life in God, coming to us as our very redemption. Marriage is the permanent union or bond or covenant of love; and God is love. Therefore, God *is* marriage; God *is* eternal union. To be married means to participate in divine relationality; it means to image union back to the Unified One.

Being male and female—are we not made therefore for marriage, the most significant union of life, the relationship which first transforms us into and then identifies us as that new creation, as that one flesh? Marriage: from male and female to husband and wife, from parts to partners—is this not the deepest longing for union with God, not unlike but somehow continuous with and even fulfilling of human marriage, is this not the inmost and ineradicable drive of the heart for the life to come? Our humanity to God's divinity—is this not unlike the opposition of maleness to femaleness, designed to lead to apposition and union? Are we not, therefore, created for marriage with God?

✠

Revelation

God speaks, but cannot be spoken. As the You of our life, God may be addressed but not expressed. God reveals, but only within the cloud of mystery. God cannot be objectified in any sense, but may be remembered. Yet not the "Who" but only the "That" of God can be retained by memory. The Who is recorded, but only by and in the wholeness of the who of the person—and that means beyond the grasp of consciousness and memory. God is remembered, not as object but as event, as unique and paradoxical time-space event of pure Being-together, as encounter of mutual revelation, of the human and divine sharing knowledge of being in their togetherness.

The self-revelation of God happens to us in moments that have therefore been transfixed, sanctified and lifted out of the flux as a time for all time, as a way in to subsequent encounters with the divine. The event sanctifies memory, donning it the living reminder that orients, the connecting link between the human and the divine. As long as the memory holds, the event has the potential to reoccur in the life of the person, and thus grants hope, faith and promise for what is to come. As long as the score is recorded, the music has the possibility of being heard anew. The Eternal has broached time, the infinite has paradoxically manifested itself in the finite. The event is recorded, however, not in the world of things but in the personal world of humanity. Yet the event stands beyond the historical conditions of the breakthrough itself; something has been revealed for *all* time—or it is not of God. And it grants a standard, a canon, by which to measure time not yet included within it, namely the *saeculum*, the time between the eternity both preceding and succeeding creation.

What is revealed? *A relationship, a divine-human We—and God and humanity in that relationship.* God cannot be known apart from a relationship which involves our own being, and which at the same time reveals our being to ourselves. We remember a relationship, which through the joint will of God and the persons involved can become formalized as covenant, as *religion.* Religion, as covenant, is binding; it is the formalized and stiltified replay of revelation, erected in the dusk, after the sun of meeting and mutuality has set. The goal of every religion is the consummation of its own peculiar and self-justifying life-form; and the propagation of that human-divine way of being together is its mission.

The relationship revealed and lived out on the plain of history becomes the unconditional model for our relationship with God—and built upon that, for our relationship with each other and the world. The conditioned and the partial, which spring from the human side of the revelation, are placed by the believers into the realm of the holy, into the sphere of the unconditioned and unchanging. What is peculiar to the human person, the "prophet," in both personal and historical terms, is now judged to be peculiar to God as well. The "wedding" of human attributes and conditions with divine is thus the direct result not of the divine, but of the human will. Divine *and* human in nature and composition, thus unconditioned and conditioned, *both* temporal and eternal, such is the reality—and limitation—of all religion.

We encounter and seek to bind the divine. We want to "own" a part of God, even at the cost of our freedom and life—and God's. We long for God's benefits, salvation, protection and all the gifts God is willing to throw our way. In turn, it seems, God seeks our nearness and allegiance, our faithfulness and loyalty, our love and obedience. An uneven quid pro quo emerges, a "mismatch" which will lead to a "mismeeting": God seeks a true relationship with us, the life of We between us, whereas we seek personal and corporate gain. Like children, we ask "What will You give me?" We are like Jacob who is called Israel: we would wrestle with God and hold on with all that is in us, tendering but one incessant petition: "I will not let You go unless You bless me" (Genesis 32:26).

How far apart are we from God in our vision of the meaning of relationship, of a possible divine-human *Us*! God becomes a means to our own ends; yet we are God's ends. And in truth, God is our one and only end as well.

✠

We encounter God in God's own "time" and "space." God is experienced in God's own sphere of Being, God's own "We," as it were. This happens through the grace-filled event of God opening an unexpected and wondrous seam between us. The sphere of meeting is neither in the world nor in the I, but in the yet-to-be-apprehended and explored realm between persons. Our meeting with God spills over—like no other meeting—into the worlds around and within us, into the It and the I domains, so that everything comes to be seen in the context of the meaning and life of the revelation. God reveals God's own Being to and in the persons, breaking through both their own time and space and that of the world external to them. Behold, everything is therein transformed and new-made, yet paradoxically, remains precisely the same, only now is seen in its true context as creation, as holy occasion and meeting place.

As we approach God and our relationship to God, we come up against paradox. The paradox, the antinomy, seems to be an ever present element of God's manifestation, of God's personal signature or calling card, as it were. Hence, in our relationship with God, we experience absolute inclusiveness and exclusiveness—both at once. We are inclusive to God in the totality of our being, including the whole of our past, present and future; we find our life and substance in the Spirit of God. At the same time, however, we experience God's radical and eternally incomprehensible otherness, the divine *ganz andere*. Even in God's nearness, there is unbridgeable distance; even in the divine light, there is hiddenness; even in the awe-full intimacy of sweet communion, the mystery abides and intensifies; precisely in the depth of oneness opens wide the height of otherness.

Another antinomy: God's Spirit in the communion of revelation and prayer is at once both utterly exposed and thus seemingly vulnerable, yet wholly untouchable and invulnerable. Contrary to the human person, it appears that the tenderness and vulnerability of God are as limitless and unconditional as all the other characteristics we may attribute to the divine nature. How shall this be said, that God may indeed be "wounded" or "hurt" but never mortally so? That God as Person, in some manner beyond our comprehension but not our intuition, actually participates in the sufferings of love and openness to other persons, though not in a way which could lead to the destruction of the personal being or "soul" of God, so to speak? Behold, God reveals ultimate weakness and softness, tenderness and understanding, yet at the same time strength and invulnerability, hiddenness and incomprehensibility.

✠

I meet You, Holy One. Only of myself can I speak in this, for You are beyond human Words. Neither You nor We can be described; I may but live before You and out of Us. In the course of prayer, behold, it happens: I am drawn from the world of time and space and into a temple invisible. The world cannot enter that holy realm of Presence, but must, for now at least, stay behind, unaware. The encounter unfolds with the world somehow wrapped around the event—or perhaps only around me—untouched. While the temple is not in the world, the world is in the temple, or shall be, in a manner and mode to be seen only at the dawning of the Word of redemption.

Into an invisible, still and consecrated sphere, a temple of heightened anticipation and awareness, a place of air so rarefied as to have become reified as Spirit, I am drawn. The temple is of Spirit and Truth, and in its strangely measured silence—almost like the silent measures of music, pregnant and full of meaning—I await an audience. Behold, movement precedes meeting as I am granted wings at Your wordless call to me, Your direct address, holy and long sought. Your address is also the beginning of our embrace, and in and with my movement to You coexists a movement of Your winged Self unto me. In this air of the Spirit I am summoned forth, following with inexpressible joy and awe in Your train to the inner court where You abide, at least for this meeting.

Meeting and mutuality happen, to a depth and extent beyond anticipation. *Ecstasy.* I am outside myself and in You—or should I say in "Us"? I know You in holiness, just as I am known in totality—and know that I am known. There is an inclusivity of being, even though in Yourself You are Mystery; and even in direct embrace, You remain strangely hidden. Familiarity and absolute otherness, intimacy and distance abide together in Us, in the inexplicable harmony of our wholeness. Have I then met You, or only Your love as messenger? Yet You are in Your love, and You are love itself. Your incomprehensibility cannot be surmounted; my knowing is also an unknowing. I do not, I cannot touch You, but I am invaded and permeated by You, through and through; for a time beyond time, and in a way I cannot grasp or take back into the ordered and ordinary world, *I am included in You;* I am unified with You and with myself in one, and life is at last wholly unambiguous.

In our communion, being and knowing are one. I am what I know, and know what I am. And behold, in this knowing is also a recollection of a time no longer to be remembered, of a prior event of knowing. Was it that of my creation itself? I do not know. I only know that in meeting You, a primal memory reveals itself as well, a history of Us, forgotten until We happened again. And I sense what will become fact when I return to the world of things and human affairs: nothing of the content of this meeting and knowing can be taken across, nothing of the holy may leave the sphere of the holy. I will only be able to remember *that* You are; but the *Who* shall continue to abide in mystery and at a depth of memory I cannot lift into consciousness. Not without Your gracious nearness, O God of my life, may I remember what I know of You and of Us!

Yet the inner truth of this mystery now lives in my heart. In meeting You there was a bestowal of being. "Something More" dwells in my inmost heart, something beyond my reach or control, something more unconscious than conscious. Call it a knowledge which also bears being; call it something beyond human language which will create language. Call it a center of new awareness and life, a mutual life with the Holy One, which summons me to carry out its mandate with my life, to make it real here. Mission and meaning have been granted in this something more. It is a kind of covenant of being, the direct consequence of our shared life, of our meeting. It is both Your fire in my soul and the being in me You have awakened, my true self, my life. It *is* our relationship; it *is* what We share. This something more is our life together itself. And You are present in that life, and I not only share but am of that life; it is me in our new creation, our covenant. Is this not the "wellspring of eternal life," opened and flowing in me because of You?

Where did I meet You, Holy One? Where is this temple invisible, this consecrated sphere which no one can enter by human effort or will but only through the action of the Spirit? It is not in the world, though the world must be seen from its vantage point, from its ultimacy. Indeed, the end and consummation of the world signifies the being drawn into and redeemed by this wondrous domain hidden between us. *The temple is the kingdom of Heaven, it is the realm of the interpersonal.* It is the meeting place for love and Spirit. It is the kingdom of the We, the mutual, the koinonia, the sphere of knowing and being known in one, of finding and being found, of action and passivity. All of history is moving toward the revelation of the world between us, of the kingdom we are to share, the common realm of the inter-human, which is also the meeting place of the divine-human. Behold, the temple is here, now! We are called to meet not only God but one another in this holy place, in this kingdom between us, the home of Spirit, of God in the world. It is our purpose and our destiny.

✠

Grace

God and necessity? The only necessity in God is that of the divine will, thus of God's own choosing. For God, can and will, cannot and will not, are one and the same. God acts in absolute freedom of will; divine intention is unconditioned by anything beyond itself. Unconditioned, but manifest in the Word of creation and revelation, the will of God is to love. God wills to love us, and in that love to bring us into the divine life, to "save" us. God's decision to love us is not conditioned by or dependent upon anything outside of God. There is nothing in us to which we may attribute God's love, nothing to draw our attention away from the sovereign will and incomprehensible decision of God for us.

The *grace* of God is God's *will to love* in action and event. It represents the unmerited favor, the undeserved good will, the decision to heal and to save, on God's part alone. The Word of grace: "I will be gracious to whom I will be gracious." Thus grace, like love itself, comes in freedom and as gift. It holds us, but we cannot hold or hold on to it. As giftedness, grace *is* the experience of the Spirit, and the experiential ground of the hope of final redemption. And what comes to us as essential gift cannot be purchased or earned later. Grace has no strings attached; no hidden law of paying back or quid pro quo abides in the absolute "giving without counting the cost" of grace. Rather, any return would have to be on the same basis of freedom and gift. And if grace succeeds in bringing home to the heart the message and fact of the love of God, there springs forth a grace-enabled response of love to God, not of necessity but of freedom, not a "have to" but a "will to." Grace received spawns grace in action and deed.

The grace of God is threefold in accordance with the threefoldness of the divine Word. The grace of the Word of creation is *prevenient*, of revelation is *justifying*, and of redemption is *sanctifying*. Our relationship with God is that of an unfolding and unfinished "love story"; and the sequence of grace signifies the stages of God's love on the Way to our promised consummation. Thus were we born in love, addressed into being by and in the love of God, carried henceforth if unknowingly by that love—prevenient grace—until such a time as that love is revealed to us—justifying grace—and we are invited by that love to make our home in it as it makes its home in us—sanctifying grace. That is, prevenient grace *prepares* us for love, justifying grace *reveals* it, and sanctifying grace *transforms* us into that love. Love hidden but active, love found and present, and love in self-fulfillment, these are the three essential dimensions of the love-grace of God in human life and history. Prevenient grace signifies what God does *to* us in creation, justifying grace what God does *for* us in revelation, and sanctifying what God does *with* us in redemption—all for the sake of what God seeks *with* us, namely our unending participation in the Eternal We.

While God as Trinity acts in oneness and mutuality, each divine Person is especially associated with one of these three graces. Prevenient grace has primarily to do with God the *Creator*, the Eternal You, and is to be grasped in terms of the *givenness* of creation, the ground of the past. That givenness includes not only all that is over against and around us, but also all that God has placed within us, especially the "law of the heart," our incarnated and unfolding future, the emerging "Christ." Prevenient grace is that action of divine love which has placed the logos within us through the Word of address. It is thus God's *Work* in creation, which also means God's ongoing "behind the scenes" labor of sustaining and building us up, of preparing and enabling us to turn our face to the Face, in desire and repentance.

Justifying grace has primarily to do with God the *Revealer*, the Eternal I, and is to be apprehended in terms of the "*givingness*" of revelation, the ground of the present. That givingness involves the dialogic of divine-human presentness to each other, the either/or of partners in self-discovery and affirmation. The poles of the relationship, the I and the You, step forward into mutual being and into presence with power and realization with life-bearing substance. Thus does Christ over against and within us become manifest. Justifying grace concerns above all God's *Word* in revelation, the actual offer of true relationship and being-together, of a forgiving and cleansing power, of a restoration of communion and intimacy made possible by a never-to-be-repeated holy deed of mutual divine and human self-sacrifice, the Cross. Through the Word, we encounter God within and over against us as Lord and Savior.

Sanctifying grace has to do primarily with God the *Redeemer*, the Eternal We, the Holy Spirit, and is to be understood in terms of the *giftedness* of redemption, the ground of the future. That giftedness signifies the work of the love of God, the way in which that love transforms us into itself, making us consistent with its life and able to abide in it, to remain true to God, to actually be capable of carrying through with our end of the relationship. It makes real the both/and, the dialectic of love, the We of mutuality in which we stand, and through which we have our life. Thus, sanctifying grace concerns God's *Way* in the heart of the person and in the life of the community. God's Way is also God's life, and that life is love; hence, this grace consummates love, and brings to maturity Christ within and between us.

Behold, grace is the will and work, the Word and the Way of God. It is God's decision and consequent commitment in action, to create us in and for love, to prepare and guide us toward it, to reveal its fact and presence and power, and to make us holy, to sanctify us in and into that love.

✠

Conversion

Conversion is a threefold process of change. It is a change *from* something *to* something *by* means of something. Hence, for instance, loneliness is converted to communion by love; fear is converted to peace by grace; death is converted to life by the Spirit of God. Conversion is usually preceded by some predicament, by the person reaching some untenable state of existence. Emptiness cries out for its eradication through mutuality; meaninglessness awaits in silent pain some purpose to pull the person out of despair; grief aches for the soothing nearness of hope and the strength of faith to carry on. Thus do we seek to be freed of something for something else, whether seen or not, and by means of some yearned for power.

Conversion is not healing but the preparation for it. It makes healing both possible and desirable; it brings hope and anticipation and a vision of new life, along with the faith necessary to go forward toward the newfound goal. The power of conversion is that of primal redress, of facing again what was denied or ignored before. It means to "change one's mind," as the central term in the Greek New Testament, *metanoia,* signifies. The underlying belief which fuels conversion is an active invitation of the heart for the Reality sought to enter into the person's soul and life. And the invitation to change is itself the beginning of change.

Conversion is a threefold movement of the Spirit of God in us. It begins by the planting of new *"in-formation"* into the heart, new insight into one's true state, together with the offer of new life and meaning. The inner "Yes" to the informing of the Spirit leads to the *"re-formation"* of the mind and soul by the power of the Spirit at work in us from the initial in-filling onward. The third and final phase of conversion is that of the *"trans-formation"* of the life of the person, brought about via the continuing work and sanctifying love of the one Spirit.

One need only look at the Apostle Paul to see the cumulative impact of the threefold work of the Spirit in conversion. His conversion began with the powerful and life-altering information that he had been persecuting no one less than the Anointed of God. Through the continuing grace of God, this led to the reformation of his mind, of his thinking and feeling. And finally, the converting work of the Spirit eventuated in the transformation of his whole life. Informed, reformed and transformed, Paul was sent forth as Apostle to the Gentiles. And through his threefold conversion, many indeed would be turned in like manner.

Conversion, in short, is a lifelong work of God in us. It is an ongoing baptism, a series of immersions into the waters of divinity and truth, all toward the attainment of our maturity and perfection in the image and likeness of God. We rise and die and rise again, over and over, until one day on arising we stand united with the Arisen One.

✠

Our mode of life says either *Yes* or *No* to God. There can be no "fence-sitters" to the truth. We are headed for either conversion to or perversion from the truth. To pervert means to corrupt something or someone, to change something from what it should be or is meant to be into something it really is not, or is not meant to be. We are ever moving toward either renewal or decay, rejuvenation or decimation. While the Apostle Paul could proclaim that "I die daily," he could also maintain that "Though outwardly we are wasting away, yet inwardly we are being renewed day by day" (2 Corinthians 4:16).

The grace of God is offered to us daily. It is up to us, however, either to infuse or refuse that grace, to convert or not to convert, to accept or to reject God—and therefore ourselves, all one day at a time. For our true and ultimate life is with God, and our life here represents a continual conversion into God.

Is there then a *will to conversion*? What else could it be but the willingness to do and to become whatever is necessary to attain to communion and union with God? The will to conversion is nothing more or less than the *will to God*. For all our life long we are in a steady state of conversion, of transformation into and unto God. We must not stop moving, any more than the cone which carries cement on a cement truck dares to stop its motion—for fear that the cement would harden, and thus become useless. So too would we become useless if we hardened within our hearts, so that God could not pour us out for God's purposes and for our salvation. Behold, we are not to harden until the end of our pilgrimage. For God intends to pour us whole into the finished mold of the Eternal I.

✠

Conversion is the transformation of something or someone from one form or state of being to another. *And an energy release always accompanies a conversion.* The manifestation of energy is in fact a sign of the conversion process. Behold fire. The point of ignition is both the point of conversion and the converter. And that which is converted, be it wood or coal, releases great energy in the heat and light of the fire. The conversion process can literally consume that which is converted and in an irreversible way. Wood once burned will never be wood again.

God is called a "consuming fire" in Scripture (Hebrews 12:29). That means, first, that God is the great *Converter* of the soul, and second that God is, so to speak, in an eternal state of *conversion*. And the Spirit is the eternal fire of God. Hence, the Spirit is God's agent of conversion. For are we not told that Jesus came to "baptize . . . with the Holy Spirit and with fire" (Matthew 3:11; Luke 3:16)? Jesus himself proclaimed that "I have come to bring fire upon the earth, and how I wish it were already kindled!" (Luke 12:49). His resurrection fueled and Pentecost actually ignited the converting flame of the Holy Spirit. For at the great and most holy event of the pouring forth of the Spirit, the Spirit descended upon the heads of those thus converted as "tongues of fire" (Acts 2:3).

The fire of the Spirit is ignited by the flint of meeting and touching each other. And the fire that can come to rage between us is love's torch. Would that we could find the raw passion and faith to say Yes with the whole of our being to becoming one with the fire we share. God is a consuming fire; and God is love. Behold, love is the fire of God, which would consume us, and would bring us its life and energy, and enable our release into itself. Our salvation is our eternal conversion with God, our life in God's fire.

O to be aflame without ever burning up or out! O to glow forever in the pure and inexhaustible fire of the love of God! 'Tis a consummation devoutly to be prepared for.

✠

Prayer

Prayer is the whole of our communication with God. And what in life is not communication with God? How can we hide anything from God? When are we not making a statement to God? Every moment and mode of our existence stands in relationship to the One ever over against us. Just as we stand always in relation to the sun on a summer day, so that our bodies are recording the presence of its rays, even to the point of burning if overexposed, so too do we stand ever before the Face, with our spirits recording both the Presence and our current relational posture. Unlike the sun, however, there is no dwelling into which we can escape from the penetrating rays of the apprehension of God. "Where can I go from Your Spirit? Or where can I flee from Your Presence?" We cannot affect the presence, but may only block our awareness of God—and for the whole of our lives.

More than our communication, prayer signifies our communion with and in God. And God seeks greater intimacy with us than we do with God. God seeks "co-union" and mutuality with us above all. In truth, *spirituality is divine-human sexuality*; it is the intercourse of the soul through the spirit, greater than the intercourse of the soul through the body. More than symbolizing the former, the latter is a sacrament for and to be fulfilled only in the former. For God is the ultimate end of all desire. The course of prayer leads to the holy marriage bed of our union and consummation in and with God. A bridal chamber exists between the soul and the Beloved; and the prayer life of the soul is towards and in that abode of meeting and communion. Our prayer life *is* the life of the divine-human We, it *is* our meeting and mutuality in fact, deed and history.

What then is not prayer, what does not belong to our life with God? Prayer is our opening to God; when, then, are we not to be opened to God? Prayer is our presence in and with God; when, then, are we not to "practice the Presence" of God, where is God not to be in our lives? Prayer is our dialogue with God; when, then, are we not to be in ongoing conversation with God, when are we to say "Good bye" to the One who is always with us? The whole of our lives, awake and asleep, the totality of our daily moments and concerns, all is to be spent with God, with our "Beloved One," our "Eternal Spouse." Therefore are we to live ever and always in prayer.

Prayer is the mode of our conversion into God. As with conversion, therefore, prayer is threefold. It begins with the "in-forming" of the heart, then proceeds to the "re-forming" of the mind, and leads ultimately to the "trans-forming" of the life of the person. These three phases of prayer are in accordance with our threefold relationship with God, namely creation, revelation and redemption. As creation is monologic, so the first phase of prayer is that of *inception,* be it from the human or the divine side. The second phase is that of *reception,* in accordance with the dialogical nature of revelation. And finally, the dialectic of prayer, its redemptive impulse is that of *conception.*

In the beginning, prayer is either speaking or listening, either action or passivity. Then it progresses to dialogue, to both a listening and a speaking, to a unity-in-difference. And, if we continue in prayer—and too few do—we attain to pure mutuality, to the birth of shared vision and insight, meaning and mission. For mutuality stands behind all manner of births, from babies to nations, from ideas to religious faith. And without prayer, the human We itself would soon become barren of meaning and purpose.

As we pray to God, God prays to and in us. Prayer in the Christian context reveals the essential triplicity of God and our unified life therein: we pray *"to* the Father," *"in* the Son" and *through* the "Holy Spirit." That is, we pray to the Eternal You in the Eternal I through the Eternal We. Strictly speaking, the Holy One, the Beloved, the You of our lives, can only be addressed but not expressed; the Eternal I is the One expressed; and the Eternal We is the context and ground of our common meeting, our "shared Person," as it were. The vision of the Eternal I-You, our destined relationship to God, is given and realized above all in prayer.

✠

Corporate Prayer: I pray for You and with You. An act of yielding begins as we join our hands together. I seek to lose myself in You and in the Spirit of prayer. Your concern now becomes my concern in the open channel of God's concern. In silent waiting, we are touched and united by the opening of the Presence within and between us, of the peace-bearing One who permeates and sees all, who hears and heals. Anointed thus, we move together into the temple invisible, the wondrous Kingdom between us, which may be entered only through the door of mutuality and love. We are heard; and the hearing has power and gracious intent, and we are changed through it. As we share in the common concern, so also do we share in the common answer. We have drunk deeply of You and of the Spirit in the "co-notation" of meaning and community.

How came we to share the One Spirit in our prayer together? How is it possible that You and I, distinct and different, could come together with the embrace of hands and hearts and find ourselves so quickly and decisively enmeshed not only in a common event, but in a common message and life, granted by the one Spirit, who responded with grace to our invitation of faith? For behold, as You and I spoke to—as I addressed for You—the common Spirit, the Spirit spoke back to us in one voice as to one person. That which is impossible for us is possible for God! And the intimacy of our common prayer exceeds that of any other form of human intercourse and mutuality. For the intimacy of corporate prayer is heightened by the common Spirit, the Spirit which goes to the ultimate depths of the soul. We share in revelation about each other in the healing and whole and holy sight of God. We are fellow pilgrims in the Kingdom of Heaven between us.

We have prayed together. We have shared in the We of the Holy Spirit, uniting our We with the We of God. Our relationship is not the same as before, for the "Something More" of prayer now lives between us, and somehow You and I are accountable to it. We have prayed together. That means, for a time beyond time, neither of us were alone; for a common space unseen yet more real than the space between us and the stars, our very beings moved in harmony with the Greater Being. In our prayer, we were one in the Spirit; now that Spirit—living still between us in common memory—calls us to be one in the world, and to allow that unity to pervade and transform the whole of our lives. For all of life is destined to be lived in and from the one life of the Spirit. Common prayer is the prelude to a common heaven.

✠

The Way of Spiritual Life

Spiritual life is threefold in accordance with the threefoldness of persons, human and divine. The threefold path is that of *illumination, purgation* and *unification.* Illumination begins as the revelation of the You, and of the I in relation to the You. Purgation is initiated by the I in response to the You, and represents the purifying of all that is not consistent with the You and the revealed relationship to the You. Unification comes as the fruit and growing fact of mutuality between the You and the I, and is the proper work of the Holy Spirit, of the Eternal We as such.

In the beginning is the Word. And the Word brings illumination of the One who is over against us; the Word calls the Truth into being in the light of its utterance. Behold, the Word is the Truth. And the Truth is of Person, Persons-in-relationship. Truth is ever of and in relationship. And the Truth of relationship emerges first as the presence of the Other and of otherness, that is, as Truth-in-externality, as the "wholly other," the *ganz andere.* In the beginning we have a relationship with that which is other than us, the Holy.

The presence of the Other calls forth the awareness of the I, and of the I in relation to the You. And from the consciousness of the vis-a-vis springs forth the primal experience of the discrepancy or difference between the two personal beings. That is, the revelation of the Holy includes the revelation of our own state, of our own fallenness from the former. We sense, in some fashion beyond our grasp but also beyond our doubting, that we are both of the Holy yet far from it, belonging to it by essence yet estranged from it by existence. The tension caused by the illumined and palpable disparity between our essence and our existence becomes a powerful internal agent for change. It mandates and authors a slow but necessary process of purging from within all that is not consistent with the Other, the You of our life, and with the relationship bestowed through revelation. All this is made possible by the Word of illumination, now working Its will in us.

Illumination thus eventuates in the interiorizing of the truth of the You, and motivates a cleansing away of that which is incompatible with who we are called to be in our revealed relationship with God. The promised end of the relationship, built into its very beginning, is the We of unity and communion. The revelation of the You and the purging work of the I are all for the sake of the consummation of the relationship in an Eternal We of love and pure mutuality. This is living context of the Spirit from the first moment of presence, the unspoken yet abiding and active purpose of the meeting itself, and therefore of everything that is to follow. The end is unification, everlasting marriage, a holy unity made possible by a holy revelation, and then by a holy work of preparation and consecration. *Spiritual life is the revelation of, the work towards and the existence in, a divine-human marriage.*

✠

In the beginning is the revelation. And not only do You reveal Yourself to me, Holy and Beloved One, but in the light of Your Presence, I am revealed to myself as well. What then have I come upon? This revealed self is almost as strange, as "wholly other" to my life and self-understanding as are You. In the indescribable intimacy of Your Presence I am addressed not only by You, but by an I also somehow over against me, the I who I am to become with You, the I anointed by Your Spirit, the I of Us. Distance and otherness, intimacy and sameness, these and other antinomies live side by side in the mutual world of the revelation.

From the revelation comes the first and the great commission: "go and become like this I revealed to You as your true self with Me." The joy and ecstasy of the illumination is followed by the profound assessment of the work that is to be done in fulfilling it. My life is no longer the same; I exist and am to exist eternally in and by virtue of this revelation, this unfinished relationship manifested as mutual presence, as Spirit. I am to become like the image granted me during the revelation; I am to purge and to hallow, to cleanse and to consecrate this I loved by the Beloved. I am to overcome the distance and the disparity between us in this first meeting. All this is in preparation for something which is to come, felt and present in the revelation, but only in the unvoiced ground of the Spirit between Us.

What is to come, Beloved One? Unbrokenness, absolute and unending. What is to be between Us? Mutuality, total and and eternal. What will this "We" be like? I will not know until it is attained through pure gift of grace and preparation of will. And note carefully: preparation for is not merit towards, but only the developing of the capacity to say "Yes" to and live out of the coming relationship, the Eternal We. We cannot earn unity by our efforts, or somehow "deserve" it; we may only—and indeed must—get ready for it through will and grace. Then when the gift comes, we will actually be able to take it and make it our own.

✠

May we attain unity with God in this life? To what extent? Only to the extent of word and deed, of spirit and consciousness, but not to that of true being. We may "practice God's presence," and live in a unity of consciousness and oneness with the inner intention of the heart. But as long as we are in the flesh, there cannot be a full unity of being. For we are body and God is not; we are of creation, but God is Creator. Until the body is redeemed by and in what is to come, unity and oneness will always be conditional—and breakable. And temptation will be an ever-present potential.

The Spirit of unity and mutuality is here and is offered to anyone who seeks—and indeed, seeking God is God's own gift of calling, and hunger for God is a wondrous grace of God preparatory to meeting. Though unity may become full, it cannot become complete—even though in a "mystical moment," we may seem to have at last attained what we seek. That event is not attainment, but embrace, not the fruit but a fore-taste thereof. For though the Spirit is willing, the flesh is weak, as it were. And this life is a preparation for but not the place of the unity which is to come. This is our time and space for growth and pilgrimage. Yet God abides with us as guest and giver, as companion and guide, as the One who unites with us when we cannot yet unite with God.

What then of the purported "union" of the mystic with God? In truth, the experienced oneness of the soul with God is that of the primal unity of the relationship with God, not of an undifferentiated union with God as such. It is a "co-union" or communion, not a union or actual merging with God. Behold, the I and the You cannot merge, but they find each other and their life in the We between them. Hence, what is experienced is the pure mutuality of that which is shared between the soul and God. It is life with and in the We, but not in the You of God. The sovereignty of the Holy One is never broached, the being of God is never invaded, the individual is not "absorbed" into the Godhead, like a drop of water into the ocean. Rather, the Eternal I-You is entered into, the temple invisible, the sphere for meeting and mutuality between us and God. In that holy place, the human person assumes the person of the I of revelation and destiny over against the Eternal You of creation in the ultimate and salvific We of redemption. In that event, the life which is to come has come indeed, but not yet in unbroken fullness. There is unity but not union, save only in the sense of a reciprocity of shared being in the relationship itself—and only in the relationship. And it is a relationship which is as absolute and unconditional as the being of God. The relationship cannot be transcended; it ever abides. Being ever faces being.

✠

Two Ways of Salvation

What is the end of the religious quest? How are we to envision our ultimate destiny? Are we to live with or in God? Is our relationship to be transformed into an undifferentiated oneness, or are divine-human distinctions to abide in unending mutuality? Is our relationship with God to be transcended by our immersion into God, the between finally giving way to the within or to the without of the divine reality? Or is the relationship as primary as the "being" of God? If the being of God is understood to be "personal," then are not persons required—and persons in relationship? If God is "Person," then must not relationship hold, age upon age?

There are two fundamental ways of salvation, determined by two primal visions of the end of the religious quest. And the end is determined by the beginning, by the originating revelation. The two ways or spiritualities are those of *Detachment* or *Attachment*. The respective ends are either, first, a transformation into utter oneness and singularity, wherein the individual self merges ontologically with the One, that is, wherein the person "ends" at the point of immersion into the Absolute Being; or second, the end is the consummation of a relationship, a "covenant," begun in this life and lived out on the plain of history. In the former vision of the end, only God is real, and only a single "God-consciousness" abides. Multiplexity and becoming, differentiation and change, are only illusions, are only indications of estrangement and fallenness into temporality, into the karmic cycle of death and rebirth. In the latter vision, the human and the divine reach a relational consummation and unity where God is "all in all" but not all, where unity abides in difference, and difference in unity. The end is the paradoxical unity of oneness and otherness through the mediation of "betweenness," as it were. The end is life with God in tri-unity; the end is eternal mutuality and "co-unity."

The respective originating revelations are either that of *"Enlightenment"* or *"Encounter."* Enlightenment represents not only the vision but the attainment of Absolute Being; encounter signifies the meeting of the human person with the divine Person. In the former revelation, individual and personal being is shown to be either unreal or merely a temporarily displaced fleck of the one Universal Being. Whether unreal or displaced, the self does not abide or remain as an individual entity, real in itself with an ontological integrity over against that of the eternal being; either way, the reality of the world and history—and that means of the Word itself—is denied and purportedly transcended.

In the revelation of encounter, however, the human person stands before the divine Face and perseveres in existence. Here one comes to know with a certitude that one's own person is in truth an image or likeness of the divine, and is therefore legitimized and ontologically vouchsafed by the fact of the personhood of God.

At the basis of enlightenment is the unconditional realization, with the force of salvation, that "knowing and being are one." To attain knowledge, therefore, means to attain being; to be means to know; we are what we know, and know what we are, at least from the event of revelation onward. The focus here is on the one who attains enlightenment, on the transformed human I. With enlightenment, *becoming precedes and is preparatory to revelation.* That is, growth and discipleship are necessary but not sufficient preparation for the event of realization; the event itself comes as grace, for it is transcendent in nature. The enlightenment usually happens as the sought for consequence of much labor, as the end of a long, narrow and rigorous road of training. And the grace of enlightenment appears as the reward, beyond all anticipation and human endeavor, for the level of preparedness attained—not in terms of length of labor, but rather of ontic perfection. One is not enlightened unless one is prepared for the irreversible event of knowing and being.

At the basis of encounter is the unconditional experience, with the power of eternal presence, that "knowing is bestowed in being-together." To attain knowledge, therefore, means to attain mutuality; truth requires reciprocal centers of consciousness; truth is mediated by and lives in relationship. The end of knowledge is "to know as we have been known." The focus here is on the gift of mutual presence, and on the divine You who reveals and is revealed. With encounter, *becoming is subsequent to and to be guided by revelation.* That is, at the point of the encounter, we are "reborn" as babes into the new truth-as-relationship. As with a marriage relationship, the nuptial ceremony is not the end, but only the beginning; the real becoming of the relationship and the persons who will live therein is merely getting under way. The life of the partners is ahead of them.

The way of detachment is thus built upon a radical *No* to the threefold world of persons. The way of attachment is founded upon a radical *Yes* to the abiding reality of the I, the You and the We. In religious and metaphysical terms, to deny one of the three is to deny the whole; to affirm one is to affirm all three. No You means no I, and vice-versa; no We means no ground of meeting, thus neither I nor You.

The question of the reality of the You is the first and most crucial issue, from which all else follows. The way of detachment must deny the reality of the You, the Other, as such—and therefore of the I and the We as well. The way of attachment, however, posits an absolute You, who is not reducible to the I of the human person or the I to the You of God. Here the I is conditional and the You unconditional. Here the I is created by and ever dependent upon the You. Here the You is not merely an epiphenomenon of the I, not merely the I with a public face. The You ever remains the Other, and the consciousness of the I is mediated by and grounded in that of the You.

The way of detachment is thus one of reduction and subtraction, of the many into the One, of the individual into the single universal. The way of attachment is one of addition, of one plus one, of the many finding common life with the One. That is, the oneness of the way of attachment is that of relationship as such, whereas the way of detachment grasps oneness in being as such, in an "undifferentiated totality beyond multiplexity and diversity." Salvation for the way of detachment means entrance into the oneness *of* the One; for the way of attachment, it signifies entrance into a relational oneness *with* the One. The riddle of how the many comes from the One—and yet returns to the One, being somehow "re-dissolved" into it, remains forever unsolved for the former. The only solution comes from the way of the latter, wherein the many is apprehended as emerging from the One with the Other, that is, from the ground of the Word between the You and the I, from the We of their mutual Spirit.

✠

The essential triunity of persons determines and is determined by the nature of the Word-event. If the persons are not real, neither is the Word itself; if the Word is real and actual, then so must be the threefold world of persons as well. Therefore, in denying the world of persons, the way of detachment cannot affirm the reality of the Word, of the speech event itself. For speech is intrinsically relational, with real and nonreducible partners. Hence, the "knowing" of enlightenment is a non-Word knowing, and the "being" of enlightenment is an impersonal being. Apart from relationship, enlightenment is an absolutely empty knowing and being. It is the revelation of the I of its own consciousness of being, which arose through the Word of address in creation. That is, enlightenment is the pure self-awareness of the I of being as such. But it is at the same time an awareness of "non-being," of nothingness. "Somethingness" comes only through the mediation of an otherness, only via the encounter with the You, and thus through the Word.

✠

The way of detachment is that of *exclusivity*, the way of attachment is that of *inclusivity*. The former begins with *denial*, namely of the world as seen and lived in commonness with community and nature. And salvation remains the exclusive attainment of the individual disciple; the world cannot be saved as the world. The latter begins with *affirmation*, namely of the reality of and divine involvement in the daily affairs of life. And salvation is ultimately the inclusive event of the transformation of both community and nature; the world will be translated as such into an eternal totality of God's design and good pleasure.

In the way of detachment, the end of the path is either the I or Self, be it understood as the Atman, Brahma or Buddha, or the It of a Nirvana, beyond all personality. Nature is neither real nor "redeemable." The self is either unreal, or it is the only thing which is real. In either case, however, the integrity of the threefold world of persons is destroyed; only the grand and exclusive It abides. For apart from relationship, the I is divested of all personality and differentiation as person. And all relationships are blown away, like a coat of cob webs in the wind, when the revelation of Being comes upon the one now enlightened. And subsequent "compassion" for is not the same as identity with, others.

In the way of attachment, the end of the path is the We in which the partners in their otherness abide, in which the I and the You continue to exist in and by virtue of the We-Spirit of their mutuality. The end is thus the fulfillment of relationship as much as the becoming of the persons involved. Being is inclusive in that there is true reciprocity and sharing, and the distinction between the persons is non-transcendable—and is indeed essential for the relationship itself. Further, the relationship includes and is to be redemptive not only of the world of persons, but of the whole of creation itself.

The way of detachment is also that of *"disinterest"* in all that is not eternal, in all that is imperfect and in flux, in everything which belongs to the sphere of "becoming"—and therefore of "ceasing." That means the renunciation of all desire, for desire spawns illusion and distance from the Absolute in the involvement it produces with the things of temporality. All relationality, all attachment to and involvement in the world of persons and things must be severed and abandoned. The word of this spirituality: "Let go and let be; be the One in ceasing all becoming."

The way of attachment, however, is that of *"interest"* and "desire." It is founded on the desire for God and the things of God, be it prior to or as a result of revelation. Desire leads to encounter, and encounter to mutuality, and mutuality to the fulfillment of the desire—in an indissolubly triune relationship. The word of this spirituality: "Receive and accept Life; become perfect with the perfect One in endless relationship."

Detachment signifies an *intra-subjectivity,* an intrinsically inward attainment and directedness. The truth of the whole is within. Attachment signifies a primal *inter-subjectivity,* an intrinsically outward reaching and other-directedness. The truth is between us; we are the whole. The truth manifests itself and is one with the relationship. Yet behold, intra-subjectivity by itself and apart from reciprocal subjectivities, eventuates in the world within, namely that of internality, becoming indistinguishable from the world without, namely that of externality. For only the world of the between, only mutuality, can allow us to maintain the fundamental distinction between the two spheres. The sphere of the between is not only the bridge between persons and nature, but the essential perspective-granter for the whole of existence. By positing an either/or as ultimacy, the way of detachment dissolves the difference between the two worlds, and they cave in and merge together. Only by the maintaining of the absolute status of the both/and, can the truth and interrelatedness of the whole be seen and vouchsafed.

✠

The way of detachment is seen most clearly in the life and work of Siddhartha Gautama, the Buddha. The way of attachment is seen most dramatically in the life and ministry of Jesus of Nazareth, the Christ.

The "Buddha" as "enlightened" and the "Christ" as "anointed" speak powerfully and succinctly to their respective significance and apprehension of Ultimate Reality. To be "enlightened" focuses on the I and the truth it has realized; to be "anointed" focuses on the We of a relationship and the One who has done the anointing. The Buddha attained Being; the Christ was baptized by and into eternal relationship with Being. The Buddha denied the existence of the self and was silent on the question of the reality of God. The Christ legitimized and fulfilled for all time the "I Am" of both God and humanity, together with the holy "We Are" of his relationship with God. With the Buddha the attainment of enlightenment was and remains the consummation to be sought for; with the Christ, the entrance into the kingdom of heaven, into the realm of pure relationship with God, was and is and will continue to be the life and substance of his mission.

In truth, only the coming Word of redemption will demonstrate with finality which of the two ways leads to salvation.

THE DIALECTIC OF SCRIPTURE

The Bible

The Bible is the written form and record of the revelation, through the Word, of the persons of God and humanity. *Through the Word*—that means in and through the *logos* of both divine and human speech, of dialogue and mutual encounter. *Of the persons*—that means in essential threefoldness. The Book bespeaks the source, present reality and destiny of the I, the You and the We of the human person.

The *inerrancy* of the Bible has to do with the faithfulness of its representation of the state of affairs between the divine and the human persons, as captured within the three interwoven relationships of creation, revelation and redemption. The Bible is not only the "official" record of that relational state; it is inseparable from the revelation itself, ongoing and living, light and life bearing, all in the Word, to which it attests with a singularity and faithfulness like no other book. Indeed, the Bible *is* the current state of our relationship with God, in terms of God's twofold marriage with humanity through the covenants of *Torah* and *Christ*.

The Bible is not only a record— *the* record—of the *dialogue* between the divine and human partners, the divine and human I-You relationship. It is also and above all, the testimony of the divine and human *We*, of our mutual life together, of the human We vis-a-vis the divine-human We, of covenant and open-ended *dialectic*. Behold, the Bible is the singular witness to the emergence of the human person in the context of the divine-human relationship. From the first letter to the final period of the Book, every word of the dialogue takes place strictly within the setting and life of the covenant of the We, of being-together in a historical drama of cosmic consequence. And the promised end of the Book, and of the relationship it proclaims, salvation, is nothing less than the consummation and eternalization of our mutuality.

The Bible, consisting of the "Old" and the "New" Testaments, is the living testimony of two marriages, of two concrete and historical covenants between God and humanity. The second builds upon and is inseparable from the first—so that if the latter fails, the former loses its very ground and hope as well. Both unions have three essential elements or dimensions, in accordance with the triplicity of God as such. The first and archetypal marriage between the human and the divine persons, is that between *YHWH* and *Israel*. The dimension of the between, the covenant as such, is called *Torah*. Thus, as is said, "Israel, YHWH and Torah are one." The second and eschatological marriage between God and humanity, is that between *the Father, and Christ*. The dimension of the between, the covenant as such, is called the *Holy Spirit*. Thus, as is said, "The Father and I are one."

The Father is the second and more intimate revelation of YHWH; Christ is the individual and personal revelation of Israel; the Holy Spirit is the revelation of the ground, purpose and life of the Torah. The first covenant revealed the category of the We for all time, as the "extensive" We of a people, created for the sake of and to live ever before its God, YHWH. The second covenant revealed the category of the We in its "intensive" mode, the We between God and the single person, and ultimately, between God and God—that is, the Eternal We of the Trinity.

✠

The category of the We finds its birth in Israel—as does indeed the category of the You and the I. For the revelation of the whole of personal existence is given from the beginning. The revelation of God to Israel created the people Israel as an *extensive We* before the Face. For the first time in world history, God set apart a whole people to be God's own—"You will be my people, and I will be your God." Thus does the revelation include the manifestation and "naming" of God as YHWH, the manifestation and naming of the people as Israel to and for YHWH, and at the same time the manifestation and naming of the relationship as Torah, through which YHWH and Israel abide together in a solemn union. The We of the people exists in and by virtue of the Torah, that is, the human We in and by virtue of the We between God and humanity.

In Jesus of Nazareth, the category of the *intensive We* is revealed in its eternal and therefore eschatological mode. In Him, the Holy We of God is opened and available to us unto the end of the age. In Him, the category of the We reached its consummation, wherein humanity attains its end: unification, "marriage" with God. This is not, however, to the revocation of the Oneness of God, of YHWH, but rather reveals a new kind of unity, namely the oneness of love, the life of Spirit. In the oneness of their love, of their Spirit, God and humanity are both unified and distinct, and loved precisely in their distinctness. Unity and diversity abide in the mystery of the mutuality of God.

The *intensive We* of God and a single representative precedes and underwrites the *extensive We* of God and the people. God chooses to become present to and covenant with the people in and by means of an individual person and relationship thereto. Thus does God choose Abraham, and from him give rise to the whole people. And God's relationship with Abraham becomes the model for the whole and every individual within the whole, as symbolized and sacramentalized by circumcision. The spirit of the intensive We between God and Abraham permeated the people as yeast the dough: the promises given to him became the people's own promises; his stance of persevering faith in the face of the non-fulfillment and even abrogation of those promises, became their own stance.

The pattern continued into the next generation. The intensive We between Issac and God offered assurance to the clan of God's continuing presence and favor. Then came Jacob, who was called Israel. Behold, the individual representing the whole, and his wrestling with God, and refusal to let go until the blessing had finally been received, became—unto this very hour—the identifying model for the people who live under his name. Jacob is yet Israel, is yet wrestling with the Holy One, for the bestowal of that which was promised.

With Moses the intensive We between God and humanity attained the mountain peak of revelation in the Hebrew Bible. The name of God given to Moses became the name for the people, and the law which came through Moses the binding law for all. Israel truly became a people through being granted the Torah, and through vowing to the now named God, YHWH, the solemn words echoing still in the life of Israel: "all that YHWH has spoken we will do" (Exodus 19:8).

Through the intensive We between YHWH and David came forth for the people the identity with Zion, with God's choice of Jerusalem and the temple for a holy center, from which to reveal to the nations that YHWH is God, and Israel the chosen nation of priests. And from David and YHWH came forth the concept of the Messiah, of the one anointed by God to establish God's kingship and reign—not only in Israel, but throughout the peoples of the world. Through the *Messias*, or *Christos*, the promises to Israel and David would be fulfilled; through him, the world would come to know that YHWH is King; through him would come salvation for the peoples and vindication for Israel.

In Jesus of Nazareth, who is the promised Christ to the nations, the intensive We between Israel and YHWH attains in itself the status of revelation and salvation. With Jesus, not only has the medium become the message, but the relational medium of the messenger the message of salvation itself. That is, the revelation is not only the *Who*, but just as much the *Where* of Jesus. He could legitimately announce the presence of the kingdom of God *because He lived in it*, in all its fullness and healing power. His relationship, His We-Spirit with God *is* the kingdom of God, *is* the destiny of the human person.

✠

The intensive We between Jesus and YHWH was too great to remain within Israel, as was indeed the extensive We of believers it spawned. Where those who stood in the name of Israel became but one people, those who found their life within the name of Jesus could not be so historically and culturally contained. The We of the Torah forged a visible people in the world, singular and unique, like their God. The We of the Spirit created a temple of human pillars, present to the world yet unseen by it, like their Lord. And that temple invisible cannot be linked to a single people and land. Rather, it happens where two or more gather in His name, meeting in Spirit and Truth. The We of Torah is of creation, of past and present, held together by a common history and promise. The We of Spirit is of re-creation, of future and the presence of eternity now, held together by a common cup and faith therein.

The We of the "Christ-ians" is founded on an exclusive and intensive We of faith between the follower and Jesus. To be a Christian means to have an individual relationship with Jesus, and, in and through Him, a relationship with His-God-now-my-God, the Father, Abba. One becomes a Christian through confession of faith and baptism, both intrinsically personal events. What the believer has in common with other Christians is the intensive We with Jesus, through the one Spirit of their relationship. Salvation comes through personal relationship with Christ. Indeed, salvation consists of participation in Christ Jesus' own relationship with God; it is having that relationship with God that Christ came to announce and in His own life reveal as present with healing power and actuality.

The We of Israel, however, is founded upon a historical event at Mt. Sinai. The giving of the covenant establishes a whole people as God's people, an entire nation as priests. "You will be my people, and I will be your God." And the covenantal ratification of "All that YHWH says, we will do," forges a common commitment and the ground of a specific peoplehood before God. To be a Jew means to be born into and of the people Israel, it means to belong to a concrete community with a holy history. To be a Jew means to have a relationship with the people, and, in and through them, a relationship with their-God-now-my-God, YHWH, the Lord, the Holy One. By virtue of identity alone, and the existence of the promises and covenants with the preceding generations, the individual already has a place in that fulfillment which is to come. Salvation comes through the people; indeed, it means to participate in the one eternal feast given for the whole. It means to receive what they receive in one long-awaited event.

In the Israel-event, the meaning and destiny of the extensive We of humanity is pronounced and charted out. In the Christ-event, the meaning and destiny of the intensive We of humanity is revealed and the Way opened henceforth. The two convenants are inseparable and complementary. And the promised consummation of both is to come as the same event.

✠

In Israel the category of the We first emerged. Subsequently, and through the dialogical and dialectical processes set in motion by God and the Torah covenant, the category of the individual surfaced with decisive clarity. And at the time of God's choosing, a single individual arose as a light to the nations to reveal, and actually implement— on the Cross—the eternal end point of both categories. As the revelation of the eternal I-You, the Cross is the center of history, the beacon promising and through faith beginning the process of the salvation of the historical individual. But what of the salvation of the historical people? The destiny of the people Israel has not yet been revealed. Their story is still unfolding, *and the whole of history hangs in the balance.* For the consummation of the category of the extensive We of a people, of the covenanted community of Israel, *will mean the salvation of the world.* The history of the We begins and ends with Israel.

✠

The Christ

In the beginning is the Word. That means: in the beginning is the Person of the Word, the logos. Addressed as You and responding as I, the Person is one with the Word. Before the foundations of the world, the Word was uttered, and from the First, a Second Person had been begotten of and in Word. The "eternally begotten" means the "eternally addressed," for from the beginning was the Word. The First Person is apprehended as Person only in and by virtue of the response of the Second Person of address. From the vantage point of the Second Person, the First Person is the eternal You of address.

Between the First and Second Persons are the Word and the Spirit of the Word. For Word and Spirit are one. The Spirit is the speaking and that which is present yet not spoken in the Word—and that includes the Persons of the Word as well. For Persons live in Spirit. The Spirit is thus the relationship of Word as such, and represents the Third Person of the life of God, the eternally shared Person, the We, the unending I-You. The Spirit is the "Us" of God, as it were. And the Second Person, begotten of the Word, lives wholly in the Word and is one with the Word and the Spirit of the Word. The First Person, the primal Speaker of the Word, has come to stand in that Word, yet is ever beyond Word in unfathomable mystery. Hence an eternal distinction emerges between the I of the First and the Second Persons: The I of the First is prior and the Second subsequent to the Word. The First conditions and the Second is conditioned by the Word.

The I of God the Speaker is both disclosed and hidden in divine address and speech. Yet in the address which begets person, the I is in a real though derived way "transferred" through and "translated" into the Word itself, so that a "residue" or "echo" of the I of the original Speaker abides in both the hearing and in the responding. It is the I which hears the Word of creative address, and the I of the Word which responds to the Speaker in and through the self-same Word. It is the I which is the end point and agent of the Word, the intended One, who as a part of that original intention of the Addresser is to address back, to live in that Word between the Persons, and to grace the Speaker in the Speech. The I of the addressed and begotten One retains, then, something of the "substance" of the I of the Speaker, so that they are, in the Word, truly like one another. And behold, in the Spirit of their mutual Word, in the communicative arc between them, they are of one substance. Or else communication and communion could never attain true mutuality and consummation.

Note carefully that the whole of creation, from the Second Person of the Trinity to the cosmos, all stem from the Word issued, and exist in the movement of response. God as Creator, as Eternal You, can be apprehended only from the point of view of the "other side of the Word," as it were. That is, it is the movement of the logos back to God which generates consciousness itself. So that all awareness of the self and others, including that of the Eternal You of our life, is "post-pole," happens subsequent to and precisely along with the God-intended orbit of the Word back to its Author. In short, we come into consciousness already standing and interfacing with the God of our existence, all this by virtue of the impact and work of the Word of address. An unbridgeable gap exists therefore between the Original Speaker and all that has come to be in and by virtue of the Word. Yet, through the Spirit of the Word—and only through the Spirit—a substantial mutuality persists in the Trinity; and, through Christ, is offered now to the human person.

✠

Echoing still within the I as its Word-center of creation: "Be You . . . You are." This Word cannot rest within the person as a passive kind of knowledge; rather, it ceaselessly summons us to consciousness and action, to respond both to it and to the One who has so addressed us. The address at the base of our being has a pulsating incompleteness, as if it posed our existence as a question we must somehow answer. And the answer begins with the one response seemingly given by and intrinsic to the addressing Word living in us: "I am." How comes the person to make the extraordinary extrapolation from the second person to the first person singular? What is present but not spoken in the Word that could warrant and motivate such a category-creating transition? Behold the wonder of God's own creation: from the Word the I is ever summoned forth.

"I am" is said with the life and being of the person. And this answer to the riddle of the sense of a prior address becomes itself a greater and more vexing question. For it is uttered not only to others of our kind and kin, but to the universe which seems neither to care about nor be responsive to such a personal existence. The cosmos is simply not Person; it either does not hear or has no way of responding to our assertion of being. Did it then address us into being? Wherefrom came the Word, and wherefore? The "I am" of personal existence seeks confirmation, longs to meet and be heard by the sensed Addresser, and in being heard, to be brought into endless relationship, that is, to be saved.

Comes the revelatory Word of response from above: "I Am." The revelation of the personal existence of God amplifies, affirms and offers final confirmation to the meaning of being a person. The ultimate ground of person is revealed in the highest moment of divine self-disclosure. The I of God is the ever-mysterious, never to be imaged basis and guarantor of the human I. The human I is created in the divine "image," that is, as an I in response to the creative Word of address from the I of God. Thus is the I of humanity vouchsafed for all time. It is as if God said in our creation: "Because I Am, You are and shall be as well. You shall be a person to Me because I Am a Person to You. Apart from Me, You have no I. Your I exists in and by virtue of My I addressing You into being. You cannot transcend personhood or the moment of Your address. You are inexorably locked into and located in the moment and mode of My address, of My Word to You, in You, and of You. My will is in that Word; Your deepest will is to carry out My intention of You."

But what is God's true intention of us? How are we to bring to conscious clarity this I that is planted within us, this Person we are to become? The revelation remains incomplete, and the "law" of our being-together does not have the grace to bring us life. The Spirit is needed, and the concrete model and Way necessary. In brief, revelation without incarnation cannot save and direct.

"And the Word became Flesh and dwelt among us." Behold, God spoke a second Word, attesting to a second creation, one bringing the first to completion. God spoke the Eternal I of the Word, the second Person, to us and in us. The first Word was consistent with the First Person, the Eternal You, the second with the Second Person, the Eternal I. The first Word gave us the image of God as You, the second the likeness of God as I. Where the first Word of creation addressed us from the outside in with the Person granting "Be You . . . You are," the second Word addresses us from the inside out with the Person confirming "I Am . . . in You."

The Christ is the incarnation and revelation of the second Word, the divine Word-Person, the I eternally addressed by the You of all life. And the Word brings to pass that which It announces; hence, the Christ came to proclaim and reveal the presence of the "I Am" within and among us. Christ's message and Person are one and the same. The Kingdom of God is the life of God, the Eternal I-You. Christ came to confirm the eternality of the I over against and with the God already known as YHWH, as the Eternal You. And further, Christ came to offer us participation in the life of God through and in Christ's own I: "I Am the Vine, you are the branches. Abide in Me, and I will abide in You. Apart from Me, You can do nothing. Eat and drink Me; ingest Me into yourself. I Am Your eternal life."

✠

The Christ is the same, yesterday, today and tomorrow. Both male and female, this One is the I ever addressed by God, and ever responding. And in the responding, Christ is ever addressing God. Absolute communion, "co-union," exists in the eternal reciprocity of the speech-movement of Spirit. The word "Christ" means anointed, and that is precisely who Christ is: the I under the anointing of the Word of address and the Holy Spirit of love. Behold, the end of *anthropos* is *christos;* Christ is humanity under the baptismal impact of the Spirit-drenched Word of love. Thus Christ represents the apotheosis of the human person into the Holy We of God. Christ is the personal position we are to occupy in our eternal stance with God. "In My Father's house are many rooms. I go there to prepare a place for You. And I will come back and take You with Me, that where I Am, You may be also" (John 14:2,3).

Jesus of Nazareth arose as the Christ in God's time through the anointing of the Word and the Spirit, the Word of address as "Son," and the accompanying Spirit of love, peace and power. Henceforth ever to be identified with the Christ, Jesus is in truth the author and perfecter of our eternal relationship with God. Jesus revealed and brought to actualization on the plain of history, the ultimate I of the human person, the I we shall become with the You of God through the Spirit-We of our life together. For the Christ is the ground of our being, the internal being-agent we call the self. The Christ is the "law of the heart," the Torah of God, planted within as the basis of our being—of our being-together with God.

Jesus Christ came to reveal the eternal relationship, which *is* the Kingdom of Heaven. And in the Person of Christ, we shall become one as individuals and as a people. Christ is indeed "the Way, the Truth and the Life." Apart from the Eternal I-You, there is no salvation. For salvation means life with God, the life of Spirit, the Eternal We.

Through Christ we are addressed anew by God. God's eternal address to Christ is incarnated by Christ and repeated to us. This address of the You of God through the You of Christ is the "Good News" of the presence of salvation in the Person of the Messenger. To be so addressed means to be "elected" or "chosen." For God's address in Christ *is* eternal life. Christ Jesus calls us as individual persons to enter into relationship with Him and the One who sent Him. And behold, in the call of Christ, the address of God is heard as well; in the I of Christ the You of God is transparent. For Christ is not only perfectly addressed by God, but He responds with the same perfection. And in the response, Christ perfectly mirrors to God—and to us—the You of the first address. Thus is Christ the true image of the invisible God; thus do the "Father" and the "Son" speak with one voice, and share one Spirit. "To have seen Me is to have seen the Father."

Not only are we addressed by God in Jesus Christ, we are also summoned to respond in His Name and likeness. Called, we are to call; reconciled, we are to reconcile; receiving, we are to give. Few are willing to hear God's address; fewer still, upon hearing, to respond. And to be as Christ means both to hear and respond as Christ. Christ is as Christ does.

In Jesus Christ all three Word-events of God are present and summed up. The Word of creation: "You are my beloved Son." The Word of revelation: "I Am He." The Word of redemption, begun only in Jesus' priestly prayer, for this cannot be voiced, but may only be intimated in the holy and mutual atmosphere of prayer, of intimate divine-human address: "We are one" (John 17:11,22). For in Jesus' life and ministry the unutterable has broken through into history; that which cannot yet be said with the fullness it represents has emerged as present with power, though not with visibility and finality: the Kingdom of Heaven is at hand.

The "Christ-event," then, is the center of history. As the essential revelation of the ultimate nature and destiny of the human person, of the I with the You of God in Their Holy We, the event of Christ sets the proper context of meaning for the whole sweep of history. The "Alpha and Omega," the beginning and end, gives meaning to the on-the-wayness of the now, of the *saeculum*. From the revelation, the fact and hidden purpose of creation is finally made known and in that One already actualized. From this revelation, the meaning and end of the history of the human person, of the I, is brought into the sphere of world history. And through the presence of the Spirit, that future is now; now may it be sealed in the heart and the heart in it. In the beginning is the You; in the middle is the I; in the end is the We.

Christ thus represents the Mediator between God and humanity. Christ participates fully in the We of God and in the We of humanity. From the human side, Christ constitutes the end point of the human I. From the divine side, Christ restores the image and likeness of God, by perfectly mirroring the You of God to and for us—as well as to and for the Father. Christ is at once for us and for God.

✠

The You of God and the me of history: The You of creation, of divine address, is the ground and living foundation of the human I of history and personal consciousness. We have all been addressed by God—as our actual creation as persons—and therefore we both know God and exist by virtue of the Word-relationship to God. The You-Word initiates the I, the inbreaking the outreaching. The divine image of the You is the source and implanted center of the I. Beneath the emerging I of personal consciousness, however isolated and lonely it may come to feel, is the You of divine-human relationship. And hidden within the primal You-Word is the knowledge of God and the intention of God in the very utterance of the person. And that intention is both common to the species and unique to that named person. It is, as it were, the RNA and DNA of the soul.

Jesus Christ incarnates, reveals and for all time represents the true You we are called to become in our creation. Not only that, Christ also manifests the second Word, begun in the first, namely, the perfect response to the Word of creation, to the Word of address: the "I Am" of revelation. Jesus Christ represents the true You and ultimate I of the human person, within the eternal context of the We of God.

Yet the You I am addressed as being in creation is not the same as the me of my personal knowledge and history. For who can bring to conscious remembrance the personal call of creation? The You I am to God is almost as great a mystery as the You God is to me. And the me I know myself to be is only a temporal being of this world, born and destined to die here. How then is one to hear and integrate the You of God into the me of humanity? I cannot even absorb into myself the

You that I am to others, nor can others see and experience the me that I understand myself to be.

Further, I cannot see the I that I am, but only the I of another coming to me as the You of meeting. What I may apprehend is only myself-as-object, not myself-as-subject. That is, the me I know is only the I as object in the world, as person to myself and others. Yet the true I is the one who says: "I am who I am." The true I is the knower not the knowing, the observer not the observed, the subject not the object. The true I lives ever with the true You over against it. For the You is the only image of the I. Knowledge of the I is mediated through the direct encounter with the You, and is apprehended as being shared, as being both unique and mutual, both exclusive and inclusive. Whereas the I cannot be separated from the You of meeting and mutuality, the me cannot be other than an isolated object belonging in and to the world.

The distance—and therefore tension—between the You of creation and the me of the human world-spirit is that of the "Fall" itself. The Fall is the loss of the You and the knowledge of the I in its relationship with the You—hence the loss of the We. And the You of creation is the only foundation for the authentic human I. For the I exists as I only in and by virtue of the We, of the primal I-You relationship. Hence, until the me is at one with the You of creative address, the human person will know neither self nor fullness.

What then of this distance between the I that I am in the truth of creation, and the me of personal knowledge and history in the world? Wherein is the unity of the mysterious agent I am and am becoming, and the me that I know and have found as inner object and center? Behold, Jesus Christ is the bridge between the I and the me, between the self-as-subject and the self-as-object. For He represents the vision of the invisible, who reveals to us our hidden depths, and our hidden life—past, present and future—with Him in God. Christ is not only the image of the imageless God, but of the imageless I as well. In Christ, the You of God and the I of humanity find their reconciliation and unity—as does, conversely, the You of humanity and the I of God.

In Christ Jesus, the You of creation and the I of divine intention are one and the same. The within is perfectly at one with the without. In Him, the me of history is brought back and restored into the I of destiny, all through the ground of the holy We. Until we come to know the way in which God sees and addresses us, we will not know who we are. Christ restored the You of divine address by His perfect receptivity to God's call; He restored the unity of the You to the I of divine intention by His perfect response to God, by carrying out God's will in absolute purity of heart. And He restored the human participation in the We of God by His perfect faithfulness and obedience, even unto death, death on a cross.

Christ, in short, is my true me.

✠

What then is the "Good News" of Jesus Christ? What meaning does the Kingdom of God have for us, which Jesus so wholly and consistently proclaimed as arriving in His ministry? The answer is Jesus' own relationship with God. He dawned in the Kingdom as the Kingdom dawned in Him, the Kingdom which signifies the time of God's active reign in God's own "personal space" of being. He announced where He was and what He lived: Jesus is the first human to break through the veil and enter into the inner sanctum of the Holy of holies, the Eternal I-You relationship. The revelation *is* the relationship, and *who* Jesus is in that relationship. For who He is, we shall be as well; His God will be our God, His life our life. Christ is our life in and with God, our destiny, opening to and embracing us, so we can open to and embrace it. The Persons of God in the Relationship of God—that is the revelation in Christ, that is the Kingdom of Heaven.

✠

The Divinity of Jesus

Is Jesus Christ "God"? Are there then two—or even three—"powers" or Gods? If Christ is the Eternal I to the Eternal You of God, all within their Eternal We, is Christ therefore "fully God"? Yes and No. We enter paradox once again—which will always be the case when we seek to objectify God. Christ lives wholly in the relationship with God; and God is relationship as well as Person. Therefore, in and by virtue of the relationship, Christ is fully God. Yet Christ is also "fully human." Born of woman, Jesus was "adopted" by the Spirit into the realm of God. In that realm, God as You is ever sovereign. God is greater than Christ, and is forever over against Christ. Bridged only by the Word of address and the Spirit of love, a chasm forever separates not only all creation from the Creator, but even Christ from the One who eternally addresses.

Christ is the End, the destiny of humanity as such. *We will become precisely as Christ.* Who that One is, we also shall become. For, as Scripture teaches, we will all "becomes as gods." We will enter into the life of God, into the We of God, in the second Person of the Trinity, the I of the Word. But the Word cannot be equated with the Original Speaker, any more than the potter can be identified with the pot. *Christ cannot simply be termed the "same substance" (homoousia) as the Eternal You, but as the Eternal I is of "like substance" (homoiousia), derived from the Word, in which all creation and all persons have their life.* That is, *the "being" of Christ* is a *"being with,"* begotten wholly from the Word uttered by the Eternal You. Whereas *the "being" of God* is *"being itself."* God alone has and is being itself. All other existence is derived from and absolutely dependent upon God, in accordance with divine intention and speech.

Yet, paradoxically *in being with God,* in Their relationship of Spirit, in Their We, *Christ is of one substance with God.* The oneness is that of mutuality, not of internality or externality. Though derived of Word, in and through their love, Christ is One with God. "The Father and I are one."

✠

What of the "pre-existent logos," that is, the Word before Its utterance in and as creation? It is impossible to conceive of the logos apart from the means offered by the logos. In what "form" did Christ exist prior to creation? That cannot be answered any more than the question about the pre-natal whereabouts of a neonate. Whether Christ existed only in the "mind of God," like an idea awaiting expression and actualization, or in the form revealed in the resurrection, will not be known in this life. Let it only be said that it is difficult if not impossible to conceive how God as Eternal You could ever have been without a Person with whom to live in love. And further, as the sages warn us: it is forbidden to discuss what is "before and after, above and below" the Word.

✠

The Cross

The Christ-event is the center of history. And at the heart of the event, as the holiest moment in the human—and divine-human—story, towers the Cross. Before our story is over, each of us must in some way stand at the foot of the Cross. Each must see who God is, and who we are in God, at this most precious and never-to-be-repeated event of the great Self-giving, the ultimate Love-moment. Come therefore and see the breaking of the Beloved, when the Mystery hidden before and after was poured forth as the water and blood of our salvation! Come to the mercy trough, bathe and drink in God! Encounter directly the treasure revealed in the sacrificial rending asunder of the earthen vessel of Christ's visitation among us. "Truly, this is the son of God."

Why is the Cross the holiest moment of history? Behold, it is the actual *wedding ceremony* of the long-sought marriage between heaven and earth, God and humanity. It is the *binding enactment of the covenant of pure, mutual and total self-giving love, God to humanity and humanity to God,* both through the one man, Jesus. Jesus, our undeserved proxy for all time, what You wrought for us in your final excruciating moments among us! You were and are a joint gift from above and from below, in one and the same Person. In your ultimate sacrifice, in your being lifted up and poured out, You draw all of us unto yourself, there to meet God—and ourselves. And all in the context of the covenant between us You are, the new covenant of and in your blood.

The Cross reveals as no other event ever shall, the deepest truth of the nature of the human and the divine persons. That truth, which lives as need at the base of our being, is to give ourselves entire for love. The Cross is thus the very moment at which for all time and eternity, humanity gave itself to God and God to humanity. All for love, and in love—therefore for and in God, who is Love. Jesus, the "God-

Man," represented both the human and divine persons in one. From the human side, and in direct substitution for each of us, Jesus completes with perfection the offering of His life for the sake of the restoration and consummation of our relationship, our "We" with God. This self-giving, this absolute self-abandonment reveals the full potential of human love, love reaching unto God, love carried over into divine love, love becoming at one with the Love with which we are loved.

All of us share in His Cross, all accompany Him to Golgotha. Jesus died for all of us, as our very We before God. The eternal Adam is brought forth and dies to the world that He might live to God; He dies that through Him all might live as He lives.

✠

Like Abraham, Jesus believed in God even unto the apparent abrogation of His mission through the sacrifice of His life, precisely at the point when He was to have been crowned from above as YHWH's Messiah. Instead of a crown, a crucifixion. Instead of a feast, an offering, pure and unblemished. Jesus offered all in anguished faith, and God took all in silent love—as the earth mourned. The love offering, begun with Abraham and Isaac, was now to be completed. Isaac was spared when the faith of Abraham was born out. Point proven, command withdrawn, peace granted. Yet, even though His Father was God, Jesus was not spared. For His faith had to be born out unto death. Only by dying could God birth Him anew, as the reward beyond all rewards this earth can bestow. A man had to prove out all the way, to give all in faith, in order to receive all in love. "Father, into Your hands, I commend my spirit."

From the divine side, Jesus at the Cross manifests the love and very nature of God. Behold, God *is* self-giving love, merciful and long-suffering. And in Jesus' self-giving as a man, God's own self-giving is perfectly incarnated and poured forth for all time, and with the absolute clarity of His own blood. In Christ's Person, His solitary and seemingly forsaken I upon the Cross—forsaken by God and man—, God's Person is given for and to us. Note that blood *and* water came from Christ's wounded side, signifying both His life and God's, both lives offered to us in one, life in God and with God, the I of the blood and the We of the Spirit.

The ultimate prophet speaks the final Word of God to and in history, with His own life. And the one Word of the Cross is at once a Word of judgment against sin—look what it has cost God!—and of forgiveness and reconciliation to sinners—look what God is offering us! The countless cost of the death of His Son, is transformed into the pearl beyond price of eternal life. Who but God could work such a reversal? Who but God could turn the worst fate for a man into the greatest destiny for humanity? The worst rejection into the ultimate redemption?

The Cross represents the precise moment at which human and divine history merge. The Cross is therefore the meaning and fact of God's history among us. And it is a history of covenant-love offerings and rejection, of not being seen or understood, of thirst for us in the face of our non-response, of continuing forgiveness for our cruelty and barbarity to ourselves and to God. In the Cross the Word of God breaks through our insensitivity and blindness, our deafness and egoism. The Word hovers about us, echoing still; and from that height, It continues unto this very moment to address us, awaiting the opening of our minds and hearts, our eyes and ears, that we might finally turn and live.

"Father forgive them, for they know not what they do." The Word is that of forgiveness, and the sacrifice of love is for the sake of bringing that Word to the human heart with the power of God's own Spirit. Truly, no Word speaks with the power of the Cross, for both God and humanity are in this Word of self-giving love. It is their ultimate joint statement to history, as it were. It is their final Word of forgiveness and invitation to an awakening and to true life with them. Their next Word will transform history into the redemption—and the judgment. Listen now, therefore, while there is still time and history to be lived!

✠

The Cross also symbolizes the sum total of all the refusals of a humanity inexplicably deaf to the Word of God's love and offer of life. And Its non-rejecting presence in the heart must be encountered before forgiveness and redemption can become real and their glory seen. In truth, the pain of the Cross bears death, death to sin and the sinful self, to the one who could say naught but No to God, this self mortally wounded by and inescapably acting out of the ongoing apostasy and self-serving of the world. Yet the pain of the Cross also bears redemption and rebirth, a new life in the very blood of the One who gave His being so that we could hear the Word in its truth, as that of eternal love.

✠

The Cross bespeaks for all time the fact of the eternal divine-human We. It is the breaking open of that relationship for all to see, the manifestation of the love of God in the context of human opposition and rejection. In this respect, the Cross is both oppositional and appositional to the life of humanity. It speaks a divine *No* and *Yes,* a No to sin and rejection, and a Yes to love and forgiveness. The Cross is therefore also the judgment of God brought about by human hands, the revelation of our state of sin and spiritual deadness in the light of God's love and self-offering. Yet the Cross is at the same time appositional to the human condition it reveals. For it is the Word of reconciliation and forgiveness, of understanding and healing. It offers in Itself the corrective to our fallenness, the healing in His name and blood, the healing of His walk and Word, His very Person.

How God prepares for our opposition! The Cross reveals that God is after all God, and that therefore nothing can defeat the divine Word of love and salvation, no human response—or lack thereof—can annul God's decision to be gracious to those to whom God would be gracious. Hence, the poison we gave comes back to us as God's healing potion, the blood we shed is revealed as our very life, the life we took is given back as God's life for us. God cannot be thwarted; the Word that is uttered will not return to God empty. The greater the magnitude of our resistance to God, the greater the force of the revelation. The more that sin ensues, the greater that grace pursues. The Cross reveals, then, that absolute failure has led to absolute success; out of total defeat, God has pulled total victory. In everything, God works for good. And Jesus Christ is our good. And the Cross is His chalice, offered to us. Who will drink?

✠

The Cross signifies the actual holy moment that the human I gave itself to the divine You, a giving without any preconditions and even in utter defeat and in the seeming abandonment of the Holy You. "Even if You have forsaken Me, I nevertheless yield Myself into Your hands—and only Your hands." History stops, and the eternal covenant is sealed and revealed. The end of the human I is the divine You. And it is in self-giving to the You that the I fully regains what was lost of openness and obedience. Only in the Cross is membership in the eternal relationship restored—and for all of us.

The subsequent *Resurrection* represents the revelation of the actual and concrete reestablishment of the eternal I-You, the Holy We. And *Pentecost* signifies the beginning of the restoration of the human I—and We—and the entrance of the Holy Spirit, God's We, into human history. Through that outpouring, the intensive We begins the baptism of the extensive We of humanity. The church was born as the symbol and concrete vessel in the world of the Holy We, of the life of God.

Behold, from the Cross to Pentecost is one continuous outpouring of the Spirit, of the life of God. The vessel is broken and the fountain gushes forth. Only who will accept Jesus' baptism? Who will come forward to the Cross, to be washed with the blood and water of the life of God?

✠

Holy and Healing Community

From whence comes our healing? From the one Source of love. And the Cross of Christ provides the symbol of and way to reconciliation and new life, to the restoration and consummation of the We. For the Cross represents the climax of both our rejection of the We relationship with God—and indeed, of the accumulated crucifixions of love itself by our own hands—and God's holy offer of forgiveness and redemption. The Cross of Christ: the depth of brokenness and the height of healing in one historical event and symbol thereof.

The way to the healing of the We relationships in our life is first through the healing of our relationship with God, the vertical dimension of the Cross, representing our holiness. This in turn and in time opens up the way for forgiveness and reconciliation with other persons and relationships, past, present and future. The latter is the horizontal dimension, representing our wholeness. Both dimensions are required for the healing and wholeness of the life of the We. But note that the way to wholeness is through holiness, not holiness through wholeness. It is the Holy Spirit of our life with God, which constitutes the ground and home of all our We-spirits with one another.

And at the nexus of the Cross of healing? The holy community of divine-human covenant, the body of Christ. The heart of the healing and wholeness offered to us by the Cross—and by the Person on the Cross—is the establishment of the community of those seeking and redeemed by the Love brought home by the sacrifice itself. Apart from the community of faith, neither healing nor wholeness can be realized in individual life. The holy community offers us a visible and supportive connection between our relationship with God and with other persons in our life in the world. Healing is a rebirth of mutuality, made possible and symbolized by our communion with God.

The We of holy community is created by the Spirit of holy communion with God. It is *holy* because it is "set apart" by God and for God, as God's own community. It thus actually anticipates and presages the ultimate community of redemption to exist between God and humanity in the world to come. The Cross is the true symbol of this community in the world, for it represents the union between God and humanity—a union revealed and sealed in an actual event in the world, the holiest event in the history of the world. As the sign of ultimate self-giving and commitment, the Cross is also the pictorial representation of the ultimate We of divine and human mutuality. Revealed in dramatic defeat, this We will one day conquer the world.

Where two or more have gathered to invite and celebrate the presence of God in their midst, there is the Cross formed and actual. That is, the group gathers at the precise nexus between the vertical and the horizontal beams of divine and human relationships. They make their camp there, as it were; they together risk God and each other. *In being open to the holy together, they become holy and wholly together.* The desire for God has power greater than that of the universe to bind us fast together. Nothing can separate us from the unity of the longing for and the love of God.

The holy community therefore is that body of persons mutually committed to live in God. It is that community of persons committed to being open daily to God, and in God being open to each other. Each person's relationship with every other person in the community is based upon and rooted in the I-You relationship of that person with God.

✠

You and I meet in the context of the You and I of God; our We is grounded firmly and covenantally in the We of our respective lives with God. The Spirit between God and I—as between God and You—moves also between Us, not only in our one-on-one but between us as a whole community. In our shared will for God and for living together in God, the Holy Spirit permeates and cherishes us, cleanses and heals us, guides and provides for us. Through our will and God's grace, the vertical life of God is wedded with the horizontal life of humanity. The depth of the life of God, and of the faith life of the individual with God is invited to abide in the total life of the body of believers. Thus is God all in all in the community. The breadth of our communion takes its stand in the depth, as together we abide ever before the Face of the height of God. The sacred blood of the life of God has mingled with and seeks to become wholly merged with the blood of the life of humanity. And as we let that sacred blood wholly disperse through the blood of our common life, we attain as gift the holiness of the Holy One in our midst.

In holy community, it becomes especially clear that the human I-You relationship of the intensive We is the exact image of the divine I-You relationship, the eternal We. Here we see that being made in the image of God means not only as individuals in our being an I, not only as being a You to God and to each other, but also as participating fully in the We of mutuality and communion, one with another. And as we are open to God in our relationship, the I-You of God can pervade and nourish and underwrite Us. God's verticalness, together with our own respective vertical one-on-one with God, become the sanctifying and protective foundation for Us—and for all other I-You relationships.

Holy community then is a network of I-You relationships with God and with one another in God—the vertical dimension— brought into living connection with each other by God and human commitment, for the mutual support and celebration of those relationships—the horizontal dimension.

✠

The Body of Christ bespeaks the unity of individual persons in the Spirit of Jesus Christ. The "Body" refers to a "mystical" organism, the second Person of the Trinity as an actual concrete presence in the world. Christ's is a corporate Body, an inter-human configuration of divine origin and destiny, in an ongoing participation in the life of God. The Body of Christ signifies those persons who share in the Spirit, and through the Spirit, in the psyche and soma, the soul and body of Christ. The Spirit brings to maturity the planting of God; It transforms the soul and ultimately will transform the body, individual and corporate, into the soul and body of Christ. For "Christ" means "anointed"; and humanity becomes Christ under the anointing of the Holy Spirit. This is the inner meaning of Communion: becoming as Christ. And Communion must be preceded by baptism, by the initial anointing of the Spirit.

Where the Body comes together, where two or more gather in Christ's name, all the gifts and fruits of the Spirit are in evidence. They are present in individual souls, but given life by the Spirit between the members, by the life of Christ in their midst. The Spirit grants power and motivation for the utilization of the gifts and graces accorded to Christ by God. When this Body, this We is constituted and consecrated in the name of Christ, it *is* the presence of Christ in the world. And it shall offer the only concrete presence until Christ's return. And when the community is together, the power of Christ is sufficient to carry out the work of conversion, reconciliation and healing. How the enemy therefore seeks to divide and disunify the Body, so that it cannot carry out its God-given mission! Where there is no unity, there is no power, and the message of love is contradicted by the messengers. The Kingdom seems unreal.

Such is the state of the Body today. And the unreal world laughs at the unreal church, as if to say that, as the church goes, so goes the Kingdom. Yet the Kingdom will arrive, and with unmistakable decisiveness, even if the church is not prepared to greet it.

The Blood

"The life is in the blood" (Leviticus 17:11). The blood is the common, and sustains the members, requiring the integrity of the whole to maintain itself. The blood cleanses and nourishes, nurtures and protects, heals and strengthens the parts. The life is in the blood: that means the true locus of life is not in the individual segments, but in their commonality and life together. The Biblical center of attention is on the common, the covenant, the shared basis of individual life, not on the individual as such. The attention to the individual is given only vis-a-vis responsibility and participation in covenantal life. The common does not, however, undercut the reality of the individual parts, but rather constitutes their life-ground.

The life is in the blood. That means: the life of the whole is shared by each and every member. For what segment of the body can exist without the blood and all that it provides? The physical body demonstrates the importance of blood, in that when there is thirst and dehydration, the last fluid to be affected is the blood. Hence, individual cells will dry up and perish before the blood becomes mortally affected. For with the blood goes the life; the life of the blood must therefore be protected at all costs. Cells can be rebuilt, or the organism can learn to function without them; blood cannot be lived without. It carries the life of the whole within itself.

Biblically, the blood came to symbolize covenants that were "cut" between God and humanity, as indeed between humans. The sacrifice of an animal and the spilling of its blood represented, first, the seriousness of the oaths being taken, and what the gods were henceforth authorized to do to one or more of the partners, should they break the covenantal vows. "May I be as this animal if I do not remain faithful to our binding covenant." The blood ratified and implemented the covenant and the conditions specified and promised therein. Frequently a feast would follow, with the sacrificed animal often being the main course.

Second and more importantly, the blood also symbolized the "new life" which the covenant brought into existence, the new state of commonness determined and defined by the covenant. Hence, the blood of the covenant signified the very life which its ratification brought into being, the actual unity and mutuality it granted. The blood *is* the life of the covenant, which all the members share, and which must be protected at all costs. And like the blood of the body, the integrity and intactness of the body is necessary if the blood is to maintain its life, and the life of the individual parts. A breach in the body can lead to the spilling and defilement of the blood. And ultimately, it can eventuate in the nullification of the covenant itself.

Exodus 24 presents the covenant ratification ceremony between YHWH and Israel. After the people verbally commit themselves to YHWH, with the binding promise that "All the words which the Lord has spoken we will do" (vs. 3; cf. vs. 7), blood from sacrificed oxen is poured over *both* the altar and the people. The blood symbolizes their new and common life together, the uniting of God and humanity in a covenantal relationship. The life is in the blood; the blood represents their marriage spirit, as it were. Note carefully that the blood is poured over both the people and God, *binding both by mutual consent.*

Behold, God in sovereign freedom becomes solemnly committed to a common life with Israel. Both parties are now to live together in the fullness of their marriage-covenant. God is no longer merely God, but YHWH to the people; a disparate band of ex-slaves is now a strangely corporate being called Israel, existing before and with YHWH. The covenantal relationship sealed in blood, is called the Torah. And the blood actually represents the "life-spirit" shared by the parties, their mutuality as such, which cannot be reduced to either party's responsibility or subjectivity. The members exist in and by virtue of the life of the whole.

✠

The blood also came to represent and be used as the atonement for sin, for the breach of the covenant. Within the covenant itself, YHWH made allowances for human transgression, and mitigated the harsh call for the blood of the sinner by accepting the blood of a ritually pure and unblemished animal *substitute*. The sacrifice serves as a propitiation or peace offering to God, and as an expiation or making amends of the sinner. Through the divinely offered cultic statutes, it is as if YHWH said to Israel, "Better this animal should die and its blood be given up to Me, than your blood—and therein the blood of the covenant. The blood of the covenant must not be defiled, for My blood is mingled with it. And I want you to live for another day, that we may yet reason together, and find the way to reconciliation and communion."

Yet this kind of sacrificial cultus could only atone for specific *sins*, not for the general orientation *to sin*, as definitively discerned by the Hebrew prophets. Something greater than an animal sacrifice was necessary in order to bring to pass the prophetic promise that Israel would "will with its God," would have YHWH's "Spirit" within them, making them thereby both desire and succeed at walking in, the divinely ordained Way of the Torah. "New blood" was needed; a "spiritual transfusion" had to be performed by God, the great Physician, so that a blood would be given which could bring about a once-for-all at-onement, which could re-establish the divine-human We for all time, and beyond time.

Enter the New Testament, or the "New Covenant" in the blood of Jesus Christ. In Him, the whole of the sacrificial cultus is consummated and transcended. In Him is the blood for an eternal atonement offered, and indeed brought to pass. His blood is offered to God—by God—for our blood, as our ultimate and once-for-all sin offering. God imputes to Christ all our sins, and spills His blood as the direct substitution for our blood. Hence, in His blood is both our judgment and forgiveness.

Not only forgiveness, but Christ's blood is also the symbol of the very life of God, our redemption and new covenant, our salvation offered precisely in the holy blood shed for our sins. O the wondrous enconomy of God! How a single event can pronounce judgment, forgiveness and salvation! Christ's blood represents above all the divine life to be given and received, as a holy cup to be shared between us and God, as well as between us as disciples. Only this time instead of being poured over the participants, the human partners are to ingest the blood, as well as the body given for their sakes. "This is My body; this is My blood....My body is real food; My blood is real drink." Where the water of the Spirit baptizes the believer, the blood and the body of Christ become the very life and substance of the person. Christ's *psyche* or soul is to become our soul, His I our I. The blood of Christ atones, that is, makes us at-one-with God; it brings us into the eternal relationship with God that Christ came to offer us. For Christ's psyche, Christ's "soul-life" is our destiny; Christ's Person is the Person of our ultimate end and destiny (*telos* and *teleios*).

✠

Thus, and as an absolute paradox, the blood of Christ is offered to us as the "concrete universal," the "corporate individuality," the common home or eternal dwelling place of the individual human I. Hence, for instance, Hal Green truly becomes the Hal Green of destiny only in and by virtue of the blood of Christ, of Christ's own eternal soul-life. I have found my true and ultimate person in Jesus Christ, my Lord. In His common blood my uniqueness finds its basis and guarantee, its cleansing, nourishment and protection. In Him the profoundly personal and private life of my soul is wedded with that of God, with the You of my life. In His blood, God and I are one.

✠

Symbols of Corporateness

Sacraments of the We

Our God is a God who covenants. A divine-human *meeting* eventuates in a new *mutuality* in the world. Revelation is not only of God, but also of humanity, and of a *relationship* of the human with the divine Person. That is, revelation manifests the henceforth existence of a new *We* between heaven and earth. For revelation, like the Word itself, brings into reality that which it uncovers. And subsequent to the actual encounter, yet authorized and consistent with the "logic" or logos/ Word of the revelation, comes a binding commitment to that which was received. Subsequent to meeting comes "religion," comes the being "bound back" into the mutuality now presented as the basis of our life in the world. And in truth, that which is "received" in the meeting is more than a mere Presence—as if we have nothing to say to each other, and nothing in common but our unbridgeable differences!—, but as mutual Spirit between the divine and human persons, represents a new life together. What is received is a whole new way of being, of being-together, a "Something More" not only within the person, but between that person and God, in which they have mutually taken their stand. Call it their eternal "co-incid-ence."

As Spirit, the relationship is yet to be voiced, but is creative of word. For Word and Spirit are one. That is to say, *all three dimensions of meaning are present and active in the sphere between the divine and human persons.* A divine *intention* stands directly behind the meeting itself—or it simply would never have happened. An unforgettable though non-verbalizable *connotation* or "co-notation" of the actual mutuality in all its specificity abides in the heart and in memory. Further, a life-changing *denotation* was present, clear and distinct as the address of God, inseparable from the persons themselves. The persons—divine and human—are denoted in their relationship of revelation. They are themselves the *objectum* of the meeting.

Any other possible "information" which may seem in retrospect to have been passed directly between the partners during the revelation itself, arises from deep within the human person, still in the grip of the Spirit of the meeting. Such content, be it law or decree, promise or plea, may be "God-breathed," but it is nonetheless of human substance. It attests to a relationship in which the human is not a passive vessel but an active participant, shaping as well as being shaped by the reciprocity. Any word or statement is historically conditioned and directed, and addresses one *Zeitgeist,* one "time-spirit," from another, namely the Spirit of divine-human mutuality. The address is unavoidably bound into the language and mentality of the time—or meaningful communication would be impossible.

Though conditioned and historically contextualized, the Word is nevertheless of God; hence, it is also transcendent and restless within the limitations imposed by time-bound humanity. The eternal struggles within the message and the bearer thereof to shape and not be shaped, to express itself with purity and directness. But its essential mystery ever abides. We simply cannot hear what the Spirit would say; It is of the future and we are present-bound, taking our stand on the common ground of the past. Mutuality between the Spirit and us is real; yesterday and tomorrow do meet at the altar of our today. But a distance of time as well as person is manifest in the heart of our intimacy: the We of our meeting, though replete with implicit promise of a coming consummation, is not yet fully *here.* What then is dialogue but our respective attempts to become fully present to each other, for creation to meet redemption in the now of our generation, in and through us? But alas, we can but hear our response. Yet God abides in response, as well as in address.

Any word, in brief, which issues from the human mouth cannot be other than a "joint statement," a "mutual communique," bespeaking the fact of "Us," of a divine-human here and now. And in the mind of the prophet lies the paradoxical awareness that the Word, in becoming word, comes from above, and yet is also built in from below, inseparable from personal being, from the I itself. More than this cannot be said.

✠

Symbols of the fact and ongoing "in-force" presence of the covenant are needed for the sake of continuity in the world, for the passing on of the relationship, with all its benefits and obligations, from one person to another, as well as from one generation to the next. Revelation builds community, and community requires visible and concrete representations— guarantees, as it were—of continuing and unbroken divine presence and justification. Covenantal *sacraments* are just such symbols. Divinely ordained as a part of the covenant itself, they characterize the relationship, project the person into it, and protect the person in it. They serve as entrance requirement and rite of passage into the faith and the community of the faithful.

Sacraments are symbols of the divine-human We, and represent God's will and human obedience, God's gift and human receptivity, God's promise and human faithfulness. God pledges to be efficaciously present in and through the sacrament, when and as it is administered in accordance with the covenant. As long as the covenant is in force, the sacraments are effective means of grace; the fact of their redemptive impact upon the person proves to faith the continuing integrity of the relationship. Without sacraments, there would be no covenantally approved means by which heaven and earth could touch, no manner in which God could propagate conversion into and growth in grace.

Sacraments, then, symbolize and bring to bear the benefits of the divine-human relationship as such. That is, and much is at stake in the realization of this point, *the benefits do not simply flow directly from God to the person, but are mediated by the established relationship.* Like money, the "currency" which is received as gift in fact belongs to a specific people and country, and its value and legitimacy is determined and vouchsafed only therein. And it is to be spent there first. Behold, the channels are set in and through which God summons forth the water of eternal life; *God moves in and through marriage*. The benefits come by virtue of the marriage, not the marriage by virtue of the benefits. God first founds a relational ground and then works within it. Though God is ever free, God chooses to operate—consistently but not exclusively—within the self-imposed limitations of specific and historical covenantal relationships. It is not as if God could not heal and save outside of marriage—and God does indeed exercise that option—but that God chooses to be faithful, as it were. Marriage Yes, affairs, No.

✠

Our God is a God who covenants. The covenant in the Hebrew Bible which truly begins Israel's history as a people, is that between God and Abraham. It comes as the third occasion in the Biblical narrative of Genesis that God sets apart or chooses one man. First, God chooses to regard Abel and his offering instead of that of Cain. This leads to the first murder. Later, God chooses Noah and his family to be the sole surviving humans from the flood of divine wrath. God subsequently covenants with Noah—the first true covenant of the Bible—for the sake of the whole human family, with the rainbow serving as "nature's sacrament" of God's perpetual peace and promise never again to destroy the world with water.

Then God calls Abraham. Abraham is commanded to leave his home and country and become a wanderer on the way to a now-promised land, and for the sake of a now-recognized seed within him of a promised progeny in number as great as the stars. God calls Abraham: that means, Abraham is set apart as *holy*; he is set apart as God's own man, and Sarah as God's own woman. Without explanation, God establishes a covenant of promise with Abraham and Sarah. An open-ended *We* is entered into by the eternally inexplicable act of God in the selection of this one man and this one woman—indeed, this one *marriage*—to serve as the personal and relational host for God's inscrutably minor and undramatic entrance into human history. The whole of history and nature itself are ultimately to be redirected and transformed by the thinnest of threads, by the simplest—and therefore most mysterious— of story lines. The God of all picks a single couple to become the single source for the whole of God's own people.

A divine-human mutuality comes to exist around this selection and promissory process. God speaks and Abraham believes, he trusts the God of his life above all and in all. This trust or faith-in-stance constitutes the spiritual ground for what is to follow, for the actual covenant is yet to become *flesh,* literally as well as figuratively. For twenty-five years Abraham and Sarah wait for the beginning of the fulfillment of the promised seed to be born between them. Indeed, the faithful waiting seems a divinely desired preparation—if not justification—for the covenant to come, for the concrete ratification of God's selection process.

At the will and timing of God, comes the sacramental twist: *circumcision.* The covenant, though long in existence in the spirituality of Abraham and Sarah, and lived through the elusive visitations of God, is now to become visible and concrete, historical and ritualistic. God speaks and Abraham listens:

> I will confirm my covenant between Me and you and will greatly increase your numbers. . . . You will be the father of many nations. No longer will you be called Abram; your name will be Abraham, for I have made you a father of many nations. . . . I will establish my covenant as an everlasting covenant between Me and you and your descendants. . . . This is My covenant with you and your descendants after you, the covenant you are to keep: Every male among you shall be circumcised. . . . As for Sarai your wife, you are no longer to call her Sarai; her name will be Sarah. . . . I will bless her so that she will be the mother of nations; kings of peoples will come from her. (Genesis 17:2ff).

At the point of its historical confirmation, the covenant of God's promise adds a single and most significant requirement on the human's part. The requirement is non-negotiable: "Any uncircumcised male, . . . will be cut off from his people; he has broken My covenant" (Genesis 17:14). This act of obedience, to be carried out in perpetuity, is the visible sign of *both* human faith and God's direct intervention into human history. Thus, it is a sign of the *mutuality* between God and Abraham. It is the sign of the transformation of Abraham's biological and sexual being by the promissory—though present and powerful—Word of God. Circumcision says, in effect, *"This one belongs to Me, this one is holy, set apart as My inheritance."*

Through circumcision, the meeting and mutuality of God and humanity are made manifest and their relationship sealed. Further, through the same event nature and history are granted their now finally common and unified destiny. For their respective ends are herein joined; the transformation of nature and the consummation of history are inexorably linked by divine-human covenant. Nature and natural functions—especially those concerning the wondrous drive of *eros*—are henceforth to be understood and lived through in the light, spirit and life of the mutuality between God and humanity. History is henceforth to be grasped as grounded in divine intentionality, and as unfolding in accordance with divine promise and will.

Note carefully that nothing is destroyed here, but rather a transformation of meaning—and one day of substance—is begun in both nature and history by the presence of the Word-Promise-Covenant, by the infusion of the "marriage Spirit" between God, Abraham and Sarah. God covenants with them in and concerning their own marriage covenant, and the fruit thereof. The future is determined by the present mutuality of divine-human meaning. *Meaning is mutuality, and mutuality,* ultimately, *is marriage.*

✠

The sacrament of circumcision signifies the transformation of nature into the context of divine-human relationship, into the meaning of the We in their history. The two fundamental sacraments in the New Testament, *baptism* and the *Lord's Supper,* supplement the first one and move humanity toward consummation in God. That is, the latter two sacraments build upon and complete the action of God upon the threefold nature of the human person, bringing thereby the whole person into whole relation with God. Circumcision hallows the human *soma* or body; baptism frees and redeems the human *pneuma* or spirit; the Lord's Supper works toward the transformation of the human *psyche* or soul—the last and most difficult metamorphosis. Hence, the final sacrament is not a one time event, like the other two, but must be faithfully appropriated throughout the whole of the one's life.

Circumcision sets the natural apart for existence in the covenanted life with God. Baptism represents the twofold action of God to cleanse the human spirit and soul—the "water baptism"—and to rebirth it into the family-Spirit of the Eternal We—the "baptism of the Holy Spirit." The Lord's Supper concerns our identity with Jesus Christ himself, in the most personal I-You terms. Through the body and the blood, our person, our soul, our very I, is to be transformed in the image and likeness of Christ. This twofold transformation is into the *being* of Christ—as "image"—, and the *actions* of Christ—as "likeness."

Thus, the Biblical sacraments reveal the sequential promissory actions of God upon humanity toward the goal of our eternal relationship in the Holy We. For the sacraments symbolize not only our life with God, but also and especially *God's work in us*. They are signs that God is at work in us "to will and to act according to His good purpose." And when the work is finished we will all be like Jesus, body, spirit and soul. The first two sacraments represent the action of God *from the outside in*. First the body is to become holy— and our life in the body— through its separation from pure nature into the new creation of a divine-human history. Then the human spirit is to be cleansed and reborn into an eternal mutuality of Spirit. And finally, and *from the inside out*, the human soul itself is to be transformed, degree by degree, into the new or "second Adam." That is, into Christ, the Eternal I. In the I of Christ, the I of humanity attains its final and perfect actualization.

Note, then, the divine actional sequence: first the body, then the spirit, and finally the soul are to become holy. God intends to redeem and save all that we are, that we might know and love all that God is.

✠

Torah and Christ

The two fundamental Biblical symbols of our being set apart for and actual entrance into a life with God, which characterize as well the meaning of that mutual existence, are circumcision in the Old and baptism in the New Testament. The Way of our daily life with God however, not the entrance into but the unfolding relationship itself, not the nuptials but the marriage as such, is that of *Torah* in the former and *Christ* in the latter covenant. Torah and Christ constitute the context of meaning and modus operandi of the life-together, the living ground of the covenant itself. Torah is deed-centered and behavioral, seeking to transform the person from the outside in—as if to say "doing leads to becoming." Christ is person-centered and interior, and seeks to change the heart and then the whole of the person's life, working from the inside out. The covenant in Christ would seem to say that "becoming leads to doing." Where the former would maintain that "you are what you do," the latter would assert that, in Christ, "you do what you are."

The inner logos or Word of Torah, hence its daily goal or telos, is "Be holy, for I your God am holy." The essential logos of Christ, hence the goal or telos of the Christian faith, is "Become perfect as your heavenly Father is perfect." Holiness of life and perfection of person, these constitute the overriding relational ends of our life with God and with one another. And they dialectically complement if not necessitate each other. For in truth, *Christ does Torah to perfection*; and *Torah is the holiness of Christ*. In Christ, Torah is fulfilled. Holiness, which means separateness from the world and unity with God, and perfection of person, which both results from and enables the perpetuation of a life of holiness, together represent the height and depth of the human person before God. They signify, in sum, the unification of the outer and inner persons. They are our end: total consistency and "unblemished" wholeness through and through. And that end will come only as the fruit of long-term commitment and fidelity.

Torah represents God's loving instruction on the divine Way in the world and through life, that is, through *this creation*. It tells us what to do and not to do, how to be and not to be in this world and this life. Christ is God's loving revelation of who we are becoming through the Way of Torah, that is, with God and in the *new creation*. The revelation tells us who we are to be and to be like. Hence, Christ is envisioned in the Hebrew prophets in terms of the Torah of the heart, that is, the new covenantal act of God, wherein God's Way will be written into our very core, so that a personal transformation will take place. This signifies a "second Word"—and therefore creation—, through which we will be enabled to will what God wills and to do—on the basis of who we are, rather than what we are commanded to do—what God would have us do. Being shall determine and fulfill doing. But the doing will nevertheless get done!

At the same time, we are promised not only a new heart, but a new spirit as well, which will permanently affect our wills and walk, our feelings and behavior. The new heart is to give us inner and direct knowledge of God and God's will; the new spirit is to give us the motive power and desire to act on that knowledge and carry out that will. For Christ and the Spirit are one, even as Word and Meaning are one.

Torah is God's eternal Way for us to live; Christ is God's eternal Person for us to become. The Way and the Person, the walk and the "soul-life," must never be separated—any more than the Hebrew Bible is to be separated from the New Testament. As they are One Book and story before God, so we are one day to become One People, with One Way and in One Person. Would that that day were finally here!

THE THREE COVENANTS

Judaism, Christianity and Islam

Coming from a common Source, and as the three primary religions of attachment, Judaism, Christianity and Islam revolve around the three realities of the world of persons. Both Christianity and Islam are dependent upon Judaism, and emerge as two distinct yet related streams. In Judaism the *You* of God is revealed for the first time in history. God as You is Creator of nature and Lord of history. As a new act of God's first creation, one which establishes a historical relationship, this eternal You, through an initial "hallowing," chooses a specific individual to become the father of many people. With Abraham—and Sarah—"religious history" begins, in, with and under world history. God appears through specific call, and therein founds a relationship of absolute obedience to that call, and radical faith in a twofold promise of progeny and land, incomprehensible as regards merit and vastness of consequence.

Obedience to call and Caller—which signifies "faith-in-action" (*deed*)—, and *faith* in promise and Granter—which signifies "faith-in-stance" (*perseverance*)—these are the two fundamental elements of Abraham's relation to God. And in the subsequent trans-generational unfolding of the relationship begun between them, obedience would come to be associated more with commandment and "law," faith with promise and "grace"; the former more attuned with "justice" and "righteousness," the latter with "mercy" and "love." The former is covenantally specified and lawful; the latter is unconditional and spiritual. Obedient is what we are to be for and before God; faithful is what we are to be with and to God.

Judaism, as the primal religion of attachment, thus begins with God's attaching, God's *hallowing*, or "making holy" or separate that which is of the God's own inscrutable choosing. God as You enters history as "jealous" Lord and Creator. Obedience and faith are the required responses to the gracious choice of the Holy One. At the center of Judaism is God's hallowing and *holiness*. God's own special people are chosen, and many generations after the initial selection, a kind of historical marriage ceremony is performed on a mountain in the desert. With the covenant in their memory and hands, the people are commanded to "be holy, for I your God am holy."

Judaism as a religion, therefore, has essentially to do with a divine-human marriage, along with the covenantal requirements of separation and holiness, of purity and fidelity. The holy and eternal You specifies the conditions and nature of this separation through the wondrous gift of the *Torah*, God's own teaching in the way of holiness and divine-human reciprocity. Through the Torah, together with the prior promises to the patriarchs, God establishes a *unique* people in accordance with the divine *uniqueness*. Separation for the sake of God, holiness and uniqueness are inseparable covenantal requirements and consequences.

Add to the holiness of God primal and eternal *oneness*. God is one: there is one God, and God is one—in terms numerical, ontological and qualitative. The single creedal statement of the Hebrew Bible, the *Shema*, proclaims: "Hear, O Israel, the Lord our God, the Lord is one" (Deuteronomy 6:4). The God who calls, chooses, and covenants with a people, self-named YHWH to Moses, is *one, unique* and *separate*. In short, YHWH is *Holy*. And God's own people are to become like their God in and through their covenant. The one God requires one people for one covenantal life, one divine-human We, one marriage. "Be holy, for I your God am holy."

The hallowed people are to hallow in response, to love in response to being loved, to serve in response to being served, to follow in response to being graciously led. As the people are transformed through being lifted up and separated, through being thus chosen and loved, so they are in turn to lift up and separate for the sake of YHWH; they are to become partners in a joint venture of transforming history and nature, by hallowing and therein bringing life and history into the sphere between themselves and their God. A *holy We* is thus established between YHWH and Israel through the Torah, and a joint mission of making holy is embarked upon. Ultimately the whole of nature and history is to be redeemed by being brought into the relationship between God and Israel. The essential task of the Jewish soul, the *mitzvah* or deed to be done, is thus to hallow and redeem.

✠

The eternal You is first revealed in Israel. The revelation comes through the call and choice of a people to be God's own, a human We before the Face. And through the covenant or marriage ceremony at Mt. Sinai, the giving of the Torah, a divine-human We comes into existence in world history. Over the centuries subsequent to Mt. Sinai, the concept of the individual, of the I, first emerges clearly within Israel. The individual steps forth decisively in the prophetic consciousness as a responsible agent, as the personal being held accountable to God for the carrying out of the commandments and the law, the *mitzvot* and the *halacha*. The demands of covenantal and ethical responsibility, religious and cultic accountability, with their attendant rewards and punishments, led inexorably to the discovery of the individual, of the I, the single one, the person. First the You of revelation, then the We of covenant and promise, and from within the We, came forth the I of agency and personality.

In the Psalms, yet another mode of the I first emerges: the I of prayer life and personal devotion—*devekuth*. In the Psalms, the holy I-You relationship between the individual person and God first steps forward and is canonized. From the Psalms it becomes apparent that the consummation of religious life must not only include the individual, but must indeed have individual life at its center. The I and the You become the focus of piety and concern, but never in Israel to the exclusion of the We. For Israel is first and foremost the people of God.

But each person is responsible before God, and to each is assigned a specific portion in the world to come. The religious I-You remains nestled within the history and corporate life of the people as a whole. As goes the latter, so goes the former.

The intensive We must not be separated from the context of meaning of the extensive We of Israel. To do so would transform mutuality into mystification. To do so would "privatize" and spiritualize the covenant and promises to the point of their utter meaninglessness, if not annihilation. For Israel, the concrete divine-human mutuality called history must remain the living and legitimate ground for all modes of relationship and spirituality. Not only the story and fulfillment of Israel are at stake in this, but the reality of history itself.

✠

Judaism is the religion of holiness. Its essential Word: "You shall be holy, for I your God am holy." And that holiness shared between the people and YHWH through the Torah dictates the transformation of all of life into that mutuality. Holiness calls for hallowing for the sake of the end, the *telos*, of covenantal existence—namely the redemption of the people Israel, and with them of nature and history.

Christianity, built upon and inseparable from Judaism, is the religion of perfection or maturity, *teleïos*. Its essential Word: "You shall be perfect, just as your Father in heaven is perfect" (Matthew 5:48). Where the essential Word of holiness speaks directly to the people as a whole, the Word from the mouth of Christ speaks to the depth of the soul. The former Word prophesies the end of the people, on the basis of the covenantal existence of the extensive We between YHWH and Israel; the latter Word prophesies the end of the individual soul, on the basis of the covenantal existence of the intensive We between Christ and the Father. The covenant of Torah is of this life, and is centered in the redemption now entering history through Christ. The former reveals the status of the "eternal people" before God; the latter reveals the reality of the "eternal person" with God. It is therefore from the eternal people that the eternal person is chosen to step forth into the relationship of all relationships, into the Eternal I-You of God. For salvation comes from the Jews.

✠

Note carefully that perfection or maturity is built upon holiness. We must be holy—in corporate terms—before we can become perfect, in personal terms. The "social holiness" of the extensive We of God with Israel is the "sacred root" which supports the personal maturity of the intensive We of God with the "Christ-ian." Persons need a covenanted community of God in order to grow into the personal wholeness intended by God. Hence, to seek to separate the Old from the New Testaments would mean literally to pull out from under Christianity the spiritual ground upon which it stands.

In the Apostle Paul's understanding, the function of the "law" or Torah in this context was one of a guardian and teacher of God's child, until the child reached sufficient maturity to no longer require it. That point is attained in the internalization of the law, the completion of the "law of the heart" planted within by God's action. Then the "You shall" and the "You shall not" of the commandments become the "I must" and "I must not" of the will. Then religion ceases to be a yoke laid upon a person from the outside, and becomes something from within, yearning for expression and realization. Thus is the yoke of Christ "easy and burden light"; thus does one find rest and fulfillment for the soul. Yet the law is not dispensed with, but completed by the Spirit, not abrogated, but finally carried out all the way.

For, behold, the end of maturity will be holiness yet again. Beyond the holiness required of Israel with its YHWH, the holiness to be attained in Christ is that of God's own. "You shall be holy, *for* I your God am holy," leads to "Become perfect, *as* your Father in heaven is perfect." All this is for the sake of the time when God will be "all in all"; and the human person becomes, in God and with God, *"holy, as your Eternal Beloved is holy."*

✠

For *Judaism*, God is above all holy. And the two fundamental attributes which flow from the divine essence are those of *mercy* and *justice*. *Christianity* bases its revelation primarily upon God's mercy, specifically on God's *grace*, the "Good News" of the offer of forgiveness and salvation in Jesus Christ. *Islam* takes its fundamental stand upon God's justice. While Allah is indeed the compassionate and the merciful, the whole structure of the Quran is built upon God's *righteousness*.

Allah is righteous—and fair and just— in granting to the Arabs the Book, the direct revelation of the untranslatable Quran, through the prophet Mohammed. Their half-brothers through Abraham, the Jews, had their Book, and the spiritual heirs of the latter, the Christians, had theirs. Now the righteousness of God is revealed in the offspring of Ishmael at last becoming a fully legitimate partner of the covenant-minded God.

Where the Christian through the apostle Paul came down on the faith of Abraham as the primal stance before God, the Muslim through the Prophet opted for obedience. Hence, Islam means "surrender," surrender to the righteous and merciful One, Allah. The people are to become a *righteous We*, an obedient nation in response to the righteousness of Allah. Islam concerns the whole of the nation in its legal, social and political structures as well as those of religious practice, ritual and obligation. And the Quran incorporates the Jewish concern with this life with the Christian focus on the coming end of history.

YHWH called Israel into existence as a people and established the covenantal life of the Torah together with them. Allah revealed the divine Person and will through the Quran, and therein gave legitimation to a people already in existence. Allah, the Quran and the consequent Islam all belong together, in the same fashion as YHWH, Torah and Israel. With both Israel and Islam, the creation of peoplehood in response to God's graciousness is absolutely essential to the revelation and covenant itself.

With Christianity, however, the issue of peoplehood is built upon and secondary to the personal relationship with Christ, and through Christ with the Father—and through Them jointly, with the divine We of the Holy Spirit. The people of the Church represent an eschatological community of those who stand redeemed in a salvific relationship to Christ, who proclaim or witness to the Lordship of Jesus of Nazareth. What is common to all Christians is, first, this essential relationship of faith with Jesus Christ, and second, the gift of the Holy Spirit. The Spirit establishes community and is the ground of We, just as Christ is the ground of the new I of the believer. The We of the Christian community happens where two or more gather together in name, Person and Spirit of Christ. Hence, the Christian We, like that of the Eternal We of the Trinity, is not and cannot become an institutionalized social structure in the world. For it actually represents the divine We, and is called to reveal the spiritual presence of the Kingdom of Heaven, until the final consummation arrives with the return in power of the Messiah, Jesus Christ.

The covenant with Christ is not on the plain of history in the same way as that of YHWH with Israel and Allah with Islam. For though it was offered by a historical person, and implemented through the historical event of Golgotha, the covenant concerns eternal life. It is a covenant not of law but of Spirit, not of nature and history but of water and blood, soul and rebirth. The kingdom of Jesus is not of this world but of the world to come; it is not of the structures of creation but of re-creation and redemption. That is, Christianity is centered in the intimate and intensive world of persons, of the I, You and We. And the consequent and necessary social and denominational structures in the world serve as carriers of the Book, the traditions, and the memories of the moments over the centuries when true Church erupted and affected history. The institutional church has the vital role of protecting and repetitively proclaiming in word—even if not in deed—the revelation and story of the Church, *so that at the timing of the will of God, true Church can happen again.* Surely now is such a time.

THE FALL : EVIL, HUMAN AND BEYOND

Original Sin

And the Lord God commanded the man, 'You are free to eat from any tree in the garden; but you must not eat from the tree of the knowledge of good and evil, for when you eat of it, you will surely die'. . . . 'You will not surely die,'the serpent said to the woman. . . . When the woman saw that the fruit of the tree was good for food and pleasing to the eye, and also desirable for gaining wisdom, she took some and ate it. She also gave some to her husband, who was with her, and he ate it (Genesis 2:16-17; 3:4,6).

"Original Sin" is present in all of us, and comes to be repeated by each of us in our lives. It signifies both an innate "predisposition" at the base of our hearts, and an active fact of the world into which we are born. That is, original sin must be located both within and between us. Our heart contains a "dis-ease" at birth, a "spiritual virus" present as an ineradicable potential for evil. And society enflames the virus. Thus must the age-old "nature-nurture" issue of which preceded which be answered in both/and rather than either/or terms. Even to purify society would not therefore resolve the predicament of sin, for the human heart must be purified as well. And only God can do that.

As sin signifies the willful transgression of the law of love, *original sin* represents the *primal event,* both within the human I and carried out in the relational world, of *our disobedience to and "disavowing" of, our covenantal existence with God.* That event initiated the "Fall" from the divine-human We of creation, from the mutuality, the intimacy and peace with God depicted as the "garden of Eden." The sin must not be understood merely as the violation of God's *law,* but of God's *relationship,* and the conditions of and for that consecrated state of being-together. For the original sin was of the I against the Eternal You in the context of the betrayal of the We. The commandment was transgressed, the law broken; that means, the unity and integrity of the Spirit-We was rent asunder, and the You—as well as the I—afflicted as the direct consequence of the breaching of the whole.

The real issue of sin Biblically is not that God establishes the rules and binding conditions of the "field of play," and that humanity fails to stay within the guidelines—as if God were some kind of arbitrary rule maker, and everything had to move in accordance with some inscrutable Ego's "game-plan." Rather, *what is at stake in human sin is the startling inability of the human person to persevere in the divine-human We*—and from that, to persevere in any We at all. At issue is the human I in its predicament of not being able—or willing—to trust the You of its creation. Without that trust the I is unwilling to surrender its own life for the sake of the entrance into that true Life of mutuality God has intended from the beginning.

Self-interest, self-serving, self-preservation, the me above and before the You and the Us, this primal attitude of willfulness instead of willingness, this "Me first" predisposition of the heart, effectively prohibits the self-giving and abandonment required for genuine mutuality. The I simply cannot get beyond itself to discover the You, and in that meeting to become the true I. And even if the You is discovered, the I is unable to persist in the relationship, and claim daily its identity as the I of their We. The I cannot take up the Cross of its We.

The context in which this fatal human flaw of egoism is presented biblically is thus not in terms of God's law for us, but God's life with us. God's law constitutes the vows of a kind of marriage; to violate the vows means to violate the marriage-Spirit, and therein the Person with whom we are married. Sin is the breach of our shared life. The You is offended precisely in the context of the stripping away of the common life supporting both the You and the I. The betrayal of the You is the betrayal of the We.

Thus the biblical understanding of the immediate consequences of the original sin upon the I of the perpetrator centers upon the fall of the We. In violating the We, the I automatically undercuts its own life in that relationship. And in relationship with God that means the I wounds itself mortally by cutting itself off from the very ground of its sustenance and life. Thus does our existence become estranged from our essence. For our essence is true and unending relationship.

In the dawning consciousness of sin comes the realization: "In disavowing You, I first disavowed Us, and thus myself. For I have severed our life together, the life which fed and supported both of Us. In wounding You, I have poisoned my own life as well, for You and I have been bonded in an unseen commonness. But how I see it now in its loss! By dis-easing Us, I have become dis-eased as well. O God, save me from the consequences of my sin!"

✠

The "Fall" from the garden of Eden despoiled the peace or *shalom* of the prior divine-human relationship of creation. Only with and in God do we have our true shalom—which means that wondrous harmony within us and between ourselves and all others, which comes as the direct consequence of being right with God. The Word of our peace: "All is well *with* me because *I am with God.*" If the "with God" is missing, there can be no peace with ourselves and with others.

Hence the immediate consequence of the disobedience of Adam and Eve, of the rupture of their We with God, was the seemingly irreversible disruption of their relationship with each other. Upon the ingestion of the fruit of the tree of the knowledge of good and evil, "the eyes of both of them were opened, and they realized they were naked; so they sewed fig leaves together and made coverings for themselves" (Genesis 3:7). Prior to that they were one flesh, and though "The man and the woman were both naked, . . . they felt no shame"(2:25). Oneness gave way to shame, fear and hiding. The I distrusted and clothed itself from the You—divine and human. The No to the divine You led to the loss of the ability to say Yes to the human You. The I and the

You now began to "miss" each other, in fact and in feeling.

In hiding from the Eternal You, they relinquished their participation in the Eternal We of their beginning. Consequently, they lost the true ground of the human We in which God joined them at their common birth. Isolation and unfilled space between them came into being, and the *saeculum*, the secular was born. The saeculum signifies the time/space interim between divine-human mutuality, the time and space apart from God. The Fall was therefore the entrance into the void. And in that void, not God but darkness abides. And non-mutuality with God *is* our mutuality with darkness. *Evil exists* precisely and literally *in the gap between ourselves and God*. And how wide is that gap! And how dark that darkness!

Behold, in the Fall the Holy We was the first to be lost, and will be the last to be regained. For is not the restoration of pure mutuality the meaning and promise of redemption? And has not that redemption already begun with the offer of Jesus Christ, the "second Adam," for our full participation in the Eternal We of His relationship to God, the Holy Spirit?

✠

Idolatry

> You shall have no other gods before Me. You shall not make for yourself an idol in the form of anything in heaven above or on the earth beneath or in the waters below. You shall not bow down to them or worship them; for I, the Lord your God, am a jealous God.... (Exodus 20:3-4).

Idolatry signifies the addressing, with the whole of our being, of anything other than the You of our life. And in as much as only the You of our life can be addressed with the fullness of our being, idolatry is self-deception as well as God-deflection. Only the Eternal You can apprehend and love us in truth and totality; only the Holy We of the shared life of our I with the Beloved You can ever gift us with fullness and fulfillment. Only the You and the Spirit-life of our commonness can save us. To respond to anything other than the Creator You with the whole of our life and substance means to deny both God and

God's life with us. It means to divert the Word in which our I has its life from returning to the One who called us into being. And to divert the Word, even for a time, is to divest it of its power and purpose.

"Seek Ye My Face"—thus speaks the Eternal You. "Thy Face, Lord do I seek"—thus responds the Eternal I. To seek another face, or to treat another reality as if it were that One Face, and to respond to it as if it were worthy of devotion and total obedience, this is idolatry. And it takes many forms, from the self-worship of the I to that of money and power. But in all cases, idolatry absolutely prohibits the life of the divine-human We from becoming a present reality. The blind alley of false attachment blocks our being from God's, and God's from ours; it blocks *us* from happening and being-together.

What then of the human You? Is it idolatrous to love another person with the whole of one's life and being, to the breadth and depth our soul can reach? If it were possible to so love another human, then it would indeed be idolatrous. For there is to be no You before the You of God; no other person is to stand between us and the ultimate Person of our lives, the One from whom we come and unto whom we cannot do other than return. No human marriage can supplant the divine-human marriage; our days and nights can in truth and in fullness belong to but one Beloved.

Only the You of God can be loved with the fullness of the human I. When the I speaks love to the "You" of its life, God is always addressed, even and precisely through the human You thus addressed. The human You is loved in the divine You—whether the I is aware of this or not; the divine You is ever honored and revered in the human You. And paradoxically, neither You is lost in the other, but loved with one love, just as they are addressed with one word. Thus though we may seemingly yield ourselves to another You as the one and only, the exclusive You of our life, we do so only in the illusion of the "romantic moment," only drunk with the imagery of the "great love," the love which God alone can offer.

Comes therefore the divine plea: "Abide in My love." Only God's love can avail us in our hour of going under. Only the love which can surround and encompass us through and through can save us. No human You, however sweet and wondrous, precious and fulfilling the We of our communion may be, can reach all that we are with all that they are.

Yet God is love. Therefore all love is of God and in God, just as God is all love. Hence, to love You means to love You in God and God in You; it means to reach and embrace You through God as Medium between us, just as to be reached and embraced by God through You. In our mutual loving presence, we mediate God to each other, we re-present and incarnate the Eternal You. And where there is love, there is the Spirit, as the living fire which holds Us as we hold one another.

What a miracle, that through You and in Us, I may yield myself to God even as I abandon myself to our love! Is this then idolatry? May it not be so! Let us rather call it our very purpose, to give ourselves to one another in love and in God. For we are created to give ourselves over to the You of our life through each other, and to the love of our life in our love for one another. What is essential is to live for love, for love is of and leads to God. God is love's self-fulfillment.

✠

One of the most significant forms of idolatry is all too often overlooked. Yet it may be one of the most prevalent and insidious. Let it be called, simply, *relational idolatry*. It means to continue to respond to a past mutuality, and to the person of that meeting, as if they were still in the present. If I do not see You as You are in the now, but only as You might have been in the way back then, if I thereby "miss" You in the open-ended here and now, I become idolatrous toward You—and *Us. For we can be idolatrous of relationships as well as the persons therein.* To respond to an internal *form* of You as if it were the present You, and to a *form* of Us as if it were Us now, is to seal myself off from the life of Spirit between us, and the Word within me seeking expression and dialogue.

Treating the forms of meeting and responding and knowing from the past as if they had a sufficiency for You and Me today, denies us any real presence today. And it precludes new meetings and deeper discoveries of one another and Us. For the Spirit is our tomorrow, breaking into our today, ever open and novel. The past at best gifts us with channel markers to get us out of the bay of the self and safely into the waters of the infinite Now of the Spirit of mutuality. There I can encounter You as presence and as gift; there I can become presence and gift to You—and to myself.

What then is the need of this, as of every hour, and the one antidote to the relational idolatry now raging not only among humanity, but especially between humanity and divinity? To restore the life of Spirit and the Word itself, we must step forth and meet the You of our life afresh; we must encounter God in the eternal newness of the We between us. That will mean as well the rediscovery of ourselves. "Seek Ye My Face. . . . Thy Face, Lord, do I seek."

Uncleanness

It is of great significance that the same adjective in the Greek New Testament, *akatharos,* means both "unclean" and "evil." And in the Hebrew Bible, uncleanness emerges as the direct opposite of "holiness." To be holy means, first, to be set apart by God as God's own. That is God's "branding," as it were, God's active work of choosing, in which the human is passive—save but to accept the gracious election with the whole heart. Second, to be holy means to be faithful to the conditions and guidelines of the covenantal event of being included with God, and at the same time excluded from that which is not of and for God. It signifies humanity's work of a disciplined life within the relational parameters of the covenant. In short, to be holy means to be *"married" to God.*

The entire "Holiness Code" of the Torah, with its numerous and seemingly insignificant laws and statutes for the maintaining of holiness or cleanness before YHWH, constitutes the logical—the "logos-ful"—working out of the cultic and cultural consequences of the mutuality between Israel and its God. Israel is to be faithful to YHWH with the totality of its life; everything that is done is to be done for the sake of God and in the holiness of the covenant. Israel is to be "clean" before YHWH; that means, it is to abide, minute by minute and deed by deed, within the specific conditions of mutuality. Thus is a casuistry born, for the protecting, maintaining and perfecting of covenantal life. For YHWH is a Holy God—therefore a "clean" one; that is, One who is absolutely true to and consistent with the self-imposed conditions of the covenant. And YHWH expects and demands the same from Israel, for "You only have I known of all the peoples of the world."

The eventual consequence of the failure to live out of the covenant could be that relational disaster called *divorce.* And with divorce, death as "Israel." Yet how God hates divorce; when God betroths, it is forever.

✠

Uncleanness is the direct and immediate consequence of the violation of covenant, of mutual life as such. That means uncleanness could be equated with sin itself. Three different dimensions of uncleanness must be distinguished: the *source* of the uncleanness or defilement, the *state* of the person, and the *spirit* or relationship which has been breached. What is the source of the sin? What antecedent conditions led to it? From whence came the initial motive power, from within or from without? What specific state of the person eventuated in the defilement? What underlying susceptibility opened the person to the temptation to breach the relationship? And finally, what is the nature of the relationship thus violated, and what are the consequences of it?

In addition to these aspects, the question must be raised regarding how both the person and the relationship can become clean again. *For relationships become unclean, just as persons.* What must be done for the sake of "at-one-ment"? The conditions for reconciliation must be built into the covenant itself. Or how could humanity hope to maintain mutuality with God, and therein with itself? And which is the greater graciousness of God, to covenant with us, or to build in the way through which we can be forgiven? And what are we, that God should even need to make such allowances?

With what then does one become unclean? What is the "dirt" which defiles? Call it a kind of "haze" or silken fabric covering the I or of a portion of the I, a subtle and suddenly appearing mask which remains always in place, and blocks meeting, behind which lurks an uncovenanted and thus unfaithful spirit. Uncleanness is itself a "spiritual substance," a form of darkness which silently breaks across and down the open path between the I and the You, directly affecting their "Us." Uncleanness is a spirit of "otherness" which severs all or part of the "ourness" of common life. It is that which is not a part of the covenant, but which now lives between the partners as an unholy "guest" in their spiritual home. And whether it comes initially from within the heart of one of the covenantal participants, or from the outside interference of another, it is as real and damaging to the soul as a virus or germ is to the body. Though unseen and seemingly microscopic, the unclean spirit present within the guilty one, and through him or her present between the partners, can be lethal to the spirit-bond of love, and to the souls who have taken their stand in its life.

Uncleanness in relationship is preceded by uncleanness in personal intention, that is, by the will or the heart. It is the desire which renders the soul unclean, even if the person never actually carries out the intention. Once the process of perpetrating the deed begins, the spirit of the person, that is, their own dimension of the We of the relationship, defiles itself in ceasing to live within the spirit of the covenant. For uncleanness is of spirit before it is of law. And even if the letter of the law is not broken, defilement can still happen, due to the desires and disposition of the heart. "It is what comes out of a man that makes him unclean."

Uncleanness works from the top down, or the ground up. That is, we first defile our relationship with God, our stance of being before the One from whom all Truth, Goodness and Beauty issue. The first to be soiled is goodness, for that is of the will above all. Then we despoil the truth, in us and between us and God. For the truth is of word and deed, and uncleanness, like evil, cannot look upon itself in truth. And finally we stain beauty, for that has its life in the Spirit, which we have desecrated with our transgression. And that is the most difficult thing for heaven to forgive.

Before we sin against one another, we sin against God. With the psalmist, "Against You, You only, have I sinned." All sin is rooted in idolatry, in the placing of something else between ourselves and God. The immediate consequence is uncleanness, which means "outsideness" for the life of the covenant. Hence it means real alienation, of being as well as of affections.

Uncleanness means more than violating the spirit of the covenant; it means to actually bring something "unholy" *into* the relationship. Hence, the effects of the sin upon the perpetrator reach not only into the soul of the guilty one, and not only into the mutuality of the relationship thus violated, but the possibility looms large that the covenantal partner may become unclean as well. For instance, when one marriage partner commits adultery—which is the closest human analogy to idolatry—not only is the marriage rendered unclean by the entrance of the fact and spirit of adultery into the covenant itself, but that spirit can induce or seduce the other to commit adultery as well. This is not simply a question of "an eye for an eye" modeling, or vengeance, although they certainly can and do lead to all manner of uncleanness in response to sin. No, more is at stake: darkness has a way into the soul of the injured party, an open wound. Now the formerly unacceptable can become the secretly desirable, even if never carried out or acknowledged consciously. The enemy can now "legally" enter into the marriage spirit, and by that means, into the heart of the wounded party.

Woe to us this day, we who as a people treat adultery as "natural" or "understandable," if not downright acceptable and even desirable. We stand before the Covenant Maker unclean and dead to the distance between ourselves and God, and between each other as marriage partners. True life comes only with the commitment to clean life-together. And so few among us find life together in our unclean world.

✠

Intuition and Evil

Intuition is the apprehension of spirit and the spiritual state of the soul. It is our "third eye," so to speak, the inner relational sense of the heart. As our inner ear senses our balance and total physical orientation, so our inner eye experiences our spiritual uprightness and orientation. The intuition discerns right and wrong, good and evil directly and immediately in persons and relationships. As such it is to be trusted and listened to at all times. It is also that which evil seeks to close at all costs. For our intuition is the spiritual truth seer. And evil is the spiritual untruth, which, in masquerading as the truth, would bind us in its web of deception.

Intuition first appears biblically in the drama of the garden of Eden. When Adam and Eve eat of the fruit of the tree of the knowledge of good and evil, the text states that straightaway "the eyes of both of them were opened, and they realized they were naked" (Genesis 3:7). *What opened*? The eye of the intuition. They also experienced fear for the first time, due to the sudden new awareness of vulnerability, of their exposed state. To what did they feel exposed? The realities of spirit: of forces within and without, the present possibility of rejection as well as acceptance, of evil lurking as well as good shining, of darkness as well as light, of weakness as well as strength. The first thing they needed to do therefore was to clothe themselves—which meant from each other as well as from the elements. For in clothing themselves from that which threatened them from outside the relationship, they clothed themselves from the relationship as well.

The second and even more relationally disastrous thing fear drove them to do was to hide from God. Their newly-awakened intuition did not help, but rather hindered their relationship with God and one another, and with the truth open to them in the garden. They intuited spirits, but they could not trust in the Spirit. Their knowledge was incomplete, and with their now disobedient and doubting hearts, faith in the goodness of God was simply beyond their reach. Yet what was it in them—and in us to this day—that so biased them to believe in the bad before the good?

While the mystery called "evil" engineered the Fall by leading Adam and Eve to their disobedience, and thus to their spiritual awakening, its primal task unto the present is to deaden the awareness of itself. Evil seeks to close the third eye, the eye of spirit; it would desensitize the heart to its presence and poisonous influence. It does so through deception and seduction. The work of evil is to name—that is, "pseudonym"—the good as the bad and the bad as the good, the beautiful as the ugly and the ugly as the beautiful. It works on the temptations that the heart and the flesh are heir to, seducing the imagination to play out a sin-fantasy, and to do so as if the deed could be carried out to advantage and gratification—and with minimal negative consequences.

Once conceived, the will can be aided by the evil present to it—by its own unconscious invitation—toward the planning of how to do the deed. *Once the deed is decided upon and acted out, a spiritual deadening, a closing of the eye of the intuition follows immediately, if not automatically.* The will, strengthened by evil, covers the eye of truth within. But like the physical eye, the darkness may last only for a blink, as it were. For the spiritual eye will seek to recover its vision. And at the point that it does, a spiritual battle ensues, an inner struggle between the good and evil living within the heart. Is the person to face and repent for the deed or to repress the inner consequences, to continue in the deed or seek to walk away from the whole business? Alas for the soul, for the course of repression is usually chosen. "Out of sight, out of mind." Yet the intuition knows it is there. The intuition must therefore be permanently blinded, and like Cassandra of Greek mythology, be consigned to tell the truth but not to be heard. And only evil can so blind us. We have not the power in ourselves. But we can have the will.

✠

As a part of the drive for self-preservation stands the ever-present need to be "right" or "justified." This has been termed the need for "cognitive consonance" or "ego integrity." As persons we seek—even minute by minute, when we are up against it—to be "OK," to be right. We need this sense of rightness as a part of the very spiritual air we breathe, the environment of our souls, the context-of-meaning in which we image ourselves. Just as our bodies need clean air, so our souls need the element of rightness in order to survive and prosper.

Then along comes sin and relational defilement. And behold, evil stands ready to help us "handle" our guilt and uncleanness, if we will only listen and believe in it. But it can "help" us only through lies and the desensitization of our intuition. This is made easier in the wake of our sin, for we are then actively seeking justification for our deed, so it can be rendered consistent with our value structure and self-image. We stand all too ready to believe that the worst was really the best for us and the one we hurt—and the relationship we transgressed. Would we not call "cow pies" "field steak," and do our very best to enjoy a meal of it, if it could succeed at getting us off the hook of guilt and self-recrimination?

Though we would blind and deafen our intuition, its wakefulness and memory abide nonethelesss. In us and beyond our reach is the knowledge of our true state, and of the presence of evil. And we cannot rid ourselves of its vision; we may but choose whether or not to allow it to surface into the light of consciousness. And one day it shall yield to God all that we have said and done. The deed of sin remains within us as memory and point of alienation, as the place in the road where our being veered off God's highway, into the jungles of darkness and silent despair. The deed abides until, through forgiveness received and repentance carried out, God—and God alone—erases the "tape" within. And at the same time, God restores the inner eye of the soul. "Go, and sin no more."

We must therefore take this inner eye of the intuition with the utmost seriousness. Jesus does. In the Gospels He solemnly warns us against spiritual blindness, and laments the tragic blindness of the religious leaders of His day. They failed to see and hear Him; and they claimed to see when in truth they were blind. Thus did their guilt remain.

> Your eye is the lamp of your body. When your eyes are good, your whole body also is full of light. But when they are bad, your whole body also is full of darkness. See to it, then, that the light within you is not darkness. Therefore, if your whole body is full of light, and no part of it dark, it will be completely lighted, as when the light of a lamp shines on you (Luke 11:34-36).

The intuition, in sum, is the perceptual apparatus of relationality. *The intuition sees the We.* Its realm of apprehension is the world between us, the mutual sphere, and the state of persons in that sphere. Where our physical eyes see the person over against us in their physical environment, the inner eye of the heart sees the person in their spiritual circumstances.

Would that our inner eye were as opened as that of Jesus! Then we too would see the truth; we too, as "pure in heart," would see God. And the plank being removed from our eyes, we would see our way clear to reach out and heal others—and ourselves in the process.

Yet most of us remain in a self-imposed blindness. "If then, the light within you is darkness, how great is that darkness!" (Matthew 6:22).

✠

Evil

How then is evil to be understood? Is it merely the absence of good, as darkness the absence of light? So that when the light of goodness comes, the darkness cannot abide? Or is evil only what evil does, hence, human deeds perpetrated? Is it then to be located in the culture, as the accumulated evil our frailty is open to and guilty of, ricohetting still, wounding and victimizing one innocent generation upon another? So that if we could condition behavior and bring control to the environment, the evil would eventually die out?

Or shall we localize evil as a "dis-ease" within the heart, an inner impulse or drive or desire, an ever-present potential of the will for destruction? So that if we could only love the person properly, or could instill the right conscience, the evil impulse would never fully develop? But would it remain instead like an occasional mild cold which never develops into a fever, which never really gets the person "sick"?

Or shall we understand evil as something more than the mere absence of good, more than human deed or impulse—though these elements are no doubt involved in evil—but as an "objective" reality or force beyond humanity and in opposition to creation itself—and therefore God? Yes to all the above depictions of evil, to the great mystery of the darkness hovering about the light, of the unspeakable "unspirit" trailing the Spirit. Evil is at once within, between and beyond us, and must be named and faced fully in the human predicament.

As with all creation, evil proceeded from the Word—that means, it is "logical" or "logos-full." But it proceeded in direct opposition to and as the primal force of resistance against, the Word of creation. This is innately "potential" in the logic of the Word, just as "No" is always potentially at hand in the utterance of "Yes." The assertion of the one includes the logical possibility of the other. And for the Word of creation, even potential or logical existence is nevertheless a form of existence. But evil, as a kind of parasite, requires another life form—a human person. Like a grammatical sentence therefore, evil requires a living voice to utter it—and a human to carry it out it in the world. And until this creation passes away, evil will continue to have its parasitic existence.

Evil is thus the anti-Word, and like anti-matter cannot co-exist with life as we know it. Where therefore evil is present, be it within or between us, there a spiritual battle ensues, there unrest and divisiveness tax and decimate us. How telling is the spirit of the English language, that the word "evil" is the actual reversal of the letters for "live"! By its very nature evil must say "No" to life, and "Yes" to itself alone. It is the true cancer of the soul and spirit, which seeks to reproduce itself in everything it touches and affects, to destroy and replace life's wholeness and diversity with its strangely and hideously homogeneous anti-life cell structure.

Evil as anti-Word is anti-Spirit, and thus anti-We. Evil cannot by its own nature enter into the "co-notation" of Spirit, that is, it cannot participate in relationship. It cannot accept an "otherness" as such; it must bring that otherness into its own sameness and control. Evil knows not mutuality; it does not grasp the "language" of love. Though it may use our language, it does not understand the "co-notation," the life and context of shared meaning.

Evil has over the millennia been personified as a mysterious kind of being or agent. And whether such a being as the "Devil" or "Satan" or "Lucifer" actually exists is a matter of faith and conviction, not of demonstration and proof. Only evil itself may be demonstrated; and of that we have more proof than is necessary. Would that we did not have such proof! Would that such signposts as the ovens of Auschwitz had never existed!

Evil first appears biblically as "the serpent" in the story of the garden of Eden. It functions there as the tempter and seducer. It entices the woman and man into the event of the "Fall," which echos unto today. The event revolves around three essential and still operative elements—for each of us must pass through and fall from the garden of innocence. The three: *the tempter, the tempted* and *the temptation.* The tempter stands in the place of God, and is given even greater credibility than God—or the temptation could not have happened. The *"false You,"* a "characteristic voice" speaks, either from within or from without the person. The temptation is to become like God; it is the offer of an *"illusory I,"* set within the context of an *"unreal We,"* of a "secret" world between the tempter and tempted. It is thus an attempt to change the whole order of creation from a harmonious hierarchy to an "illegal"—and "ill-logos"—equality. And the tempted reveals an unexpected desire, an ambition and willfulness in opposition to the will of the Creator, of the One who had cared enough to walk openly among them.

The tempter asserts in God's stead to one who would be as God the false promise of how to become like God. And the way? Through fundamental disobedience, that means: through the direct violation of the We of creation and covenant. But rather than attaining the life of divinity, the consequence was the death of humanity. And the path to death was reduced to that of labor and toil.

In truth, through the Word in us is granted a hidden knowledge of our destiny, that we shall one day be as God, with God. And that knowledge gives birth to promise, and promise to desire. But desire can so easily be led astray. For its hunger renders it susceptible to seeing the object of its yearning anywhere. The deeper the desire, the more prone the person to ingest that which will not satisfy! Evil only need tell us what it is we are waiting to hear. And so many hear and believe the voice of the false You. So many become its victims. And as victims, in turn they victimize.

Woe to the one who would be as God—apart from God! The only way to attain the cherished "me" is through the "We." The only Way to become as God is through and with God.

✠

One of the central New Testament terms for the "evil one" is the *Diabolos.* The term comes from the verb *diaballein,* which is derived from the preposition *dia,* meaning, "through or across," as well as "by means of," and the verb *ballein,* meaning "to throw." *Diaballein* thus means literally to "throw across." And what is it that the evil one throws across our path? The object that is hurled is called in Greek a *skandalon,* meaning "a snare," or a "cause for stumbling."

The diabolos is thus the one who would create a cause for personal stumbling and relational breakdown. The evil one is the "Tempter" of persons and relationships—including and especially our relationship to God. And note that the enemy does not throw but would tempt us to hurl the word which cuts and wounds, which itself becomes a cause for "scandal" and stumbling across our path to life and each other. The enemy would have us either originate or return evil for evil, scandal for scandal.

The evil one is therefore the relationship breaker, the one which would sever the ties that unite us. And it would fill the void thus created with its unholy companions; it would bind and blind us, that our houses may be plundered and the treasure within and between us desecrated. Evil would destroy the We, would divide and conquer through turning persons against each other and for themselves first.

Evil is the primal and archetypal enemy of the We, and of the person in relationship. It would sever the We, and attack the person through the void it has helped to create between the relational partners. Thus is evil first spiritual, then personal—or, technically, anti-spiritual, then anti-personal. It is interpersonal before it becomes intra-personal, between us before it finds its way to be within us. When a vacuum is generated, evil comes—"legally"—to fill the space; for, as with nature, there is great pressure on the person to fill a vacuum. And evil is the heinous void-filler between ourselves and God, and consequent upon that, between ourselves and all others.

Evil comes to reside initially in the *"No"* to God present within the heart. This *"No"* is itself the first and greatest gap generator between us and God. In that *"No"* abides our strange darkness and hiddenness from God—and thus from ourselves. For we know ourselves only in God, and in the truth of God. Evil stands in the gap between us and God; it is the barrier to true mutuality. And the barrier evil constructs is a kind of mirror—or the illusion of a mirror—of the I. But it is the I of evil, the I of the unreal self evil would have us embrace as our true identity. Thus would we unknowingly bond with evil; thus would we bring evil across into the world.

In place of a genuine I-You relationship, evil would grant us only an I-I relationship, devoid of otherness and mutual life. The I would relate only with the "evil I," which evil would have us merge with and become. And then, evil would have us bring this I-image into the world, to draw others to it as a model. How concerned with sales is evil! And in our vanity, how many of us are only too willing to embrace the I of illusion, only too glad to feed and attend to this I, unto the death of true relationship—and of who we are in relationship! Yet we do not realize just how empty we are while, in our sleep, we only dream we are eating and merrymaking.

Alas, one day all shall awake to their true state. Blessed are those who recognize their hunger and personal poverty now, while there is time to turn to God and be filled!

✠

Evil cannot look upon itself in actuality, for to do so it must face the truth. The truth is God, and all truth is of God and for God. Hence, to face the truth means to face God and the judgment of God. That will not come for evil until the end, until the final Word is uttered, against which there can be no resistance. Evil cannot see the truth and live. That evil lives and is permitted to operate means that the end is not yet. Now is the time for tempting and testing. Now is the time when lies and deception have the opportunity to be heard, to call out that which is of evil, and to bring us to a situation of "forced choice." And not to choose is really to choose evil. For decisionlessness grants evil permission to continue operating.

The deception of evil begins with its own self-deception. In its radical narcissism, evil sees but itself—and as it wishes to be and to be seen as, not as it is in truth. For to be in truth would mean to be in God, and in relation to God. And that is precisely what evil cannot do and be. Evil is ever prideful and vain, and will clothe itself in whatever will afford it the appearance of being good, true and beautiful. Yet it is only a garment to be used and cast off when discovered. For the evil itself remains hidden behind its perpetual chameleon masks. Evil is concerned only with show, not with substance—save only as substance can serve and be subservient to it. "The show's the thing." Evil lives for the moment and for instant gratification. For in the next instant it may be discovered and have to flee; or worse, the end may come and it will have to pay. It senses dimly the truth of its ugliness and untruth and temporariness, but it fights the revelation of these facts, and the full disclosure to itself and others of its truth and fate.

Evil believes its own lies, and must deny any culpability or wrongdoing. Honest introspection would lead to its dissipation. Yet evil can never fully believe its lies—for even in its opposition to, evil is still a creature of, the logos, the Word, and is thus unable to finally eradicate all awareness of the truth of its unholiness. It must therefore constantly seek to convince others of the truth of its lies; it must ever persuade and seduce. But it can never succeed, for it can never find escape from the Word of truth. It must seduce and silence the opposition. Woe to those who will not be seduced or silenced; evil must discount, if not destroy them.

✠

What then of "evil spirits" or "demons"? And what of "possession"? There are indeed "evil spirits" between us. They are beings of the anti-

Word; that is, they are specific "spirits" of unholy language, which can invade and pollute the soul, which can surround and imprison the person. Though not "persons"—rather "anti-persons"—these "demons" have a certain intelligence, which is the seemingly self-conscious content of their specific "logoi," of their meaning within the anti-Word. In short, like cancer of the body, they are perversely lawful. And like a cancer of the soul, they come to replicate themselves and take over the whole system.

Yet these demons have not the power to possess, but may only harass the one who remains open to their darkness. True "possession" can come about only when the will of the person welcomes and even desires it. Thus for instance, in hatred one may seek the power and "wisdom" of a spirit of vengeance to use against another. But it is vengeance which does the using, and the one who invokes it who is the used. In choosing evil, we will become its victim. And in time the heart can become hardened in its unholy choice, and the person seemingly lose the freedom to say "No" to evil. Then only the Spirit of God can free the soul. Then One is needed to "set the captives free." And in Christ, that One is actively among us.

As there is a spirit to every word, which is its unuttered but present meaning and connotation, so there is an unclean spirit to unclean language. In using and embracing words, we invite in the spirit or spirits associated with them. Words are not "only words"! To say "I hate you" opens us not only to something ugly within us, but also to the "logos"—or "anti-logos"—of the meaning of hatred itself. Unclean spirits hover about the soul—and the We-spirits of love— like germs and viruses about the body. Where there is an opening, there do they enter. Even if they already have a kind of presence within the body, which the body is able to hold in check, the entrance of a superior force and fresh reinforcements can throw the balance of power over to the enemy. And then it is that the enemy comes to hold sway.

Anger, jealously, fear, these and other elements of darkness already exist within the human soul. Evil is already germinally present and "crouching at the door," awaiting an opportunity to express and develop itself. And when we exercise any of these "natural functions" of the soul, they can open us to the augmenting power of the darkness between us and others, that is, to the anti-Word present in our darkened human world, our polluted "psychosphere." When they are exercised they automatically generate a vacuum or void between us and the one involved in the situation. Beware of these voids between us! For unclean spirits can come and abide only in the void we create between ourselves and other persons—especially and above all, between us and God. Where there is no void, there evil cannot come and set up shop.

When the final Word is spoken, the void will be cast into the outer darkness. And so will evil and all that is of evil. In its place will be the Holy Spirit, the ultimate and eternal "void-filler," the wondrous We into which no evil can ever penetrate.

In the meantime all power abides in the Name and Person of Christ, the Eternal I. Christ is the Truth into which evil dare not enter. For in that truth evil would finally see itself and die. How evil must flee from the Truth of Christ! And that Truth has dawned in the Spirit and is available to all. Yet alas, so is evil—but only for now.

THE WAY BACK : DAWNING REDEMPTION

Forgiveness

Forgiveness is a healing power within the blood of the common life of the Spirit. It can keep "Us" together—and bring "Us" back together after a falling away. Hence, forgiveness is the great "gap" remover between persons, the primal force of love to reestablish itself, to cleanse uncleaness and to eradicate the evil which can come to exist in the alienation between persons. Behold, forgiveness is the "universal solvent" of evil, the holy water of the Spirit.

Forgiveness belongs to the Word of the coming redemption. It is thus of the spirit before it is of the soul, of the future re-creation before the past creation. Forgiveness is love's agent of repair and maintenance, without which love could not survive and the We-spirit not abide in the world. To "forgive" is to "give" indeed, to give up and give into for the sake of the beloved and the future of the relationship. Love ever seeks new beginnings; forgiveness makes new beginnings possible, it keeps love young and fresh. Forgiveness clears the air, the spiritual atmosphere between persons, and bathes them in its restorative power.

Forgiveness is more than the forgetting of the past; it is the letting go of it. Forgiveness allows the past to finally become the past, without any lingering resentment or bitterness. Forgiveness thus frees the psyche for new life, often from the ashes of a former relationship. The power of forgiveness is that of resurrection; it brings back what was lost in a new form, one touched by God—for only God can truly forgive. Hence, where there is forgiveness, there is God. The relationship in which forgiveness has entered will not be as it once was; it will be as God intends it to be for the present. Some relationships will thus be deepened and more intense and mature; other relationships will never attain to intimacy again, but will fade away with grace and a "benign neglect"—with the participants able to look upon each other without malice or shame, but with compassion and understanding.

To forgive is to set free, to let go in order to let be. What then of justice? Does forgiveness merely open the prison doors after the person has served the full sentence? Or does forgiveness cancel at the point at which it is executed? If so, is forgiveness fair? What of retributive justice, what of crime and punishment, law and morality? Would forgiveness simply dispense with the order of cause and effect, of "personal karma"? If so, does forgiveness know what it is doing, as it were?

Perhaps from the vantage point of forgiveness, the question is whether law understands the nature of spirit! The "law" of forgiveness is that of redemption, that of bringing back and restoring what was lost. That means the person and the relationship. The law of forgiveness serves love above all. And God is love. Hence the law of forgiveness is a higher law than that of the derivative laws of nature and of the psyche. Forgiveness is not to be found in the strict cause-effect world of nature, nor does it set well in the soul of a humanity raised to think in terms of reward and punishment, with its system of justice established to determine the nature and limits of desert.

Forgiveness is not "fair"; it serves a different realm of law than that of nature and humanity. Forgiveness is paradoxical; it seeks to serve justice by dispensing with its very implementation. It allows—and even demands—justice to grind the facts through its instruments of evaluation, so that the truth be known and squarely faced by all concerned. It even asks of justice to pronounce guilt and the proper punishment for the offense. And finally, it pushes justice to inquire of the guilty whether there be a hard heart or a broken and contrite one, whether there be a spirit of repentance or of standing firm in the deed. All this time forgiveness waits in the wings, with justice sensing—but not understanding—a hidden movement of a holy intention deeper than the eyes of retribution can see.

At the right time, forgiveness springs forth to take the burden of punishment off the shoulders of the guilty and to bear the effects itself. Forgiveness, already as present as the Spirit of God, awaits the opportunity to be believed and received in the heart of the offender. Hence, repentance is necessary not in order to earn, but to be able to receive, the forgiveness already present in the love of God. And the sign of this wondrous divine forgiveness offered to sinners even in their ongoing waywardness? The Cross. Though we earned the Cross as punishment, the forgiving love of God is such that what we earned has instead become the fount of every blessing.

Forgiveness would allow punishment only for the sake of redemption, but never for the sake of sheer retribution. Such permitted punishment is in truth the loving discipline or chastisement of God, meant to prepare us to repent wholeheartedly, and thus to be redeemed. What forgiveness believes the person needs is not retribution but a new distribution, a new gifting of love. And if the person is ready to turn and live, forgiveness would take the whole of the remaining sentence into itself, somehow absorbing it through a capacity known only to God. Forgiveness makes redemption present, and constitutes its very announcement and calling card, as it were.

✠

Yet are there not "reasons" to forgive? Yes—but only love understands them. For they are greater than the "mitigating circumstances" of human law, beyond the scope even of the "to understand all is to forgive all" mentality. Of course because God knows all, God and only God can truly forgive. But *forgiveness happens for the same reasons that love loves*. The mystery of forgiveness and the mystery of love are one. The answer lies in the inscrutable will of God, planted in the human heart at creation, revealed in the incarnation and implemented by the Cross, brought home through the Spirit and to be consummated in the coming redemption. Forgiveness is a gift of grace and freedom; it transcends law and morality. Forgiveness is of the very sovereignty of God.

In our capacity to forgive lies our capacity for divinity, for the life of God to live in and with us. It is not that we cannot forgive; it is that we will not. The problem of forgiveness lies in the will, not in the capacity. And our inability to forgive—ourselves as well as others—is a powerful symptom of our dis-eased heart, of our fallenness, of our sin, our refusal to maintain full participation in the life of love. For without forgiveness love has no chance to set its roots deep, to take full control of the human heart. Without forgiveness, we will never attain the fullness of the Person God calls us to be.

And at the Cross the fullness of that Person is revealed for all time. "Father, forgive them, for they know not what they do." The forgiveness of the Cross is above all a forgiveness *in advance*, preparatory to repentance. It is as if God were saying to us: "I forgive You both now and in the time to come; so that when You come to discover how You have treated Me and who I Am, at the same time, instead of receiving what You deserve, You will experience the power of My forgiveness, with its new life with Me."

The forgiveness of Jesus Christ embraces all three spheres of time. We are forgiven of our past; we are brought whole and free into an open horizon of the present; we are gifted with a future where Christ already awaits us. Like the soldiers who killed Him, when we come to see the gravity and extent of our transgressions of His law of love, at the same time we will be cleansed and renewed—if we but turn and open!

✠

Faith

Faith is perseverance in the We. As such, it can make and keep us right with God and with each other. Thus does "justification by faith" refer primarily to a relational rather than a subjective stance before God. *Faith* signifies *a will to openness and inclusivity, together with a consistent commitment to and persistence in believing in the other, regardless of what outward circumstances would seem to indicate.* Faith is the unconditional willingness to trust the other and to stand fast in the relationship, no matter what may come. It is a vowed refusal to back away from the other, and thereby to generate a gap between relational partners. Faith will not reject, nor will it easily accept rejection. It maintains the unity required for mutuality to happen. Indeed, faith is the very ground of mutuality.

Such was the paradoxical faith of Abraham, such was the faith of Jesus. Both persevered in trust of the God of their life, even unto the unexpected commandment to bring to the altar the fulfillment of the promise, there to be sacrificed to the One more important to the covenantal relationship than the promise thereof. Both were chosen vessels, not only to receive great blessings from God, but especially to be tested and purified for our sakes, and for the sake of our relationship to God. The faith Abraham evidenced in his willingness to give up his only son, whom he loved, to God, and the faith Jesus confirmed by giving up His life for us, whom He loved, this extraordinary and fully tested faith, this unconditional self-giving to God, this is the model of faith for all—Jews, Christians, and Muslims.

Not only were Abraham and Jesus willing to give up that which was most precious to them—a child and a mission, respectively—; but they did so with faith in the One who called and loved them, faith in the goodness and intention of a God who is neither answerable to nor understandable by us. They did not back away and seek to withhold from God the fruit of their life, but offered it whole and without "blemish." They risked all in openness and unswerving trust; they persevered in their relational stance with God unto the end. And in the end, their faith, which justified them to God, was justified by God.

In the radical faith of Abraham, God was trusted and the divine promise of prodigious progeny was believed in despite the inexplicable delay in its fulfillment, and then with only a single heir, presented to a hundred year old man—by a ninety year old woman! And God was trusted and no movement away taken or even protest lodged when the wholly unexpected and cruel command came to "abort" Isaac—and therein the promise itself. A whole life lived for a promise, finally granted, only to be taken away! O the breaking of spirit and will to be sensed in the silence of Abraham!

Twice did God call Abraham in this dramatic chapter of Scripture (Genesis 22), and twice did Abraham answer immediately with the steadfast "Here I am." But what different circumstances between the two calls! The first call came from the still consistent God of the promise, now being fulfilled in the young Isaac. How easily could Abraham then respond with "Here I am," unsuspecting of the dark turning about to come. And the second call came to Abraham— almost too late—at the point at which he actually drew the knife from its sheath, and prepared to pierce that which he loved above all. Immediately came the answer, and with it the proof positive: Abraham was still standing fast before his God, immovable and open. Abraham had obeyed God, and persevered in trust. Thus did he remain literally "right" with God. For faith holds us in place; it keeps us open to the other, and willing to step forward and meet the other ever anew.

The absolute faith of Jesus is revealed in His willingness to go to the Cross, to carry out the will of God, in spite of its representing the absolute failure of His mission to redeem Israel. Precisely at the point at which He was to go to Jerusalem in order to fulfill His mission and actually bring in the Kingdom, the Word emerged—how and when we will never know—that the only crown awaiting the true Messiah was that of thorns, and His palace was to be a sepulcher. Rather than acceptance and joy, Jesus was to receive rejection and be most grievously crucified before His people—and the world. Rather than an army of angels coming down to meet Him, there was to be a long line of persons coming up—from one generation to the next—to look upon Him in His agony.

Yet the faithful word of response from the ultimate Person to walk among us until the end of time: "Not my will, but Your will be done." Jesus stood firm, open even to the kiss of His betrayer. So steadfast was He in His unity and perseverance with God, that He could even forgive those who, blind to who and with whom He was, crucified Him. Unto His death, Jesus held His place in the We between Him and God— and in so doing, secured that place for us forever. At the final hour, His now tested and unbreakable unity with God was to be seen by those whose eyes were open to the truth. Came the most precious moment, the last event of the story only Jesus understood, the actual self-giving: "Father, into Your hands I commit my spirit." True was He to the end and beyond, this Jesus. And in His faith, both He and we are to be eternally "justified," forever held right with God. Nothing in all creation will be able to separate us from that bond of faith and that unity of love.

✠

To be "faithful," then, means to actually be *where* and *when* one needs to be for the existence and perpetuation of true relationship. Without faith, the We cannot happen; we cannot meet and be sustained in our mutuality. Thus did Abraham answer God's address again and again with his steadfast "Here I am." And thus did Adam and Eve fail to be faithful; thus did the Fall happen with their attempt to hide from God. Faith means therefore unconditional *availability* to God and on God's terms. And God is love. Hence, faith means to be ever available for love.

To be faithful also means to be *who* one is called to be in the relationship. That is, it means to be reliably and consistently present to the Other as who one is in the relationship. Faith means therefore *dependability* for God's sake. It means to be present with an inner readiness to do and to be what God wills. "Here I am...and as who I am to you, and for you. God, You can count on me. Here I am, send me."

And faith carries with it the willingness to abandon one's self for the other and for the relationship. It is the willingness to relinquish the "me" and the "mine" for the sake of the "yours," and especially the "ours." For the end of faith is the consummation of the relationship, and in that the true and final fulfillment of the I. Faith would lead us all the Way to the heavenly city of pure and unending mutuality, where "self-ishness" has given full away to "We-fullness." Only who among us will follow faith all the way?

✠

Commitment

As we give, so we receive. As we sow, thus shall we reap. That which is needed above all to attain and maintain true life is *commitment.* Commitment means self-giving not only in the present, but in the future as well. Commitment is the one road of mutuality through all of time; it is love's rock and fortress in the world. Commitment is not of the feelings but of the will; it is the supreme act of faith-creation in which and by which the will determines the life, the height, depth and extent of our relationships, be it with ourselves, another, God and nature—with the whole itself. In this we forge our future, and lay the foundation of the meaning of our today. That means the spirit of our today, for meaning is of spirit. Where there is meaning, there is spirit; where meaning breaks down, there spirit has evaporated, like dew on the midday grass. Hence, those without commitment are without both meaning and spirit.

Where faith is the architect of love, commitment is the builder. The work of faith is to turn us to one another and enable us to persevere in openness; the task of commitment is to build the bridge on faith's foundation between ourselves and our beloved. Without commitment, love cannot find a dwelling place in the world. For commitment, like a house, is designed to withstand the extremities of weather, so that what abides within it may continue to exist and even thrive regardless of external conditions.

Faith and commitment come together as twin gifts from above. Faith is the visionary of love, commitment is the common laborer. The former sees into the future through a power of intuition we do not yet understand; the latter carves a path between that tomorrow and our concrete today. Where faith, as our foundation, needs to be immovable, commitment, as our road, needs to be unstoppable. Thus, commitment is the discipline of faith, without which our faith is empty and lifeless, without which conversion as a way of life and pilgrimage as our daily walk, become impossible.

An axiom warns us to "never put all your eggs in one basket." Yet as regards our commitment to God, we are called "to put all our person in one We," so to speak. Better nothing at all than only a part of Us; better hot or cold than lukewarm. To be tepid is an abomination before God. God wants the heart, the center and the substance. What is called for is our very self, whole and "unblemished," which is our spiritual sacrifice. The depth of the roots determines the quantity and quality of the fruit—to say nothing of the staying power of the plant through the rough times sure to come.

What then is commitment but the "drill-bit" through which we penetrate the difficult ground of the soul, opening it to the treasures of mutual life? Alas, those treasures are both gift and to be hard won. And only commitment will see through to their unearthing and development.

✠

The etymology of the word *commit* is instructive here. It comes from the Latin *committere,* meaning "to connect, entrust," and is derived from the combination of *com,* "together," and *mittere,* meaning "to send." The spirit underlying language reveals itself here. To commit means, first, to send together, that is, to will and move towards connection, even if from afar. It is a "from—to" movement of the will, from present separation toward future interconnectedness. The word of commitment: "These things shall be—together. Toward that end will I work." In this does our life have meaning and direction.

To commit means, second, to hand over to another oneself and that which is precious to oneself, and for the sake of the end, *which is the relationship,* in which and towards which one is striving. That is, the commitment is as much to the relationship or to the meaning and the pledged continuation of that relationship, as to the person. The I is not just committed to the You, but also to the We.

Further, to commit means to *entrust,* and once again the meaning of the word rings true to the spirit: the *en* intensifies the *trust;* the *en* prefix signifies the actually going into, the putting into effect, the causing to be, of the trust itself. Thus to commit means to move into trust and to bring it into full effect.

Finally, to commit means to actually *act,* to carry out or perpetrate a deed. More than word and will, to commit signifies the doing as such. And nothing short of doing is required for the life and maintenance of the We.

✠

Commitment and Marriage: The commitment of the will to the covenant of marriage is necessary for the perpetuation and survival of the life between the partners. Commitment is the strength and adhesive power of the living bond of love. The capacity of the human soul to make a commitment to another person for the whole of one's life is a sign of the divinity within us, of the image of God we bear.

The nature of the commitment of marriage is threefold, in accordance with the threefold reality of time and being, of past, present and future. The commitment is first of all to the person, and that speaks to the future; then it is to the love itself, and that addresses the present, and the willingness to meet each other daily. Finally, it refers to the relationship, the covenant, and that bespeaks the past, the ongoing history of their life together. In being committed to *You,* I am therefore saying, "I will be with You always, even unto the end of our age." In being committed to the *love* between us, I am saying "I will step forth each and every day to hold and behold You, and to share the gift of hours and space in which to be together." In being committed to the *relationship,* I am saying "I will strive to forget nothing of what we have shared and meant to each other; our covenant and history shall remain sacred and celebrated by me—and by us."

The act of committing ourselves in marriage is the most sacred and solemn vow in the whole of our life in the world. Indeed, our relationship with God is just such a vowed life, for covenant and marriage are one. The life of the We is built upon the commitment of the I and the You—in both human and divine terms. The very ground of salvation, the rock of assurance itself, is none other than the decision of God to love us, together with God's incomprehensible commitment to us, even and precisely in the face of our never-ending rejection and rebellion against such wondrous grace. Apart from commitment, love and salvation have no chance of survival. God's commitment alone will bring about the coming redemption.

✠

Marriage

"And the two shall become one flesh." The We of marriage, the spirit between husband and wife, is the highest and holiest form of mutuality in the world of humanity. We are in fact created for marriage, divine as well as human. We are designed for true and unending union, for participation in an Eternal I-You, a Holy We. And human marriage replicates the Trinity itself. Like the Trinity, marriage is a three-in-one state of being. The I and the You find each other and seek to take their stand in the We of their meeting and mutuality. Thus is marriage the proper analogy of our relation to God, and of God's own "Self-relation," as it were. Indeed, the movement toward marriage is that of redemption itself.

The We of marriage involves all three primal biblical relationships, namely, that of creation, revelation and redemption. Marriage is first of all creative of the persons addressed into existence in the love itself. It brings forth the persons who are to live together in its mutual realm. Secondly, marriage becomes the most profound and intimate scene for the reciprocal revelation of who we are, of our "private" self. And third, marriage promises and actually begins that redemption of our souls which will be consummated only by the Spirit in the coming Word. The spirit of marriage would seal us within the Spirit of eternal communion.

"And the two shall become one flesh." That means: the persons are in fact joined and "sealed" together by the Spirit of God. A new "estate" is brought into the world. Of significance here is the etymology of the term "estate." It derives from the Middle English and Old French *estat,* based on the Latin *status,* meaning "state or condition," which in turn stems from the verb *stare,* meaning "to stand." Marriage thus represents a new condition of standing in the world. A condition of spiritual and mutual integrity, just like the integrity of the body, comes into *private, mutual* and *public* existence. That means a condition at once subjective, objective and inter-subjective has come into being in which the persons have found themselves. They are "married" in spirit, and through the nuptial vows commit themselves to the perpetuation and consummation of that union.

Their mutual existence enters into the public affairs of a community. The marriage has impact and is recorded in the history of a people. Two persons are henceforth identified in and by virtue of this relational reality recognized by the culture. Hence, they do not just "have" a marriage, as they would children or a house; rather, they *are* married. Their actual and concrete mode of being in the world is changed "unto death." Something real has transpired, and not just in name and ceremony only; something of the greatest personal substance is publicly proclaimed and blessed—but most certainly not created—by the ceremony.

What has transpired? Is the ceremony only a solemn show of vowing, of two persons publicly committing themselves to a state of mere living together? Or is it a public recognition and blessing of a state already entered into, of something as actual as the persons themselves, there between them, silently in attendance? "Those whom God has joined, let not man put asunder." Who has done this joining, and when? And what is this uniting but the Spirit of love itself, the Spirit of God, joining and being joined in this marriage of God's own engineering? In truth, God is a Partner in all marriages.

Though silent, God is the ground of love between the marriage partners. And their shared vows concern the commitment to work that common ground of their love, to plant and to tend, to weed and to harvest the fruit of that gift of a place in which to be together. Marriage is then the earth of God, the realm of the Spirit, parceled out to each couple in accordance with a divine plan. As laborers of love, we are accountable for how we work God's own land.

Marriage is the proper analogy of our relationship to God. As we treat our spouse, we are by implication, treating God. For as the most important human You of our life, our spouse is a surrogate for the true and ultimate You of our life. As is said in theater: "We do in performance as we do in rehearsal." Thus, as we are to our earthly spouse, we will be to our heavenly Spouse in the marriage to come.

Better therefore, to learn now how to love and accept and compromise! Better to work out our salvation with our spouse in fear and trembling—for God is at work in our marriage, both to will and to work for the good pleasure of the coming relationship.

✠

The We vs. the Us: The We of meeting and mutuality is the ground of love and marriage. You and I meet, and We happen. There is openness and reciprocity, a knowing and a being known in one. In the We of our sharing, the Spirit between us is the only law, and freedom our only path. In the togetherness, our actual communion *is* our covenant. But in memory and over time, the "Us" of common history and tradition emerges. And it is to the Us as well as to our We that we commit ourselves in our marriage vows; it is to where we have been and found each other, as well as to where we are going and will find each other yet ahead.

A tension can come to exist between this Us of covenant and tradition and the We of meeting and mutuality. It is in essence the tension between the meaning of the past and the openness of the future, between yesterday's understanding and tomorrow's unfolding vision.

Where the Us demands dependability, consistency and fidelity, the We requires freedom, novelty and openness. Where the former is conservative and cautious, the latter is liberal and risk-taking. In point of fact, the Us and the We should not be separated. A good marriage needs both. Marriage should function like the double-faced Janus head of Greek mythology, with one face looking to the past and the other to the future. For only through the fresh meetings of the We will the deepest dream of the Us be realized.

If the Us and the We are separated, the former comes to be the "law" of marriage, the latter the "spirit"; the former the known and has been, the latter the mysterious and the could be. If one or both of the marriage partners seek to live only with the Us, and to force the other and the relationship into the refracted molds of the prior "living arrangement," a legalism sets in which could in time kill the spirit. Yet on the other hand, a marriage cannot consist only of the We, for that would lead to the opposite of a legalism, namely to an antinomianism, to a relationship which would never settle down and grow up.

For marriage is the growth relationship par excellence. Not only are we to grow in and into marriage; marriage is to grow into us. Relationships grow, just like people. And the marriage relationship does not grow backward nor tarry with yesterday any more than nature does. Would that we could keep pace with the changes in our marriage with the same sensitivity and ease that we do to the changes in the seasons! Would that we had enough faith in ourselves, each other, and in love itself to say "Yes" to those changes, and to find in them the fruit of our marriage! Like us, marriage changes; nothing stays the same. The appearance of sameness is only deception and dream. God alone abides unchanging.

We grow in marriage as marriage grows in us. That means: the marriage partners must stay current with each other, must love one another in the changes and metamorphoses of their souls, must walk together as pilgrims toward the holy city. And that means: standing square upon the rock of Us, the partners must daily seek to meet anew, that We may happen ever again, that love may embrace change as its most honored guest. For change will ultimately bring us into the final transformation: the marriage with God in the coming redemption.

Woe to those who refuse to grow, or to see the growth in themselves or in their marriage partners! Woe to those for whom marriage is a binding agreement, which once entered upon must be reenacted every day without change—like a long running theatrical production. Is that not precisely what it would have to become if they are to get through it? Woe to those who would seal the Spirit from the marriage, rather than to allow the Spirit to seal them ever afresh, with each new meeting, into loving closeness. Marriage for such a legalist is not a home, not an ever-unfinished but always under loving construction cloistered place of heart and spirit. Rather, it is a prison of discontent and "mis-meeting."

✠

"The two shall become one flesh." That means: I am no longer my own, nor are You your own. Rather, we are "ours." It is not that I belong to You or that You belong to me, but that You and I belong to each other, to *Us*, to the marriage spirit of our experience and commitment. In the context of the relationship—in which we are to abide daily—we are "ours." And the marriage spirit is given of God, and like ourselves, belongs to God. Hence—and so much rides on our recognition of this point that I will speak for myself— I am accountable to God not only for myself, for this person of God's making and will, but I am also accountable for this "second creation" of the marriage spirit.

That is, God made me, and then re-created me again in the "Us" of marriage. The second time, it is the love itself which brings me new life, just as it is the Holy Spirit which brings new and eternal life in the coming marriage with God. Love is creative of persons. And the Holy Spirit *is* the love of God, the mutual love of the Divine I for the You and the You for the I. Thus, God's own Marriage-Spirit is creative of the ultimate I we are to become, namely the Eternal I of Christ. For *Christos* is *Anthropos* under the anointing of the Spirit, the human person in the unending life with God. Christ is who we shall all become in the coming marriage, the wondrous union called redemption.

And they become one flesh. That is, the Spirit of love actually seals the marriage partners together in a common realm known only to the two of them. Call it their "private mutuality," a "sanctuary" between them, there as the place for their protection and meeting. There are they to meet not only each other, but God, as with them as their love, from the beginning unto the end of their age.

And that marriage seal must not be broken. What God has joined, we dare not sever. For once broken, the marriage seal requires spiritual therapy and re-consecration to ever be restored again. The seal and the sanctity thereof are as real as the marriage and indeed as the people themselves. And when that seal is broken, the persons become prey to all manner of evil within and between them. The point of rupture becomes like an open sore, painful and exposed and vulnerable to viruses destructive of unity, from the demon of infidelity to the spirit of unforgiveness. And many are the forces which lie in wait of wounded marriages!

Yet the healing Spirit of the God who marries is ever available to those who will it. And human love, unlike the nerves of the body, can be regenerated through the power of God's love. That which is impossible for humanity is possible for God.

It is of the greatest importance that as individuals and as a people we come to see the living parameters of the marriage covenant, this most important of all human We relationships. Only by so doing can we hope to turn the current tide of our cultural disintegration, for which there is no more potent and poignant symbol than the radical breakdown in the cultural view of the permanency and sanctity of marriage. Marriage for too many is strictly on a "trial" basis, and fidelity only an option. Yet our level of commitment and consistency determines our level of fulfillment. In all truth, adultery is relational idolatry. And as a people we have become idol worshipers.

Does not this fact bespeak our need for a religious renewal and revolution of the first magnitude? Nothing short of that will restore the vision of marriage given by God in our creation.

✠

What does it mean to be married but to always be available to each other? It means to abide unmovingly before the beloved face ever changing throughout the course of a shared journey. Marriage is a willingness to meet and to share unconditionally. And the meetings that do come about, the precious moments of discovery and fresh bonding, form, in memory, a kind of spiritual "add-a-pearl" necklace. We wear that necklace around our souls, and we remember. Each of these memories, these pearls of great worth, are in truth *charismata*, gifts of grace.

And such memories of meeting and communion can hold us steady and believing through the barren days of distance and dissonance, which visit all marriages. How sustaining to finger these moments which none may take from us in the tough times, the times when we may wonder whether marriage is real or even possible.

Behold, those pearls of the memories of past meetings and mutuality apply as well to our marriage with God. Real moments of concrete breakthroughs of the Spirit of meeting and mutuality have happened. And the marriage has been secured by those who have preceded us—for the Christian by Christ Jesus Himself on the Cross. Now is a time of seemingly great distance and dissonance, of disbelief and mutual silence, if not indifference.

How comforting, then, are these pearls of the divine-human marriage! It is all we will have until that final Word is spoken, and the necklace completed and revealed as stretching from dawn to dawn.

✠

Rebirth

> Unless a man is born again, he cannot see the kingdom of God (John 3:3).

Rebirth is the entrance into the We of God. It is the "baptism" of the Spirit Jesus came to offer humanity. It signifies a "second birth," brought about through the power of the Christ's Word, Spirit and resurrected Life. It is the Love of God remaking us into Itself. Thus did Love rebirth Jesus, there at the Jordan; thus will It rebirth us.

The Greek preposition utilized in the passage above is most instructive here. It is *anothen,* which means first and primarily, "from above." It also means, secondly, "again" or "anew." Hence, Jesus tells us that we are to be born "from above," which also signifies "again" or "anew." That means: we are to have a new family of origin, and take our roots in a new We-Spirit, with a new identity. Thus, "Hal of history" was born of the flesh to the parents Don and Mildred Green, but "Hal of Christ" was born of the Spirit, and belongs to the family of God. In the Spirit I have a new point of origin, a new We of identity, belonging and intimacy—and with it a new destiny. Instead of death, mine is everlasting life, in and with my eternal family.

It cannot be overemphasized that the new birth is into another form of mutuality. It begins with a second address. The first address was that of our creation itself: "Be You," spoke the Eternal You. And behold, we were. The second address initiates a new creation and a new relationship: "I Am" utters the Eternal I from deep within us, as well as from without—both through the medium of the Spirit. The first address fixed forever the externality of the "You" and the "It." It also established a kind of incomplete "mutuality of externality," that is, a reciprocal stance of our human You over against the divine You. The second address completes the first, and sets forever the internality between the divine and human persons, the "mutuality of internality" of our human I over against the divine I.

Behold, we are born anew by this Word of address and this Spirit of Love, into the I of Christ and the We of God. For the I of Christ exists only in and by virtue of the Eternal "Us" of God, as it were. Just so in the new birth do we attain our being and life in the everlasting communion of God.

In the first address, the You of God was uttered. In the second, the I of God came to speech and incarnation among and within us. What remains is the utterance of the third address, the Word of the We of God finally being spoken. And when God speaks, the Word will bring to pass that which it states. Thus will the "We are" bring in the final redemption of the world; it will make fully present, visible and actual all that has been implied and promised through the two prior Words of creation and revelation. Will it also bring with it yet another birth? Or is our birth into Christ through the Spirit already that birth, so that the final Word is but the confirmation of that which we have already attained?

The answer abides in the depth of our hearts and in the ground of the Spirit. And though it cannot yet be stated—or even understood, until it actually presents Itself—in our faith is a "mustard seed" of the substance that is to come, which, though small, is sufficient to carry us unto that day. And the Word upon which we must take our stand: "Jesus Christ is the same yesterday, today and forever."

Note that in the second birth, as in the first, we enter into the family-We as babes, not as adults. Though in Christ and thus "saved," we are to grow into that I, to attain maturity, completion, and wholeness; we are to take hold of that for which God took hold of us; we are to personally appropriate and make true in our lives the "Way, the Truth and the Life" who is Christ. Hence, rebirth is not the end but only the beginning of life with God, of participation in the We of Spirit. And the race to perfection set before us is not easy. It is long and arduous and demands all that we are, time and time again. And it demands even more than we are, so that we may experience the presence and power of God with us on our way to the holy city.

The only way to attain the end is to keep our eyes fixed on the One who preceded us, and to follow all the way. For the path is narrow and singular. And few find it. So few ever grow up in Christ. Most prefer to remain as babes, and let God as Parent do that which, in all truth, God as Spouse awaits our active help in bringing about. Not only the end, but also the means of redemption is and must be *Us*, a holy partnership.

✠

Rebirth: what must die and what is reborn? The whole of love and the history of humanity are at stake in the answer. Does the second birth cancel the first, the second creation make null and void the first? Is the flesh of the first creation—that is, our physical existence in the world—to be crucified with Jesus, to participate unto death in the sacrifice of His life? In taking up our Cross, are we then to repeat in our life His death? For what then did His sacrifice count, save only as the model for ours? He died for our sake that we might die for His? Where is the "Good News" in this?

The way to salvation is at one with the Way of salvation. It is the Way of love. Only love can save, and only love has the vision and clarity of *what* is to be saved. The single divine condition for salvation, that is, for entrance into the Eternal We, is *the unconditional acceptance and reception through faith of the unconditional love of God, a love which crucified itself for our sakes, that we might not have to crucify ourselves for its sake.* The love of God is one with the grace of God, which comes always as gift, never as earned or deserved by anything we have or could ever do. It is the love which created us and loves us as we are, sins and all—hence, it is a *scandalous* love. It is a love which understands that *only by being loved unconditionally as who we are now, will we ever be empowered to become who we are created to be.*

What therefore is loved into new creation is this very creation. It is this life, this person who is redeemed, this very soul which is breathed through and through with the fire of the Spirit. And behold, it is this flesh, this body which is to be a temple of the Holy Spirit now, an earthen vessel of grace; and it is this flesh which shall be transformed into a "spiritual body," not made with hands, eternal in the heavens. Paradox of paradoxes—a "spiritual body"! Our rebirth in the Spirit as persons, will include the rebirth of our very flesh in God as well. In what is to come, we will be exactly the same and wholly—and holy—new, both at once. On that your faith may take its stand.

The "new Jerusalem," the "new creation" which is to come, will not signify the destruction or actual end of the present work of God, in which God was—and is—"well pleased." Rather, that which is to come will be the "saving"—as in the "keeping"—transformation of this world by and into the Spirit of God, so that God will at last be "all in all." The physical We of creation will be loved into the Eternal We of God, through the prior wedding of God with the human We of the psyche or soul. For we humans have an essential role to play in the rebirth of nature and the world. We are partners with God. The final We will be spoken through our We with God, the marriage between heaven and earth consummated through the marriage between the divine and human persons. We are marriage partners with God. If we will not do our share, the work will not get done. God will not redeem the world apart from us.

✠

The Healing of Redemption

> Now may the God of peace Himself sanctify you completely; and may your whole spirit, soul, and body be preserved blameless at the coming of our Lord Jesus Christ (1 Thessalonians 5:23).

We are three: body, soul and spirit. And in Christ, God has revealed the gracious Way and End of our healing and salvation. That healing has three inseparable dimensions, all brought about through

Christ. In Christ's Spirit is the *restoration* of our relationship with God—and therefore with each other. We are to stand where Christ stands—as authorized in the Lord's Prayer—and to participate fully in the Spirit of eternal mutuality with God. In Christ's soul is the *renewing* of our inward being into that which was intended by God in our original creation. We are to sink the roots of our soul into the soil of Christ's life within us. And in Christ's resurrected body is the *recreation* of our physical existence into the form prepared for us before the foundations of the world. We are to consecrate our body now toward that sanctified end, when all death, decay and frailty will at last be fully overcome.

The healing of redemption therefore begins from the outside in. It begins with the Holy Spirit, the eternal Torah by which we are to live, *"informing"* the human spirit with the infusion of grace, of being loved unconditionally in concrete singularity. The Spirit, as symbolized by water, first cleanses and washes away past sins and the guilt thereof, then offers the balm of *forgiveness.* Forgiveness restores relationship. And forgiving love becomes a wellspring rising up within the soul. This is the healing of *mutuality,* of the We and the You dimensions of persons.

The second dimension of healing is that of the soul. This is symbolized by the blood of Christ, which is the new covenant, the incarnated Torah of the heart. This is the *"reforming"* of the soul by the action of the Spirit and the Person of Christ. This signifies the healing of *internality,* of the I itself. The motion of healing here is from the inside out, rather than from the outside in. For now the person is responding to the healing of the water and the blood, the Spirit and the soul of Christ.

The third dimension of healing is that of the body. This is symbolized by the body of Christ, broken and raised up anew for our sake. The resurrected body of Christ is the ground of hope for the new covenant, and forms the basis for both community now and faith in what is to come. The body of resurrection represents the *"transforming"* of not only our bodies, but the whole of creation itself. As the healing of *"externality,"* of the We of nature and matter as such, it will be the final healing, for with it the first creation will be consummated.

Jesus Christ is thus the "first fruits" of the healing offered in and through the Eternal We of God. In His life and ministry the Kingdom of the We, the "healing communion" of God, has arrived. Now is the

Kingdom; now is offered the healing of our spirits, of who we are in all our relationships, especially in our relationship to God. Now are we offered the healing of our souls through communion with the perfect soul of Christ. And now is promised the healing and salvation of our bodies through the resurrection of Christ's body. Yet, while there may be physical healings now as a sign of the presence with power of the Kingdom, the final healing of our bodies must await the coming of the third Word. *And that is the Word which Jesus heard, there in the tomb, the Word of redemption.* Jesus is the "first fruit" of that final Word, which the world awaits. In His resurrection lies faith's proof of what is to be ours.

These three dimensions of the healing of redemption are revealed and inaugurated by the three primal events of the Christian faith: the Cross, the Resurrection, and Pentecost. The power of Pentecost is that of *information,* of the in-breaking of the truth of love and forgiveness, of the incarnation of the *agape* love and grace of God. In the life of the believer, Pentecost precedes and makes the Cross and the Resurrection meaningful. The power of the Cross is that of the *reformation* of the soul, first in direct response to the love of God given in the baptism of the Spirit. This motion of response back to God begins the reformation of the soul into the original image and likeness of God intended in creation. The power of the Resurrection is that of the final *transformation* of the whole of the cosmos, by the final Word, heard first—and thus far only—by Christ. Through that Word, Christ arose to the "right hand of the Father," and received all authority in heaven and on earth.

Thus, the spirit is the first to be redeemed, then the soul, and finally the body. Now is the time for spiritual and psychical redemption. And the time for physical redemption? It has begun already through the power of the Holy Spirit, but only as a sign, a guarantee and down payment of that which the final Word will bring to fruition. We do not yet know what we shall be like. We only know that when He appears, we shall be like Him.

✠

In the Person, ministry and Cross of Jesus of Nazareth, the whole sweep of redemption is revealed. It is a threefold movement of the love of God, meant to become our love. The threefold love of God is that of *receiving, sharing* and *giving*. Receiving has to do with the You of God, and grants *healing*. Sharing is of the We of God, and brings *wholeness*. Giving is of the I of God, and eventuates in *holiness*. Thus, as seen in the threefold movement of divine love, redemption signifies our healing, wholeness and holiness, all brought about through and in the Person of Christ, and the eternal relationship of Christ with God.

In the beginning is the Word. That means: in the beginning is the reception. Receiving the Word of the love of God brings healing and restoration to the dis-eased soul. The sharing of this love with others and with God makes us whole. For apart from the We of mutuality, we can abide only in incompleteness. And the giving of this love to others reveals its holiness, and our own participation therein. For the holiness of God is manifested in Christ's self-giving to us.

The Love which saves, in short, is to be received from, shared with and given to others. To miss or seek to skip one of the three movements would derail the whole. We can only give what we have received—and made actual by sharing. "We love, because He loved us first." And without giving, sharing returns to the Giver unfulfilled. These three movements are one, and in the We-Spirit of God, they form the arc of the very movement of God.

✠

Jesus Christ reveals the true and ultimate Person we are destined to become. Christ is both the End (telos) and the Way of attainment (teleios) thereto. That means, in accordance with the threefoldness of the person, human and divine, that Christ is the maturation of the I, the You and the We of humanity. Thus, in the "I Am" of Christ, the human I attains to the image of the *oneness* of God, of the great and wholly, holy Other "I Am." We are to become one, as God is One, for, "Hear O Israel, the Lord our God is One." And in Christ, the self-giving "Person for others," humanity attains true likeness to the *"whoness"* of God, to the Eternal You ever over against us. Also in Christ, in the absolute mutuality with God bespoken in Jesus' prayer to the Father in John 17, humanity attains full and everlasting *wholeness* in the We of God.

The oneness in ourselves, the whoness to and for others, and the wholeness with others—this is the maturity offered to us in Christ. This is the "healing trinity" of the human person.

Redemption

Redemption is an entrance entire into a new state, a state of being together with that which both redeems and is itself the redemption. And the very *purpose of human existence* is to enter into the relational life of God, there in the mutual Spirit *to share God with God.* We are created to love God with God's own love, made even sweeter and fuller by our own being, by our own love. That is the greatest gift we can offer God: to actually add to the reservoir of love by our own love, to bring the Complete One to greater completeness with and in us. The meaning of this gift is the deepest secret between the divine and human persons. But let this be said: as Spirit, the ground of need is a shared one.

Behold, more than our redemption is at stake in what is to come! For the reciprocity between God and us is real and may be encountered with undeniable directness. Redemption is not only a human need. The longing of heaven for earth is greater and more difficult to bear than that of earth for heaven. We know only of the hunger for God. Would that we knew also of the hunger of God! The restlessness of the heart until we find rest in God is in truth a great gift of God. And it issues from the restlessness of eternity to consummate creation in itself. More than this cannot be said. For God is God and not humanity, the Holy One in our midst.

Two primal analogies from human life can be applied to the way into and meaning of redemption: birth and marriage. In both cases, through the combined action of our will and the grace of God, we are brought by God into a new mode of relational existence. In birth, God is the Parent and we are the children; in marriage, God is our Spouse—and therefore so are we to God. The analogies are sequential and overlapping: we must be children before we can become spouses. And while both fundamental relationships involve growth, the former is toward mutuality and the latter is in mutuality. A bonding or union is at the heart of both events, which underlies and undergirds the subsequent parent-child and husband-wife relationships. The former relationship is temporary in the sense that the child is to grow up and out of the relationship. Even though the adult will still be the child of the parents for as long as the persons live, the bond between them is nevertheless to change from that of dependence-independence to mutual interdependence, from a hierarchical structure of power to that of an equality of reciprocal influence. The child grows up and becomes more or less like the parents. Hence, the parent-child relationship is to lead to friendship.

Friendship is the beginning and lifeblood of marriage. Yet marriage is more than a friendship: it is the ever-evolving state of a life-long union. In the covenant with God, the marriage union is eternal. There is to be no end to marriage, but only growth in the grace of the relationship. Marriage is a state of mutual interdependence and commitment; it is a transformation into a state of love which is to abide for the entire life of the partners. Marriage is for the whole existence of the persons, their bodies and their lives. They are married entire, body, soul and spirit.

While marriage is to endure through sickness and health, it is conditional nonetheless. For divorce, be it only in soul and in spirit, or in flesh and in legal standing as well, always exists as a possibility. The responsibility for the relationship rests on both the partners' shoulders. In the case of the parent-child relationship, however, while rejection and estrangement are possible, divorce is not. Further, the primary responsibility for the relationship rests on the parents, rather than the child. For it is the child who is to be taken care of, not the parents; it is the child who is the dependent and passive one, and the parents who are the independent and active ones.

These two fundamental human relationships are also the primary biblical analogies to our relationship with God. God is a divine Parent; God is also divine Spouse. If God is our Parent, does that mean we are to be children eternally? So many do not want to grow up! God is always to provide for us, take care of us, be incomprehensible to us, etc. But if God is also our Spouse, are we not to be God's friend, to share in the burdens of our Beloved, to understand and support, to take care of as well as be taken care of? Are we not to share fully in the responsibility for the relationship? Too many of us want to remain as babes, and unknowingly push God towards divorce.

Where in the parent-child relationship the focus is on the child and the current state of his/her needs, stage of maturity, and the like, the focus in marriage is on the relationship itself, and on the partners in that relationship. Hence, as God's child we pray our petitions and needs; but as God's spouse, our prayer becomes that of union and communion, of embrace and intimacy, of mutuality and even ecstasy.

Mature prayer is in truth the highest form of marriage communication.

Behold, the proper analogy for our relation to God in the coming redemption is that of marriage. God has served as our Parent in order to prepare us for marriage: *God is our Eternal Spouse.* God is our *Beloved,* the One who has created us in mutuality and communion. Redemption is therefore the fulfillment of the union of marriage, the entrance into eternity of the marriage begun and grown into here.

✠

The *life between us* bestows meaning on the life around us. The circle of sharing of the We is either reaching outward or turning inward, moving either toward expanse or atrophy. But as living, the We never stays the same. And when the relationship grows, it "christens" what is brought within its sphere with its life; it "baptizes" what is within and between the partners with its own mutual being. The "it" as well as the "yours" and "mine" become elements of the "ours" through being brought into the relational life. The We of Spirit would stamp the objective world with its own peculiar seal; it would funnel the world which encircles but does not see or even know of it, through its world, and therein make it consonant with itself. For the We builds worlds and would shape what is shared into that which conforms with its own life. And one day, through the manifesting of the ultimate We in the Word of redemption, the We of God shall succeed at bringing the all into oneness with its All.

In truth, *the entrance of love into the world comes through the We, it spills out reaching for the world from the foundational arms of living and actual love relationships.* The salvation of the world finally depends on *Us,* on the We itself, in all its dimensions: human to human, divine-human, and divine as such. The love of individuals for the world may help to maintain the world, but only the love of concrete and specific relationships, of We-spirits, will save the world. For love relationships *are* the very salvation of the world, the world both of persons and of nature itself. Nature will one day be redeemed by being brought into the divine-human We and made our perfect and imperishable home. We are the hope of the world. If We will not redeem, it will not come about. Our task is to hallow everything to God, to make holy the everyday and the ordinary. We must make ready for the dawning of the final Word, confirming and fulfilling Us. Then will we see whether we have worked in vain or in God.

PORTENTS OF THE END

The Unredeemedness of the World

The kingdom of God is in our midst. It is there *between* us, offered as Spirit to transform our relationships, and us in relationship. The redemption is now available in the sphere of mutuality, but not yet fully in the other two spheres of existence, namely that of internality and externality. The I is not yet redeemed, nor is the It. The only way to that redemption is through the I-You relationship, the We of Spirit. For from our mutuality will the final Word be issued, the Word which will bring the internal and external into absolute consistency with the mutual. Then will the state of redemption exist, and the world in it.

Today the world lies in unredeemedness. The greatest and gravest sign of that non-redemption is "the void" of mutuality, in juxtaposition with the threat of "the bomb" of self-destruction. This void is writ large in both the intensive and extensive We dimensions of relationship. High divorce rates and personal estrangement on the one side, and nation upon nation defensively alienated from any sense of true commonwealth on the other, bespeak the tensions and distrust at every level of human life. Divided and therein exposed to evil, we live in a world capable of and threatening to blow itself into non-existence, or at the very least to make the "biosphere" uninhabitable, all due to the divisiveness of the "psychosphere." Our clock is surely running down: either we attain the unity of a common We or we self-destruct.

What does the world offer us instead of the *communion of the We*? The twin cancers of *communism* and *consumerism*. We are forced to choose between two forms of anti-Spirit, the It of the state or the It of the economy. Both belong wholly to this world, and thus are closed to the coming Word; both are based on a strict materialism, and are therefore blind and deadly to the We of Spirit, to the mutuality of the I and You. Things, things, we are awash with things and ideologies antithetical to persons and Spirit!

Communism and consumerism only give the appearance of a commonality, all the while demanding total obedience. Everything having to do with persons and love, with the ends of life, becomes used by these cancerous anti-spirits as means for the perpetuation of the system. While the state says "We can give it all to you," and the economy pledges that "You can have it all," the price is the soul of the person for the goods of the system. For everything must be either for the "good of the state" or for the "good of the economy." Yet material things and ideologies do not make for the good of the persons-in-relationship.

The "political Mensch" of the one side, and the "economic Mensch" of the other, interface in a war for the allegiance of persons and whole peoples. What is missed entirely—if not denied outright—is the "spiritual Mensch." Would that the We of love and mutuality were as passionate and vociferous for attention and loyalty as the twin beasts emerging from the gap between us and God! But such means would violate the end of love. For with love, means and ends are one.

In this battle, the narrow path of the between, the very ground of mutuality, is threatened from both sides. From the side of externality, the threat of consumerism is in the reducing of love and the things of love into but a part of the "natural" world. Love is devalued to desire and is seemingly purchasable, if one only has the right "goods"—that is, money and looks. There is nothing that currency cannot attain. Everyone and everything can be priced, that is, receive some relative value among the whole system of values. And what can be priced, can be purchased. And what can be purchased can be thrown away.

From the side of internality, the threat of communism is that of identifying love as an ideology, there to be debated and made consistent with the overall vision of the "natural" state. Love is an idea among other ideas, and is thus to be examined and judged, weighed and measured in accordance with the needs of the state. The state claims for itself the right and duty to determine every facet of the life of the individuals within its ideological borders. And the mutuality which cannot be subsumed within the domain of its anti-Spirit must be renounced and stamped out, like a fire the sheer existence of which the state can neither understand nor tolerate. Yet the darkness of the state will never be able to reach and extinguish that fire and the Light thereof.

Neither the state nor the economy can redeem persons. They may promise, but they simply cannot deliver. The "good" life they offer is built on sand and illusion. And though what we are fed may taste good in the mouth, it leaves the stomach strangely empty. And the more we eat, the hungrier we become. And how overweight we are in our hunger!

✠

The world is unredeemed. That means: there is a living hell here. *"Hell"* is the outer darkness into which we fall when we are cut off from the We of mutual life. Instead of taking our stand on the ground of shared being, the ground of hell is the burning blackness of unmet need never to be fulfilled, of desire turned back on itself in hatred, and in that movement incapable of either death or gratification. The hatred empowers life and prohibits fulfillment in one ugly irony half-conscious of itself.

Hell is the sphere of the estrangement from love and mutuality, thus from Spirit. It is the end point of alienation, where nothing common abides, save only the unholy commonness of selfishness, bitterness and hatred. Each soul in hell cannot but remind every other soul of the state of unending emptiness where others should have been, and of the strangely continuing "non-repentance" or "hardness of heart," which each sees in the other and detests in themselves above all. That immovable and unhideable hide of hatred encasing each one is the curse which brings the person into hell; and it is the fire which keeps them there.

Hell is the experience of the inability to love, to share one's life and being with another. I am in hell in this life when I see what I need and desire, but am unable either to reach for it or to attain it. Hell is the searing revelation that the opportunity to love has passed and seemingly shall not come again; that I was not ready and able to meet it when it knocked upon the door of my soul. Hell is the realization that the woundedness of past hurts and rejections will never be healed, but will only fester and gain ever greater control over my life. Hell is the final "unresting" place of a life predicated on *No* to love, to the way of the We.

To be cut off as dead wood, as a branch incapable of receiving and sustaining the common sap of true life, therefore incapable of bearing fruit, this is the entrance into hell. And what a fire is that void! The blackness is as great as the burning.

✠

The world is unredeemed. That means: the We of one common humanity before the One God has not yet emerged in history. The world exists rather as separate pieces, as "nations," each claiming a sovereignty and exclusivity that bars identity and oneness. Rather than seeking what is common, we lift up what is unique, and take pride therein. Like the stars in the heavens we seem to be moving farther apart, after some "big bang" birth of being, recorded in our common unconsciousness but not remembered or reverenced.

And recorded in that unconsciousness as well is the promise of yet another cataclysmic event. In the faith living in our hearts, it represents a new birth, unto an eternal redemption. But in our minds and worldly perceptions, it all too easily comes to signify our final self-destruction—whether meted out by us or by God.

Which is to come? Or somehow are both to visit us? Only the coming Word will provide the answer.

✠

The Holocaust and the We of Redemption

> The Jews are enemies of God only with regard to the Good News, and enemies for your sake; but as the chosen people, they are still loved by God, loved for the sake of their ancestors. God never takes back His gifts or revokes His choice (Romans 11:28-29, JB).

Behold, in our time *a second Jewish crucifixion has taken place.* The first crucifixion was of a single person for the sake of all single persons. The second was of a whole people—and may yet be revealed to be for the sake of all peoples. The first sacrifice, carried out under the hands of the Roman State, was an attempt to eradicate the presence of the intensive We of God, the revelation of the eternal I-You. The second sacrifice, carried out under the hands of the "Third Reich," was an attempt to eradicate the reality of the extensive We of God with a people, the ongoing evidence of the presence and purpose of God in history.

Through the millennia, the Jewish people have been held accountable for the first crucifixion. The justification for such an unrelenting persecution? A single verse of Scripture succinctly voices a curse purportedly laid on a whole people: "All the people answered, 'Let his blood be upon us and on our children'" (Matthew 27:25). With the second crucifixion, however, it is the Church which is to be held accountable. As the first sacrifice constituted a judgment—not against the people but against the religious leaders of Jesus' day—, so also does the second. It is also to be understood as primarily against those Church leaders, throughout the millennia, whose attitude against Israel created the climate—the evil "gap" between the Church and Israel—that finally permitted the Nazi regime to carry out its almost unthinkable genocide. Though Rome actually killed Jesus, the Jews were blamed. And though the Reich actually killed the Jews, are then the Christians to be held accountable? Is it to be laid upon the Church, that "Their blood be upon us and on our children"?

At the very least the Holocaust undercuts forever the anti-Semitism of the Church's history. The issue now is not Israel's right to exist as Israel, but the Church's to exist as the Church—without reconciliation with Israel.

✠

Jesus lived and died as a Jew. When He comes back, will it be as a Christian or as a Jew? We must wait until His return to find out. But let this be said: Jesus called John the Baptist, who lived and died—and remains—a Jew, the "least" of those in the Kingdom of heaven. Are not the Jews themselves the "least" of Jesus' brethren? And He warned us that whatsoever we do to the least of His, we do also to Him. Woe to those of the household of the Church who have persecuted these, the least of Jesus' own people! The coming judgment will begin there, in the very household of the Lord. In truth, the Holocaust is first an indictment against the Church, and only secondly against the culture spawned and justified by the Church.

And behold, Jewish persecution has constituted the secret "litmus test" for Christian love all this time. We can love Christ only to the extent that we can love the least of His people.

✠

Jesus identified with the "suffering servant" of Isaiah. Indeed, He was that incarnate. The sacred texts of the prophet bespeak the mission and death of Christ with startling accuracy. But Israel has also properly identified itself as the subject of those four "songs" of Isaiah, arising from and falling back into the surrounding verses with an ease that belies their extraordinary significance. Israel is spoken of in the prophets in both singular and plural terms. For Israel is Jacob, and holds onto God as but one person until the blessing it still seeks is finally received. The people are treated as one by virtue of the one relation with their one God.

And in light of the Holocaust, the servant songs, especially the final one of Isaiah 53, speak with a power and poignancy that brings us to utter silence in the face of what transpired over and over during the long days of the War:

> He was oppressed and afflicted, yet he did not open his mouth; he was led like a lamb to the slaughter, and as a sheep before her shearers is silent, so he did not open his mouth. By oppression and judgment he was taken away. And who can speak of his descendants? For he was cut off from the land of living; for the transgression of my people he was stricken (Isaiah 53:7-8).

History, quite simply, has repeated itself. Not just history, but sacred history, has happened all over again. Only it is not, thus far at least, a part of the "Heilsgeschichte," not a new chapter of God's "saving acts" on our behalf. Rather, for a black time and space, the suffering servant again walked and died among us. Only this time it was as a whole people, as men, women and children. Whole families and communities were decimated; whole traditions and sacred elements of Spirit were removed from the "psychosphere." As a sign of our fallenness, God's own people were almost completely wiped out. God once—and once for all—permitted His Son to die; has God once again permitted that which is precious to be killed by the secular powers of the world?

Note carefully: permitted does not mean willed. It is unthinkable that God would have willed either the death of Jesus or that of the Jewish people. The sacrifice took place both times because of the conditions existing in the world. Yet God, religious consciousness cannot help but believe, permitted it to happen both times. Towards what end this time? The whole of history is at stake in the answer to that question.

What will be God's response to the Holocaust? For the meaning and significance of the sacrifice must be seen in terms of Jewish history before world history. If it cannot be reconciled with tradition, if there is no divine purpose for this tragedy beyond all measure, or at least divine plan to "work good" from the murderous deeds of a fallen people, then the whole of religious history loses its very ground. Something unexpected and unaccountable has happened. What of the God of Israel? Where is YHWH? What of God's response to this destruction of almost the whole of Israel—let alone God's "prior knowledge," and seeming acceptance of it? Where is God, and why was God so incredibly absent at the very hour of Israel's need? "My God, my God, why have You forsaken us?" How, Holy One, can You possibly justify Your Way among us this time?

Behold, the first crucifixion was as unexpected as the second. Who among Jesus' followers and contemporaries anticipated a "suffering Messiah," one who would die for His Kingdom rather than bring it in triumphantly? A Deliverer of the extensive We of the people was expected, rather than what Israel got: the Deliverer of the intensive We between God and the individual person. At the point at which Jesus was to have completed successfully His mission, came the wrenching paradox: "You will fail and die." Just so, with the people Israel, especially with German Jewry, at the high point of the "Haskala," the enlightened integration of being both German and Jewish, came the equally wrenching paradox: "You will be singled out and killed."

And what was God's response to the first crucifixion? The resurrection of Christ and the offer of individual salvation. Behold, *the only possible response of God to the second crucifixion is the resurrection of Israel and the offer of salvation to whole peoples*. That is, as the *first sacrifice* was for the sake of the establishing of the *intensive We* of God among us, the Kingdom of the Spirit, so must the second sacrifice have been permitted for the sake of the establishing of the *extensive We* of God with the whole world. In other words, the only possible response of God is the final redemption itself. Either the redemption is at hand, or the whole of religious history—and not only that of Israel, but also of the Church and Islam—goes up in flames as well. Then the Holocaust was total. All was found wanting and all lost at the altar of the world.

Now is a time of waiting upon that Word, that response. And behold, it has already begun. Israel has already been resurrected as a nation, as a people of a land. Wait until Israel is resurrected as a religion, as a people of the Book! Then at last, "The Lord will be King over the whole earth. On that day there will be one Lord, and His name the only name" (Zechariah 14:9).

✠

God is a God of covenant, of marriage. And whether known in a marriage as YHWH, Abba or Allah, the sentiment of God remains: "I hate divorce" (Malachi 2:16). At least three marriages exist between God and the peoples of the world: with Israel, with the Church, and with Islam. All three are both in force yet unfinished, both of the truth and promising salvation, yet not the whole truth. All three in fact look for the same event to consummate history and their respective marriages. All three streams, initiated and tended by God, will end at the one Sea.

"Those whom God hath joined together, let not man put asunder." It is not for one covenantal stream to seek to dam—and therein to damn—the other. Unto the end, the three faiths are to learn to live together as the respective and respected "spouses of God," each loved by their God, each members of a living and inviolate We-Spirit with God. Rather than jealousy and "one-upmanship," there is to be harmony and co-operation. For each faith has its particular vision and mission.

Let us be fully aware, however, of the crucial and unbroken mission of Israel. First, *Israel* is to be the *primal model of the extensive We with God* in the world—just as *the Church* is to offer to the world the *primal model of the intensive We with God*. In this, Israel is to be a "light to the nations." The legitimacy of the other two faiths is dependent upon the ongoing legitimacy and standing of Israel. As the Apostle to the Gentiles well recognized, Israel is the "holy root" which supports the ingrafted branches of other peoples. It is not the branches which support the root, but the root the branches. Thus, if the root is destroyed, everything that depends on it will die as well.

The second, and little understood role of Israel in the world is to be that of the "early warning system" for the arrival of the actual Word of redemption. When Israel says the redemption of the world has come, it shall have come indeed, it shall be here not only in Spirit and in faith, but also in flesh and in nature. Until then, Israel shall function as the guardian of the truth, that none may be swayed to believe in a false redemption—therefore in a false god.

No wonder Hitler and the "Third Reich" had to attempt to destroy the Jews! For the "secular messianism" of the Nazis could never have been acceptable to the people awaiting the Messiah and the transformation of both history and nature! The very existence of the Jew called the Nazi regime into question—and with a decisiveness the latter could not overcome, short of the eradication of the "evidence" of God, and of God's prior choice of a people to be God's own. Thus did *"Die Endlösung der Judenfrage,"* the unspeakably evil "resolution of the Jewish question" present itself: total genocide. The extensive We of the Reich could not allow the extensive We of the Jews to exist. And behold, if the Reich would have succeeded with the extermination of the Jews, the Christians would have been next. Ultimately, only the We of the Reich would have been allowed to exist. The cancer of Hitler's totalitarianism would have destroyed everything not of itself.

But the We of God with Israel—and with the Church, and with Islam—cannot be so eradicated. They will abide unto the end of the age. But the "Third Reich" did not, nor will any other extensive We which seeks to exclude or deny the We between God and humanity.

Let us therefore, unto the end of history, uphold the holiness of Israel, love the perfection of the Church, and bow before the righteousness of Islam. And above all, *let us stand together now as the One People we shall be then.* Let us await the final Word in a unity anticipating the *"We Are"* which is to be ours with God. And may that Word of redemption come in our day and in our generation!

EPILOGUE

A Vision and a Response

I know a man in Christ who fourteen years ago was caught up to the third heaven. Whether it was in the body or out of the body I do not know—God knows. And I know that this man...was caught up to Paradise. He heard inexpressible things, that man is not permitted to tell (2 Corinthians 12:2-4).

It was about fourteen years before this book finally came to be written that I, too, knew a man in Christ who was caught up to Paradise. A man who saw that Truth which cannot be described, yet lived. And it took many years and much incubation and labor, before the meaning of that which was encountered with absoluteness came to be grasped with decisive clarity. Yet how grossly inadequate is the depiction in comparison with the holy event, the meeting itself. Call it a "revelation of the Revelation."

It happened in a dream. For I do not believe I could have witnessed in wakefulness what was revealed and lived. I was wrestling in earnestness—I do not know why—with what looked to be a series of gold rings perfectly in order from the smallest to the largest, each one nestled within and next to the succeeding one, like the yearly rings around the trunk of a tree, if about a six-inch cross section were taken from it. As I wrestled with this singular reality in my hands, I came to be aware with calm assurance that I was having a "vision," one with utmost importance for my life.

By and by my wrestling gave way to a short interval when nothing seemed to happen, save time elapsed. Then, behold, instead of the body of rings, immediately before me was a single candle, lighted and burning still. The fact and light of this candle seemed to guide me beyond itself. As I looked up from the candle toward the horizon of the dream environment, the next thing I saw was what appeared to be an old-fashioned and quiet city block—seemingly from "Ourtown, USA." It was evening and the street lights were on, as were a few lights within some of the homes. Judging from the darkness within the majority of the houses, it was fairly late in the evening.

Then I looked ahead and beyond the city block. And behold, there was nothing, absolutely nothing. It seemed an infinity of dark space. As I continued my glance outward and upward, I finally saw It. It was the original and actual reality of that "perfect" model I had been wrestling with of the gold rings within gold rings. The brightness of its gold was wondrous. It was like a heavenly city, beautiful and eternal, beyond change or corruption. And I could gaze upon it at length with peace and comfort.

It was when I looked beyond and to the left of this heavenly city, that it happened. What I saw cannot be put into words—at least not yet, and not here. Let it be said that it was the "city of God," as it were, holy and pure and beyond all description. The place where nothing human and worldly will ever enter. The colors were not of this world, nor were the infinitely complicated yet wholly simple shapes. I knew as soon as my eyes focused upon this One, that I was apprehending the Truth, the Holy One, the Beloved. As I saw this I was met by holiness, a power awe-ful to encounter. My heart seemed to both stop and burst, and I was blown at once shaking into full wakefulness.

Two cities thus presented themselves, the city of humanity and the city of God. Over the years I have come to understand that the two symbolized the The Eternal I and the Eternal You. The first city represented the ultimate fulfillment of all the divine-human marriages, that is, the end point of humanity, the Eternal I we are to attain. The second city signified the exclusive city of God, the Eternal You, the Holy One ever over against us.

What of the Eternal We? It was present but unseen; It came upon me as the very holiness of God, and carried me safely back to wakeful existence in the world. And to this day, that Spirit guides and guarantees my return to that home my heart in faith promises shall one day be mine.

Epilogue

Our end is life in the Eternal We, the Trinity. Entering into this Life through and in the I of Christ, we shall all be married with Christ to God. Eternal shall we be in the heavens, there with God, the All in our all.

✠

O God,
Enter into my heart
And burn me, open me, cleanse me
With Your life and love,
Your love which is better than life.

Be ever over against me;
Speak me in Your Word of address:
"Be You!"
I am in Your Word;
Apart from Your Word
I am not.
In Your Word I say
The holy unexpected wholly unjustified
"I Am" of Your life in me,
The anointed Word of eternal being
With You, in You, through You.

Behold, emerges now
The ground of all in All:
"We Are."
The life of Word of love of mutuality
The life of Spirit of shared breath
The life not seen but seeing
Not spoken but speaking
Not felt but feeling.
The life of Oneness
Opens wide and We Are in It
And It Is Us.